The Politics of Curriculum Decision-Making

SUNY Series, Curriculum Issues and Inquiries
Edmund C. Short, editor

The Politics of Curriculum Decision-Making

Issues in Centralizing the Curriculum

Edited by M. Frances Klein

State University of New York Press

Published by
State University of New York Press, Albany

Printed in the United States of America

For information, address State University of New York Press,
State University Plaza, Albany, N.Y., 12246

Library of Congress Cataloging-in-Publication Data

The Politics of curriculum decision-making : issues in centralizing
    the curriculum / edited by M. Frances Klein.
        p.   cm. — (SUNY series, curriculum issues and inquiries)
    Includes bibliographical references.
    ISBN 0-7914-0487-0. — ISBN 0-7914-0488-9 (pbk.)
    1. Education—United States—Curricula.   2. Education and state—
—United States.   I. Klein, M. Frances.   II. Series: SUNY series in
curriculum issues and inquiries.
    LB1570.P59   1991   90-30939
    375′.00973—dc20   CIP

10   9   8   7   6   5   4   3   2   1

Contents

Introduction

M. Frances Klein

*T*he question of who makes curriculum decisions is a fundamental and timeless issue which has received continuing discussion and debate throughout the history of the curriculum field. The answers to this question have changed over time and are certain to change in the future, given the increasing rate and complexity of change in the world. It is one of those fundamental questions that will always need to be reconsidered as new social contexts, pressures, and knowledge come to bear upon it. The array of participants who are officially designated or who function through default to make curriculum decisions is complex enough, but the question centers around not only *who* makes them, but also what type of curriculum decision is under discussion. Thus, the question is very complex and multifaceted, but the complexity is not often recognized when debates about curriculum are held in public and educational forums and when operational answers to it are formulated.

In recent times a definitive answer has been given to the question of who makes curriculum decisions by the increased power that is being vested in the state for curriculum responsibilities. Congressional legislation and cases heard by the Supreme Court also have played an increasing role in curriculum decision making at the federal level. This book discusses the current answer to the perennial question and documents the impact of how it has been answered on the curriculum, educators, and students. In addition, it identifies some related educational issues, such as the education of teachers and the new roles different educators are expected to perform, which must be addressed now and in the future when the question is reconsidered.

Each author was invited to contribute a chapter to this book because of his or her special expertise and unique perspective on the question of who makes curriculum decisions. All of the authors wrote with the current movement toward centralized curriculum decision making as a frame of reference, but each wrote from his or her own value perspective as to the impact of the movement upon American education and what will and should be done about it. No author formally defines that nebulous concept of 'curriculum', but each focuses upon a rather common definition, since the shared perspective of all the authors is the current movement to centralize curriculum decisions. Thus *curriculum*, in these chapters, is implicitly defined as decisions dealing with the goals, content, materials, and evaluation procedures, at least in part, that students experience while they are at school. If each author had been invited to define curriculum as he or she chose, this may not have been the preferred definition for many of them. But it is clear that many assume that this is what curriculum is, especially as decisions have become increasingly centralized.

Each chapter reflects the beliefs, expertise, and style of the author. Since the authors were invited to contribute a chapter because of their national stature, no attempt was made to force each one into a similar style of writing through extensive editing. Thus, not only do the chapters reflect the differing perspectives on the question of curriculum decision making, but the intensity of each author's beliefs and position on the issues is preserved.

The book does not intend to portray a unified discussion on the question of who should make curriculum decisions but rather to suggest the diversity of issues which relate to it. Each chapter helps identify the different issues, value contexts, and complexities that surround the central question. It should not be surprising, then, that each of the authors discusses the question in different ways. In spite of the uniqueness of each chapter, however, all of them collectively contribute to an increased underderstanding of the issues.

Some educators are suggesting that a new wave of reform is beginning—a movement to school-based management and curriculum reform. How this will affect the current trend of a state-dominated curriculum is not clear. It may be that the pendulum will swing once again to local control over the curriculum; it may also be that the state will continue to have dominance over the basic curriculum decisions, as Pipho suggests in his chapter. Whatever answer is given to the question of curriculum decision making in the future, this book will remain a resource because of the curriculum-related issues discussed in it. The perennial question of who makes what type of curriculum decision is made much clearer for future rounds of discussion—as they undoubtedly will occur—because of the contributions of these authors and their unique perspectives.

In the opening chapter of Part I, John Goodlad, University of Washington, places each of the succeeding chapters within the current social and political context of curriculum decision making and provides his own view of how he and other thoughtful educators must act within that context. He emphasizes the importance of the question of who makes curriculum decisions and suggests that it cannot be answered simplistically as a question of who has the power to make them. Goodlad argues that the question must always be answered within the political context and on the basis of normative criteria. Further, the basic decisions about curriculum must be made when the ground rules usually are not clear. The question must be answered consistently, however, through the process of inquiry and must always be made for the common good.

Frances Klein, University of Southern California, presents a conceptual framework for describing and examining curriculum decision making which helps to document and interpret the confusing array of potential and actual participants in the processes of curriculum development. The framework is a matrix consisting of levels of decision making and the types of curriculum decisions which ultimately must be made. The interaction identified through the matrix clearly identifies the complexity of the question. The assumptions inherent within the framework are identified, the potential role of it within curriculum development is discussed, and the complexity of the concept of curriculum is made clear.

Tyll van Geel, University of Rochester, discusses congressional legislation and the role of the U.S. Supreme Court as major forces in curriculum decision making at the federal level. He presents two visions, traditionalism and liberalism, and analyzes the ever-changing struggle over the federal role in education as conflicts between the two visions. The differing educational goals of those who hold the two visions are reflected in both the legislation of Congress and in Supreme Court decisions. In his conclusion, he notes that although liberalism has been the dominant vision in many instances, the tension between the two visions will continue to shape federal decision making about curriculum, and that the current tension may be reshaped by just one Supreme Court appointment in the future.

Chris Pipho, Education Commission of the States, discusses the recent decisions made by the states which focus upon curriculum. The number of decisions made by the states clearly point out the degree of state control being placed upon local school districts. Pipho agrees that the states have a significant amount of control over the curriculum, but there is much variation in how that control is exercised from state to state. He further notes that the movement to increased state control over the curriculum occurred with the support and agreement, or at least acquiescence, of local educational leaders. The trends he identifies suggest that state control will continue in the future and even will be likely to increase.

William H. Schubert, University of Illinois at Chicago, places the current movement of centralized curriculum decision making in a historical context by discussing past answers to the question as well as the forces which have helped frame the answers. He discusses the current movement to centralized power, but he also identifies current forces opposing the move to a centralized and mandated curriculum. He insightfully notes that each succeeding generation within its own unique set of circumstances must answer anew where control over the curriculum will be located. Schubert's discussion clearly documents the persistency over time of the question of who will make curriculum decisions.

Part II presents the unique perspectives of five leaders in American education on the impact of centralized curriculum decision making and the critical issues related to it. Gary Griffin, University of Arizona, analyzes two competing orientations to teaching for which teachers can be prepared in preservice and continuing professional education: teachers as paraprofessionals and teachers as professionals. His examination of each reveals how the current trend toward centralizing curriculum decision making forces the paraprofessional role upon all teachers and restricts the professionalization of teaching. He also makes clear that if teachers are to function as professionals, they will need a broadened body of knowledge and skills, including what is necessary to be informed and effective curriculum decision makers. He highlights the importance of the orientation taken in preservice teacher education since it is at that level that teachers begin to be socialized into professional norms and educated for the role they ultimately will play in curriculum decision making. Specific suggestions are made for improving teacher education in order to ensure that teachers will function as professionals who are skilled in curriculum decision making.

Martin Brooks, assistant superintendent for instruction of the Shoreham-Wading River Central School District in New York, discusses the impact of state decisions regarding curriculum upon the local school district from his perspective. He presents seven messages received by local districts as curriculum development becomes centralized at the state level and suggests some strong effects this movement has had at the district level. Brooks proposes some alternative actions which could be taken by the state, actions that build on the history of the school district rather than simply assume that the current trend toward centralizing curriculum decision making is appropriate for all school districts. His discussion of the pressures on and the responses from local districts brings into sharp focus the impact of the state's heavy involvement in curriculum decision making.

Audrey Schwartz, University of Southern California, analyzes from a sociological perspective how the roles of the local school board, the superintendent, principals, teachers, and students are modified with externally imposed curriculum reforms. As a basis for her analysis she uses two metaphors which affect the view of education and curriculum that people hold: the machine metaphor and the organic metaphor. After a brief historical review of how these metaphors have been reflected in educational policies and practices, she places into perspective the current attempts to improve American education by state and other external mandates regarding the curriculum. The tensions among the various professional roles of educators caused by the two differing metaphors are illuminated by her discussion. She concludes that both metaphors are competing for attention at the beginning of the 1990s, with the machine metaphor driving the pressures for state and national policies affecting curriculum and the organic metaphor driving the policies about classroom practices. The impact of the next wave of reform is expected to flatten the bureaucracy as teachers become empowered to develop curriculum at the local level.

Robert McClure, National Education Association, discusses the centralization of curriculum decision making from both a historical perspective and from the current perspective of the largest professional organization for teachers in the nation. His organization has long supported local curriculum development, as it continues to do today. Four issues are discussed regarding how the shift in power to the state has had an impact on teachers and educational practice. In each case, he concludes that the shift has restricted the efficacy of both teachers and educational practice. In conclusion, he describes a current project sponsored by the National Education Association which challenges the centralization of power in the state for curriculum development and places the responsibility for it in the hands of informed local school faculty.

Finally, Frances Klein, University of Southern California, discusses the characteristics, assumptions, and impact of a state-dominated curriculum from her viewpoint as a curriculum theorist. Although there is a base of support for the movement among some curriculum scholars and practitioners, others are not supportive of the type of curriculum which results from state control. Four issues from curriculum theory are discussed which relate directly to the type of curriculum which can be expected with centralized curriculum development. The contributions of curriculum theory to an enlightened debate on the centralization of curriculum are then placed in a context of broader educational issues.

Two persistent themes emerge from most of the chapters. One is that there has been a significant increase in the centralization of curriculum, particularly at the state level, over recent years. The second theme is that, by and large, the changes in curriculum and educational practices which have occurred as a result of this centralization of decision making have not produced desirable results for teachers or students. Most authors express these two themes, although they differ in how they reach that conclusion and the intensity with which they express their conclusions. Each author, however, makes clear his or her value screen for the evidence presented, and readers will be challenged to consider whether or not they agree with the individual authors.

Through the contributions of each of the authors, it is hoped that readers will evolve a clearer understanding of the timeliness and timelessness of the question, the complexities of the issues involved, and the tremendous impact upon the curriculum, teachers, and students which occurs as a result of the possible answers. The book should be a continuing resource to all those interested and concerned with the question of who makes curriculum decisions as it comes under debate in the future.

Part I

Current Trends and History of Curriculum Decision Making

1 Curriculum Making as a Sociopolitical Process

John I. Goodlad

*F*ew matters are more important than who makes curriculum decisions for the nation's schools. Students of the curriculum-making process not only study who does but also inquire into the question of who should. The first question is answered much more easily than the second.

One need probe into the question of who makes such decisions only a little to realize that state governors and legislators have a deep interest in what is taught and should be taught in schools. Their desire to be key players has been heightened in recent years by the degree to which our schools are seen to be instrumental in worldwide economic competition. Indeed, many politicians perceive themselves to have a public mandate to intervene in the goals and content of the K-12 curriculum.

Most are aware that, in aggressively pursuing national or state interests in the quality of schooling and particularly in what is taught, they ultimately will bump up against both the rhetoric and the substance of local interests and control. Nonetheless, national goals, national standards, and national tests are now part of the rhetoric of educational reform and are being seriously discussed as necessary by a diverse group of actors. "Education for economic well-being" has become a sufficiently powerful rallying call to transcend more subtle issues of who should participate in determining school curricula.

This circumstance heightens the importance of a book addressed to questions of authority and responsibility in curriculum development.

Unfortunately, the chances of it being read by major players in the political arena are slim. It is important and exceedingly timely, however, for the entire range of these questions to be thoughtfully addressed. This is what succeeding chapters seek to do. Perhaps some of their content will be picked up and used productively in the socio-political discourse and action now ongoing.

Overview

The chapters that follow pose a tension between the centralization and decentralization of authority for curriculum decisions. Writ large, this tension arises out of differing views of education, the role of education in a democratic society, and the nature and locus of control most appropriate to schools charged with serving simultaneously the often-conflicting interests of both individuals and the polity. Most of the authors deliberately seek to put a distance between two alternative positions while recognizing areas of cloudiness and even overlap between differing conceptualizations and their implications.

Schubert paints a nineteenth and twentieth century picture of alternating ebb and flow regarding both the issue and dominance of local or state-developed curricula. Massive expansion toward universal schooling was accompanied by vastly expanded bureaucratic controls. Consequently, the tides of central control have flooded to higher and higher levels and fluctuated within an increasingly narrow range of high and low. Leaving the metaphor, one ought not seek centralization or decentralization in curriculum development, Schubert argues. Rather, there should be a careful and ongoing exercise of judgment in an effort to determine the blend most suited to each curriculum situation. In Chapter 2, Klein joins Schubert in raising at the outset the question of who should make what curriculum decisions. Such a question could keep curriculum theorists busy (and perhaps even happy) for decades while, Schubert observes, curriculum centralization increasingly dominates.

In 1987, Calvin Frazier, then commissioner of education for Colorado, wrote the following: "The twentieth-century governance cycle for American education has brought the mantle of power back to the state level after twenty years of leadership by the federal lawmakers and executive offices. It is doubtful that a further shift to another governing base will take place in the remaining years of this century."[1] He went on to argue for the role of the state to be one of sensitively sharing power with others in the educational system.

But Pipho's summary of the increase in state control over education since release of *A Nation at Risk*[2] portrays something other than Frazier's vision of an energized team comprising government officials, the state board of education, the local school district, and the individual school unit. Interestingly, Pipho views the swing to more state control as not a one-sided grab for power but as part of the public mood for reform with which some local school boards, administrators, and even teachers were empathetic. Once again, the author makes clear that the issues of curriculum control do not divide all the actors at state and local levels into two separate, neatly divided camps.

As assistant superintendent of a school district, Brooks sits at a point where one might hope to see the beneficial consequences of the blend of expertise discussed by Schubert, the careful allocation of decision making argued by Klein, and the sensitive sharing recommended by Frazier (1987). Instead, Brooks perceives ironies in state mandates designed to remedy educational ills resulting in the exacerbation of these same ills. The historic balance between broad state guidelines and local determination of how best to meet them is being interfered with dramatically, he writes, "through the growing phalanx of state-mandated tests." An irony lies in the contradiction between the degree to which mandates stifle teacher initiative at the very time that reform reports argue for expanding the role of the teacher and enhancing the status of teaching as a profession.[3]

It is to this and other ironies that both McClure and Griffin address their chapters, and it is to a much-strengthened teachers' role and profession of teaching that they would turn for improved curricula and a better educational system. Whereas several of the other authors appear to view sound curriculum decisions representing a kind of rational balancing of local and state interests—in Schubert's words, a "blend of external and internal expertise"—McClure and Griffin view the legitimate role of the external as one of supporting decisions made close to students. McClure's basic assumption is that every decision about learning and instruction that can be made by a local school faculty must be made by that faculty. Griffin deplores the popular conception of teachers as technicians which has excluded their role in curriculum decision making, and then calls for a much closer collaboration between precollegiate and higher education in preparing professional teachers and creating professional roles for them.

Schwartz is much less interested in the issues of who makes and should make curriculum decisions than in the impact on educational quality of alternative conceptions of education. Her review of the *machine* metaphor as contrasted with the *organic* metaphor parallels to a considerable degree Schubert's depiction of the rise and fall, rise and fall again, dominance of top-down as contrasted with grassroots approaches to curriculum development. The machine metaphor leads to the paraprofessional role for teachers deplored by both McClure and Griffin, and the organic to the greater teacher autonomy and professional status they both endorse.

I have left to the end of this summary van Geel's two visions of federalism because it is this chapter that brings most to the fore the complexities of serving equally and simultaneously the democratic state and each of its citizens through a system of public schooling. The fear of tyranny pushes the traditionalist vision toward a conception of government as an agency with limited powers. The fear of chaos pushes the traditionalist to embrace tradition—and it is the local community which is to serve as the "keeper of the flame." But this view of the community does not keep the traditionalist from specifying the basic skills, books, and traditions for children in schools, who are to be citizens imbued with virtue, and mandatory tests in these basics.

In a democratic society, according to van Geel, government must preserve equality of opportunity and promote equitable distribution of wealth. The right to liberty and equality points toward a vigorous, active, central government that should not be, however, all-powerful. Regulatory authority must shape the educational enterprise to ensure that programs will serve the twin goals of liberty and equality—but must not indoctrinate children in the ideals and ideas of virtue and justice it is hoped they will come to uphold. At times, the visions of the traditionalist and of the liberal appear to virtually cross over at the level of some specific educational practices and policies. It should not be surprising, then, that ameliorative decisions addressed to certain kinds of problems either exacerbate them or result in unintended consequences.

One of my conclusions from reading the following chapters is that addressing the centralization versus decentralization of curriculum decisions from the perspective of who has or should have the power will not be very productive. (The several writers address the issues from rather different perspectives.) In popular educational parlance, the words *site-based management* have surfaced, drawing attention more to questions of power than of how best to ensure sound educational practice. The notion of shifting power from one locus to another has perpetuated the myth that power is finite—one party gains power only at the expense of another's power. Theories recently gaining increased attention in the business and corporate world promote the concept of creating power, and, in so doing, help everyone achieve greater potency and increased productivity.[4]

The degree to which the authors touch only briefly on the centralization-decentralization issue, as such, and move toward alternative visions, alternative paradigms or "worldviews," and alternative conceptions of education emphasizes the degree to which state officials always will feel frustrated over their efforts to hold the system of public education accountable as to its effectiveness and efficiency. These efforts almost always invoke the machine metaphor: legislation of goal attainment is sufficient for goal attainment to occur. The accompanying mandates simply do not fit the realities of schooling, as Schwartz points out, and so the outcomes from their enactment are disappointing. But history shows that such disappointments fail to diminish the perceived rationality of the metaphor.[5] Indeed, they encourage the believer to try again—more efficiently.[6] Unfortunately, the mandate for greater efficiency tends to invoke the finite power myth: the strong (public officials) invoke their assumed sanctions (tests and the withholding of salary increases) over the weak (teachers).[7] But the organic metaphor requires that the weak be strong so as to deal with the complex problems of the school's culture and the demands of the larger social system.

Several of the authors point out that the relative fortunes of competing conceptions and interests wax and wane over time. But there is general agreement that bureaucratic restraints and state mandates have steadily increased and that the domains of teacher decision making have narrowed. It would be nice to think that "these things too shall pass," but such is unlikely. The question to be answered is not whether states will continue to exercise their perceived authority in the educational arena but how that authority can be exercised most constructively—in what parts of that arena and in what ways. The corollary question pertains to how those charged with educating the young can do so most effectively—with what freedoms, within what constraints thought necessary, in what ways, and with what conditions of support.

These questions are complex. It is difficult to answer them even out of the political context—that is, as curricula of ideas.[8] In sociopolitical arenas, however, the interests of the decision makers transcend ideas, even when debate often appears to be focused on getting the "best" decisions. The tools of power usually dominate over the rules of discourse. In the next section, some aspects of human action and conduct (praxis) in political arenas where educational decisions are made are examined. Becoming players in these arenas creates some troublesome problems for educators. But to become a bystander and to simultaneously expect decisions to be made in the best interests of children and youth and those who teach them in schools is to be naive.

Action and Conduct in the Sociopolitical Arenas

The conceptual framework provided by Klein in Chapter 2 is intended to order the task of describing curricular phenomena: domains where curriculum decisions are made, each at a different level or point of remoteness from students; the kinds of decisions made there; and the persons or collective bodies of persons making them. It is not intended to answer normative questions of should or ought, but Klein argues that it holds potential for ordering this process, too, in that it provides many of the curriculum commonplaces where the infusion of values will move the inquirer from descriptive to normative considerations. Klein does not make explicit claims regarding the usefulness of the framework for teasing out the nature of the curriculum decisions to be described, but her summary of major ones (rather closely following Tyler's rationale[9]) implicitly tells us that the framework has a potential use in this area as well.

The complexity of curriculum, noted by Klein in both her chapters, whether viewed as a field of study or of action, is apparent in her framework. Cast into a graphic grid, there would be many cells. Consequently, it is not surprising that the several authors range far beyond Klein's initial question: Who makes curriculum decisions? And, indeed, they roam beyond her normative question as to who should, which appears to be the second guiding question posed for the authors to address. Both are central to the centralization-decentralization issue surfacing in most of the chapters. Fortunately, they carry us beyond both to some consideration of the nature of curriculum decisions and, therefore, to the knowledge, insights, and inquiry necessary to making them wisely. In effect, the authors move from questions too readily answered from the perspective of power and designated authority to questions couched so as to require careful reasoning.

The complexity to which the chapters attest would be substantially reduced if the tensions pertaining to authority over the curriculum were couched exclusively within an epistemology of power with power defined as finite and the turf clearly demarcated. Kliebard has described elements of this perspective and its effects in past struggles over the curriculum.[10] With the battle thus defined, strength, cunning, and innuendo become significant tools of struggle. One need not spend valuable time in seeking to ferret out elements of truth, beauty, and justice in the arguments of one who disagrees nor, for that matter, in seeking to reveal these elements in one's own argument. Better to use time in recruiting allies of similiar vested interests and in questioning the *motives*, not the ideas, of one's antagonists.

In this kind of struggle, McClure's case for more teacher autonomy obviously is part of a predictable power play on behalf of the union he represents. Griffin's plea for professional teacher education programs, which undoubtedly would require a longer period of student enrollment, clearly is self-serving in that he is a teacher educator. Brooks's litany of ill effects from centralized curriculum decision making becomes little more than the grumblings of a middle-range bureaucrat thirsting for more power. And so it goes. Whatever value for the improvement of education may lie in their views is lost in acrimonious rhetoric. Years ago, in a memorable speech, Mario Fantini recalled nostalgically a time in educational affairs when the welfare of children was invoked at the outset by successive debaters, but, increasingly, combatants did not bother with this nicety.

Had several of the chapters been written by state officials arguing that curriculum chaos, inconsistency, and inequity often have been an accompaniment of local decision making, advocates of local control might respond with accusations of using isolated cases or distorted data to advance self-interests. The degree of truth in these sobering observations would be ignored or discredited.

There has been sufficient acrimonious debate in the struggle over control of the curriculum that moving to a higher plane of discourse will not be easy. Further, discourse requiring sound, consistent reasoning is exceedingly demanding. Why would anyone want to forego the tried and true tactics of power struggles, ways that are as old as civilization itself and that have become less primitive only in outward appearances? And why, especially, would anyone already holding a large share of power perceived to be finite want to or even be willing to make the demanding shift?

In working with individuals at all levels of the educational enterprise, and having suffered along the way the wounds of power plays, I am a little surprised to find myself convinced that all but a few connected with it are well intentioned. There are rascals, of course, as there are in all realms of human endeavor. Further, I find myself becoming increasingly appreciative of the degree to which these well-intentioned actors in the educational milieu confront disagreement verging on conflict as an honest difference of belief and perception. And I am gratified by the degree to which those faced with difficult problems and conflicting solutions seek advice. Frequently, I am asked by policy makers and their advisors to propose actions they might take to improve education. Again and again, I find myself humbled by this challenge, even when I believe my views of what should be done are clear and sound. But when I seek to translate these views into specifics, I am inclined to say, "Please, do nothing."

Is this a cop-out arising out of my failure or inability to envision the specifics of the educational beliefs I carry around in my head? Or am I reacting to an unarticulated, not fully reasoned conviction that there is a contradiction between educational enactments by designated officials and my (obviously sound) views of good educational practice? Perhaps a virtual galaxy of such contradictions perceived by the founding fathers persuaded them to get on with the framing of a constitution devoid of attention to educational matters.

Confronted with the possibility of such a contradiction, I must ask myself whether it pertains in the face of *all* legislated enactments or only *some*. If only some but not all, then I must ask myself why I have a problem with some and not others. If some legislated educational mandates are acceptable because they advance my interests, then I must ask myself whether these interests are merely self-serving or whether I believe them to be in the public interest (and possibly even counter to my self-interests). Sorting out such complexities aloof from political arenas is difficult; the task is even more difficult and complex when one is a participant in such arenas.

Klein's question as to who should make what curriculum decisions begs for answers. But one does not probe far into it without confronting a more difficult question: What does the decision require if it is to be made wisely and justly? Both normative and empirical criteria are invoked. If my interests are likely to suffer in the implied process of inquiry, perhaps I would be better served by resorting to the rules of power struggles.

Unfortunately, the ground rules for decision making rarely are neatly demarcated, whatever the political arena. In state legislatures, the stakes are high because of the dollars and public constituency involved. The role of power is accepted and refined to a high level of sophistication. In academe, where the public stakes are considerably less, the power game often is conducted with such subtlety that it is scarcely observable to the outsider (but usually understood and often even relished by players on the inside).

Since much of curriculum making is a political activity, the various players usually prefer to keep their options open. Consequently, one resorts to power when one has it or when the prospects for all parties playing by the rules of inquiry appear remote. Almost inevitably, then, the decisions seen as most important are made by resorting to power. And so, the rhetoric of empowering teachers leaves methods of teaching to teachers but may say nothing about their freedoms with respect to the selection of content and materials.

Keeping the options open with respect to ground rules creates a difficult dilemma for educators. Given the degree to which many people would prefer the good old days of a relatively passive, feminized occupation of teaching, an aggressive political stance on the part of teachers' organizations is understandable. Becoming a strong player in political arenas and then playing by the rules of power there appears necessary. Past experience with the low profile of educational issues, particularly the well-being of teachers, provides a strong incentive for warming up the arenas with respect to such matters. But when these arenas get hot and really big political players get into the action, things can get out of control. Suddenly, politicians are into decisions educators thought were theirs to make.

In the opening paragraph of his account of sixty-five years of struggle over the curriculum, Kliebard nicely set the stage for much that is central to the chapters of the present volume:

> At the heart of America's educational system in the nine-teenth century was the teacher. It was the teacher, ill-trained, harassed and underpaid, often immature, who was expected to embody the standard virtues and community values and, at the same time, to mete out stern discipline to the unruly and dull-witted. But, by the 1890s, nineteenth-century society with its reliance on the face-to-face community was clearly in decline, and with the recognition of social change came a radically altered vision of the role of schooling. As cities grew, the schools were no longer the direct instruments of a visible and unified community. Rather, they became an ever-more critical mediating institution between the family and a puzzling and impersonal social order, an institution through which the norms and ways of surviving in the new industrial society would be conveyed. Traditional family life was not only in decline; even when it remained stable, it was no longer deemed sufficient to initiate the young into a complex and techno-logical world.[11]

Persons and groups outside of the family and beyond schools believe it is their responsibility to make decisions about what is necessary to this institution. And some educators, particularly in designated administrative and leadership roles, and virtually all of their organizations, believe this to be their responsibility, too. Should they participate in some sociopolitical arenas but not others? Dare they risk endorsement of a president aspiring to be "the education president?" Should they participate only when it is clear that the rules of the game are to be those only of inquiry?

These and other questions, some quite subtle, confront educators, the answers to which will significantly impact on the well-being of both educators and education: Are there any levels and domains of curriculum where educators and their organizations may play, with impunity and good conscience, according to an epistemology and with the tools of power? The significance of this question rises out of the nature of education itself.

The American Medical Association has demonstrated its interest in protecting the people from quackery. But many people perceive some actions to be self-serving and not in the best interests of the polity. The willingness to grant high-standing and professional perquisites to the medical profession has waxed and waned to some degree according to the nature of these perceptions.

The National Education Association has been much less successful, in spite of substantial effort, in convincing the American people of its interest in protecting them against weak teachers. Governors instrumental in requiring tests of basic literacy for teachers have enjoyed a generally positive public response. The fact that objections come primarily from educators and their professional organizations did nothing to enhance the public status of either.

But teachers generally have been seen as on the side of children, their parents, the public interest, and, indeed, as angels when they are perceived to be solely concerned about the student-teacher relationship and how best to support it. Significantly, although less noted by the public, educators usually express at this level of learning and teaching a much more comprehensive view of education than is promoted by legislated, bureaucratic mandates. When Mary Futrell, past president of the National Education Association, publicly endorsed—as she frequently did—the Mastery In Learning Project described by McClure, many people perceived a possible joining of self-interests and the public weal.[12] And when Albert Shanker, president of the American Federation of Teachers, dares to question that sacred cow, namely, a highly paid professional teacher in every class and low student enrollment in each, by proposing a team of variously prepared and paid individuals, as well as extensive use of technology, the cups of many critics runneth over.[13]

What is the message here? It is not that every school district in the United States should adopt the Mastery In Learning Project. Indeed, policy makers and bureaucrats endeavoring to mandate it would be hard-pressed to define what to adopt. Similarly, the message is not to immediately restructure all schools according to the Shanker proposal. There are at least two different messages. First, the nature of the educational process is such that every decision must be kept open at the point of its making and addressed with the blend of expertise most appropriate to its nature—as Schubert so clearly recommends. The process of inquiry to be brought into play is complex and must be learned. It is corrupted by infusion of the rules and tools of power. Second, the self-interests inevitably brought into play in the inescapably political domains of decision making must not run counter to the perceived common weal.[14] In the long run the teaching occupation will achieve professional status according to the public perception that it is aligned with the best interests of the polity and only secondarily interested in "getting its share."

Toward an Appropriate Professional Role

This is a demanding message. The epistemology of the first set of perceptions pertains to both caring and technical and professional expertise. That of the second is moral and ethical. The claims of educators and the teaching profession for a larger role in curriculum decision making must rest heavily on their demonstrated under-standing and consistent adherence to these epistemologies. Other-wise, their views are reduced to unauthorized opinions entitled to no more than a place on the voters' ballot. Providing technical and professional competence and moral and ethical awareness and sensitivity is the responsibility of teacher education programs. The road to the necessary programs is long and hard.

The notion that "my opinion is as good as yours" and therefore should count equally in the final adding up is powerfully embedded in educational matters and is not likely to go away—even when teaching has gone a long way down the professional road. Consequently, educators must not deceive themselves into envisioning a day when others will defer to their perceived educational expertise in all but a few curriculum decisions. Those well-meaning policy makers referred to earlier are not seeking to give their assumed responsibility to educators, even when they seek their counsel. At best, they want to make better decisions; at worst, they want to silence opposition through cooptation. Very few operate out of a conceptual frame encompassing a wide array of educational problems and decisions. And even fewer have addressed issues from the perspective of a consistent educational philosophy. The educator seeking intellectual engagement involving substantial epistemic confluence soon will become frustrated and strident, and perhaps will resort to a power game—and probably lose (if not the immediate battle, certainly the war).

Consequently, educators must join with all relevant decision makers in an educational process through which the gap between the professional and the informed remains modest but at a high level of educational understanding. The goal is the educational good health of the community, not personal or professional aggrandizement. Slowly at first and then with growing interest, the medical profession moved from almost sole preoccupation with treatment to health maintenance and individual self-improvement through better nutrition, exercise, and the like. The health of the community benefited accordingly, and the medical profession continues to evolve in significant ways.

But anything resembling a condescending professional attitude toward the educational understandings of policy makers and other lay citizens who make educational decisions would be out of line in more ways than in impropriety. Data gathered in a representative sample of colleges and universities gave my colleagues and me little encouragement regarding the depth and breadth of knowledge and skills being acquired by future teachers.[15] We found in these teacher education programs no common lexicon, no taxonomy of educational decisions to be confronted, and no reasonably common series of cases (as in education for the law) requiring certain knowledge and intellectual processes for their analyses. Our efforts to initiate dialogue regarding the many moral issues surrounding compulsory schooling in a political democracy were of little avail. Most students (and some faculty members) lacked the necessary language and background of previous thought.

Disappointing though these findings most certainly are, they should not be surprising. For a hundred years, various commissions directed to the reform of teacher education have advocated increased requirements in the academic disciplines, often at the expense of courses geared to the contextual and pedagogical demands of teaching.[16] Many states sharply restrict the credit hours to be directed to professional education, to the point where training (and I use the word deliberately) is focused almost exclusively on didactics and classroom management. Nearly all of the cells in Klein's curriculum framework go unaddressed. Given this neglect of professional education at the initial levels of preparation, perhaps I should be tolerant of some obvious shortcomings I find in experienced educators enrolled in graduate studies. Few are able to conceptualize at some consistent level of generality the major components of schooling about which decisions are made (by omission or commission), let alone think through what each of their own decisions and justification for these decisions would be.

But I, too, am an educator and therefore must apply to myself the criteria I am applying in setting professional expectations for other educators. If I regard Klein's array of arenas and decisions as a reasonable conceptualization of those in which I will become a player, then I must be willing to abide by consistent, defensible canons of inquiry in all and not just some.

Consequently, I must refrain from aligning with the concept of finite power and resorting to the tools of power struggles when such appears to advance my self-interests—or even when I believe that I am both right and committed to the public weal. Similarly, when a power struggle is unlikely to be in my self-interests, I must refrain from insisting that the next set of issues must be addressed according to the canons of inquiry.

Further, I must hold to the rules of inquiry even when I know that many of the other players will seek to shift from one set of rules to another according to which set appears most likely to advance their self-interests. Of course, if I make no claims to professionalism and membership in a profession, then any perceived shiftiness in my behavior besmirches only my character and in no way detracts from the professional status of the teaching occupation.

Is it reasonable even to contemplate the general exercise of the implied self-discipline among all players in curriculum decision making? Is it reasonable to contemplate the general exercise of such self-discipline on the part of educators and the teaching profession? If the answer to these questions is sought simply by extrapolating from the past and present into the future, the answer is a somber "no."

Perhaps I shall be perceived as naively quaint in suggesting that educators, individually and collectively, would be better off today—especially in regard to the respect they so crave—had they demonstrated consistently in curriculum arenas those canons of inquiry they extoll for the young. To do so effectively requires more than self-discipline. It requires a breadth and depth of understanding far beyond that possessed today by tens of thousands of educators—the professional level of understanding extolled by Griffin.

Those who claim a niche in the teaching profession as curriculum specialists and theorists can contribute to the development of this professionalism in several ways. First, the proposition can be advanced, at least as a working hypothesis, that there are no curriculum decisions exclusively for professionals to make, just as there are none lying exclusively in the domains of policy makers and public officials. There are multiple participants even at the instructional level, where teachers must have extensive but not exclusive authority. The range of participants widens at levels more remote from learning and teaching.

Second, there is a particularly distinctive contribution to make in seeking to illuminate the nature of curriculum decisions and the processes to be brought to bear in making them wisely. This book joins a growing body of useful literature.

Third, partnerships must be formed between schools and universities as advocated in Griffin's chapter. Although the concept of such is growing in popularity, few exemplars exist; getting them will not be easy.[17] The professional schools of education of the future will be those clearly joined with school settings.

If these things and more are done well, it will become increasingly clear that the rules and tools of power are dysfunctional in curriculum matters—even in sociopolitical arenas. Those who employ them ultimately will be viewed as undesirable participants in the educational enterprise. Using only processes of inquiry to solve the problems and resolve the issues raised in the following chapters is at once in the self-interests of educators and the common good.

Notes

1. Calvin M. Frazier, The 1980's: States assume educational leadership, in John I. Goodlad (ed.), *The ecology of school renewal* (pp. 113–114). Eighty-sixth Yearbook of the National Society for the Study of Education, Part I. Chicago: University of Chicago Press, 1987.

2. The National Commission on Excellence in Education. *A nation at risk.* Washington, DC: U.S. Government Printing Office, 1983.

3. Carnegie Forum on Education and the Economy, *A nation prepared: Teachers for the 21st century.* New York: Carnegie Corporation, 1986. The Holmes Group, *Tomorrow's teachers.* East Lansing, MI: The Holmes Group, 1986.

4. Thomas J. Peters and Robert H. Waterman, Jr., *In search of excellence: Lessons from America's best-run companies.* New York: Warner Books, 1982. Robert H. Waterman, Jr., *The renewal factor: How the best get and keep the competitive edge.* New York: Bantam Books, 1987.

5. Ernest R. House, *The politics of educational innovation.* Berkeley, CA: McCutchan, 1974.

6. Arthur E. Wise, *Legislated learning.* Berkeley, CA: University of California Press, 1979.

7. Linda M. McNeil, *Contradictions of control: School structure and school knowledge.* New York: Routledge, 1988.

8. John I. Goodlad (with Maurice N. Richter, Jr.), *The development of a conceptual system for dealing with problems of curriculum and instruction.* Los Angeles, CA: Institute for Development of Educational Activities and University of California 1966; and John I. Goodlad, M. Frances Klein, and Kenneth A. Tye, The domains of curriculum and their study, in John I. Goodlad and Associates, *Curriculum inquiry,* pp. 43–76. New York: McGraw-Hill, 1979.

9. Ralph W. Tyler, *Basic principles of curriculum and instruction.* Chicago: University of Chicago Press, 1950.

10. Herbert M. Kliebard, *The struggle for the American curriculum, 1893–1958.*

11. Ibid, p. 1
Boston: Routledge and Kegan Paul, 1986.

12. Lynn Olson, National Education Association State Coordinators Launch Search for Learning Laboratories, *Education Week* (February 15, 1989).

13. Albert Shanker, Testimony before the California Commission on the Teaching Profession in San Francisco, California, April 15, 1985.

14. For a more comprehensive discussion of this necessary blending of interests, see John I. Goodlad and Pamela Keating (eds.), *Access to knowledge: An agenda for our nation's schools.* New York: The College Board, 1990.

15. John I. Goodlad, *Teachers for Our Nation's Schools.* San Francisco, CA: Jossey-Bass, 1990.

16. Zhixin Su, *Teacher education reform in the United States (1890-1986).* Occasional Paper No. 3, Center for Educational Renewal. Seattle: College of Education, University of Washington, 1986.

17. For a discussion of these difficulties, see Kenneth A. Sirotnik and John I. Goodlad (eds.), *School-university partnerships in action: Concepts, cases, and concerns.* New York: Teachers College, Columbia University, 1988; and Calvin M. Frazier, *An analysis of a social experiment: School-university partnerships in 1988.* Occasional Paper No. 6, Center for Educational Renewal. Seattle: College of Education, University of Washington, 1988.

A Conceptual Framework for Curriculum Decision Making

M. Frances Klein

Who makes curriculum decisions is a fundamental question which has not been answered very consistently or successfully over the years. Whoever makes the decisions has great power over what students will and will not learn at school. Some people covet this power, work to become involved in making curriculum decisions, and diligently assert and protect their right to make them. Others would like to have an influence but not be directly responsible for making most curriculum decisions. Yet others believe curriculum decisions should be made exclusively by educators because they are trained professionals, and they want little or no involvement of the parents or lay publics. These attempts to define and protect curriculum decision-making rights and privileges have produced competing participants and decisions which are not always consistent or in the best interests of teachers and students. The topic of curriculum decision making clearly needs further study and clarification.

For years curriculum scholars have documented the various individuals and groups involved in making curriculum decisions, and through their studies, have consistently identified some of the same individuals and groups in various roles because of their obvious participation: federal and state governmental agencies, state departments of education, publishers, district and county offices of education, principals, and teachers (see, for example, Eisner, 1985; Goodlad & Associates, 1979; Hass, 1987). It is very evident that these participants have had considerable, although varying responsibilities to plan, implement, and evaluate the curricula that are offered to students and that students experience. Less often identified by scholars, however, are religious groups, courts, businesses and other lay leaders in the community, prestigious scholars at colleges and universities in the subject areas of the school curriculum, the students themselves, and political groups of all kinds who organize to influence curriculum decisions.

At first glance, curriculum decision making appears to be a maze of influence and power, struggles won by some and lost by others. Yet some participants consistently get to make decisions more often, and make the more important decisions. A conceptual framework would provide greater clarity in the analysis and study of these efforts, particularly one which provides for a systematic way of examining who makes what types of curriculum decisions. This chapter discusses one such conceptual framework for curriculum decision making—it suggests the array of individuals and groups who potentially could be involved, and it identifies the types of decisions which must be made. It is an adaptation of two other models: one used to collect, organize, and interpret the curriculum data in "A Study of Schooling" (Goodlad, Klein, & Tye, 1979) and one developed by Goodlad (1979). The framework is two-dimensional, and includes seven possible levels of curriculum decision making and nine essential curriculum elements about which decisions must be made.

Levels of Decision Making

The conceptual framework identifies seven general levels at which decisions may be made about any given curriculum: academic, societal, formal, institutional, instructional, operational, and experiential. They are shown as the different rows in Figure 2.1. Although Figure 2.1 may visually suggest that the levels are hierarchical, they are ordered only in the degree of remoteness or closeness to the student, the major focus of curriculum decisions. Participants at one level do not necessarily make any better, wiser, or more important decisions than others, according to the framework, nor should one level necessarily prevail over any other until a particular value screen about what *ought* to occur is brought to bear on the framework. Thus, the framework is descriptive, not prescriptive. It only allows one to describe what *could* be the pattern of curriculum decision making and to analyze what a current pattern *is*. It does not identify what *should* occur; only a particular value or belief about curriculum decision making can do that.

Figure 2.1
Curriculum Framework for Decision Making

Curriculum Elements

Perspectives or Levels of Decision Making	Goals, Objectives, Purposes	Content	Materials, Resources	Activities	Teaching Strategies	Evaluation	Grouping	Time	Space
Academic									
Societal									
Formal									
Institutional									
Instructional									
Operational									
Experiential									

Academic Level

The level most remote from the students is the academic level, which is defined as the scholars at colleges and universities. It includes professors in the academic disciplines which typically form the bases of the school curriculum—the scientists, mathematicians, historians, and English professors, for example—and also includes scholars in other important fields, such as education, sociology, philosophy, and psychology. Other participants at this level of decision making include learned societies such as the American Association for the Advancement of Science and the National Endowment for the Humanities.

The scholars and members of learned societies often make pronouncements about what ought to be included in the school curriculum and attempt to influence other aspects of curriculum development according to their particular expertise, interests, and beliefs. From them come recommendations about new pedagogical approaches and content for the curriculum, such as the new math; substantial revisions of science content; new subject areas to be added to the curriculum, such as astronomy or sociology; an emphasis on the structure of the disciplines; more inquiry or discovery learning; or more time devoted in the curriculum to their areas of interest. These proposals were called for during the curriculum reform era of the 1960s, when scholars were particularly active in curriculum development (Goodlad, von Steophasius & Klein, 1966). More recently, proposals at this level have been made about revisions for cultural literacy (Hirsch, 1987) and the arts (Eisner, 1987/1988). Such proposals are made by scholars or learned societies in the interests of their particular area of expertise and their expectations about what the curriculum ought to do for a student regarding their disciplines.

The scholars are usually very visible and prestigious participants in curriculum development who make persuasive arguments in support of the decisions they believe ought to be made. Participants at the academic level of curriculum are usually on the forefront of change; their recommendations are generally received with considerable interest; and sometimes they generate extensive debate by all those interested in the school curriculum.

Societal Level

The next level of closeness to the student is the societal level. It includes all those in the lay communities and organized groups who are not directly involved in the day-to-day education of students but who would like to influence the curriculum, such as governmental agencies, businesses, and industries, who are very concerned about what students learn since it is they who provide the jobs and careers for the graduates. They have a vested interest in what students learn in the curriculum while they are at school. It also includes political and civic groups such as the Daughters of the American Revolution, the American Legion, People for the American Way, the John Birch Society, the Heritage Foundation, Congress, and state legislatures.

Environmental groups such as the Sierra Club and the Audubon Society are sometimes very actively involved in getting their interests into the curriculum, even to the extent of developing and distributing their own materials for teachers to use. Some religious groups have exercised significant influence over specific aspects of the curriculum in recent years regarding reading and literature materials, topics in the science curriculum, and sex education programs. Parents, too, make their wishes and expectations known through national and state organizations such as the Parent Teacher Association and through their contacts with the local school. Participants at this level of decision making such as those identified above are distinguished from other levels by being nonprofessional educators but possible participants who have a genuine concern about the school curriculum.

Formal Level

The next level of decision making, the formal level, is similar to the academic and societal levels in that it, too, is beyond the level of the individual school, where changes in the curriculum must ultimately take place. It is unique, however, since it is composed of all those individuals and groups who have some type of direct responsibility for or influence on curricula but who are not located at a specific school. It includes federal, state, county, and local education agencies; textbook publishers; and educational organizations and unions such as the American Educational Research Association, the Association of Supervision and Curriculum Development, the National Education Association, and the American Federation of Teachers, along with their regional and local chapters. These groups have considerable responsibility for or influence on the curriculum of the schools.

Institutional Level

The fourth level of remoteness from the student for making curriculum decisions is the institutional level. It is defined as those participants in curriculum development at the individual school site. Curriculum planning which occurs collectively by the faculty or by groups of teachers for more than one classroom at the individual school site are examples of the institutional level. It includes decisions by school administrators and by those who make curriculum decisions in department meetings, grade level meetings, and general faculty meetings.

Research indicates that the school or the institutional level of decision making is a very important but neglected one (see, for example, McLaughlin & Marsh, 1978; Griffin, 1979). Significant curriculum development does not often occur at the institutional level, even though it is an essential focus for school improvement.

Instructional Level

The next closest level to the student is the instructional level, and it is composed of what the classroom teacher decides in his or her planning about curriculum. Since all the decisions made at the levels discussed above are generally channeled through the teacher in order to be made operative, the instructional level of decision making is especially influential.

Teachers have options regarding prior curriculum decisions: they may decide to implement what is desired at higher levels of remoteness from the student; they may modify, sometimes in very significant ways, what others want in the curriculum; or they may completely ignore decisions which have been made at other levels. The instructional level is such a powerful one that many efforts and resources are expended to prepare teachers through publications and staff development programs to meet the expectations and to implement the decisions made at other levels. These efforts emphasize that teachers are very fundamental curriculum decision makers who often determine what decisions actually get implemented.

At the same time, teachers have their own firm beliefs regarding what the curriculum ought to be for their own specific group of students. They are not only reactive in relation to the expectations and decisions of others; they are also proactive in that some teachers develop their own curricula and work to implement their own beliefs and values about how best to educate their students. The instructional level includes all of the teacher's decisions about curriculum for his or her classroom.

Operational Level

The operational level of decision making is the interactive curriculum (Jackson, 1966), the curriculum which unfolds in the classroom as a result of the engagement of the teacher and students with the content (however it is defined) to be learned. It is evident from research findings that even though a teacher may desire and intend to implement a certain curriculum planned at any of the other levels in his or her classroom, the circumstances of the classroom and the inter-action of the teacher and students may create quite a different curriculum. For example, many teachers report that they teach higher-order thinking skills and problem solving even though the types of homework they assign, the questions they ask in discussions, the texts they use, and the tests they give usually emphasize the lowest levels of cognition (see, for example, Goodlad, 1984; Klein, 1989). The skill of the teacher in making and executing curriculum decisions, the complexities of classroom living and learning, the internal disruptions in the teaching-learning processes, the presence or absence of learning materials, the frequent external interruptions to classroom processes, and the dynamics of student-teacher interactions may operate to create a very different curriculum from what the teacher and others might have planned. Because of the pace and complexity of the operational level of curriculum decision making, it must be docu-mented by someone other than the classroom teacher, someone who is skilled in classroom observation techniques. The teacher is too involved in making on-the-spot decisions which characterize the operational curriculum to be able to describe or analyze it compre-hensively.

Experiential Level

The experiential level of curriculum decision making is composed of the students—the individual expectations, perceptions, and achieve-ments of each student. Students often have a unique view and expectation for what the curriculum is and ought to be in their classrooms, and few deny that students ultimately are the real decision makers. Any student decides what his or her curriculum will be by the degree of interest expressed and willingness to participate in it. Students, for example, may be willing to participate quite extensively and enthusiastically in the curriculum planned for them, choose to engage in it only partially or half-heartedly, try to influence the teacher to change the existing curriculum, or refuse to be involved in the curriculum offered to them. Ultimately, each student makes the decision about the degree to which he or she will engage in the curriculum, and thus molds and shapes a unique experiential curriculum.

Interaction of Decision Makers

These seven levels represent the array of possible curriculum decision makers. Each level is defined by unique characteristics of the participants that differentiate it from others, but the categories are not necessarily mutually exclusive. A participant may operate within several of the levels at any given time. For example, a teacher may try to influence decisions at the societal level as a parent, participate in curriculum development at the formal level as a member of a state committee writing a new curriculum framework, become a member of a grade level planning team at the institutional level, and function as a primary decision maker at the instructional level.

Within the processes of curriculum development at any given time, participants from several levels are likely to be active and expect to have their interests and positions reflected. The amount of political power the participants have will help determine whose ideas about curriculum will become the most influential and dominant and thus will potentially find their way into classroom practice.

Little research has been conducted on what participants at each level expect their influence to be, what it actually is, or the types of curriculum decisions they would like to influence or make. It is likely, for example, that teachers would be expected to play an important role in curriculum development; however, it is possible that they may not want a primary role until they have developed some of the necessary skills and are provided with the needed time and resources for curriculum development. Similarly, many states are now making fundamental curriculum decisions about goals and objectives, content, textbooks, and evaluation (tests) but continue to assert that the local school district has flexibility in determining how the curriculum will be taught. How much flexibility local districts or teachers actually have when so much is prescribed for them needs to be carefully investigated.

Little research also has been conducted on the roles the participants in each of these levels think they ought to, and actually do, play. It is clear to most curriculum leaders, however, that some participants at each of the seven levels are usually active and seriously engaged in trying to affect decisions made about curriculum, although perhaps in making different types of decisions. Thus, it is important that not only must decisions made by participants at one level about a curriculum be coordinated with decisions made at other levels, but that the types of curriculum decisions made also must be compatible. The different types of curriculum decisions which must be made form the second dimension of the conceptual framework.

Types of Curriculum Decisions

Participants within and across the various decision-making levels may try to influence different elements of curriculum planning and implementation, or they may try to influence a decision about the same element. Some at the academic level, for example, may want to update the content of subjects in which they are experts; others may want to increase the time students spend in studying their disciplines; and yet others may want to create new resources for teachers or improve the materials used to teach their particular areas of interest. Each of these is an important but significantly different curriculum decision.

The various participants may also want to influence the same curriculum decision. At the societal level, for example, new content may be proposed by groups from business and industry as new social forces impact us—knowledge about computers, for example. Other groups such as religious organizations may want to revise or delete content which is objectionable and add content which they want taught to the curriculum. Parents want to make sure that their children learn the kinds of skills and knowledge which will ensure opportunities for success in future schooling and in the work force. These possibilities represent some potential conflict in what content ultimately finds its way into the curriculum and are likely to be resolved in a political arena as well as in an educational one. (See the discussion of this context in Chapter 1.)

Often participants at the various levels make fundamental decisions about curriculum with little thought as to their compatibility and coordination. Within a curriculum area such as reading, for example, curriculum guides are perennially published at the formal level by state departments of education and districts to remind teachers that certain goals, content, textbooks, or teaching strategies are expected to have a prominent place in the curriculum. Teachers consistently search for new and better materials to use with their students, reflect their own interests as they choose specific content for their instructional curricula, make continuous adjustments in the time they spend on the development of basic skills, and may often rearrange their classroom space to fit different kinds of teaching strategies and classroom interactions. At the same time, students decide whether they will do their homework, become involved in classroom activities, or take tests seriously. Unless these decisions are made in supportive and compatible ways, it is highly unlikely that the reading curriculum offered to and experienced by the students will be as powerful and effective as it could be.

All of these examples represent fundamental decisions, but some are different types or elements of curriculum decision making. The conceptual framework identifies nine different elements about which decisions must be made: goals, objectives, and purposes; content; materials and resources; activities; teaching strategies; evaluation; grouping; time; and space. These are shown as the columns in Figure 2.1.

Goals, Objectives, and Purposes

Goals, objectives, and *purposes* for teaching and learning are defined as anticipated or actual outcomes of learning—the results which are expected and worked for or which come about as a result of engaging in purposeful learning activities. All three terms are included because they refer to specific but different phenomena. Goals are broad general outcomes hoped for as a result of student engagement in the curriculum. They reflect rather imprecise expectations and are often stated by most participants in curriculum development. Objectives are carefully defined behavioral outcomes for students which are carefully formulated, taught, and evaluated; they are usually used by professional educators when precision is needed in communicating about and evaluating the explicit outcomes of teaching and learning.

Purposes suggests that the results of learning may not be known until after a meaningful activity has been engaged in by the student. Eisner (1985) suggests this distinction with his concept of 'expressive outcomes'. Students may engage in a rich, meaningful, purposeful, expressive activity, such as a field trip to a museum, which leads to different learning results among the students. The different purposes students have for learning, such as in reading literature, also lead to outcomes that are likely to be very unique for each student and not predictable in advance. *Purposes* suggests that learning is deliberate on the part of the student but less controlled and predictable by the teacher than *goals* and *objectives*. All three terms are important in curriculum decision making because they reflect careful deliberation about the possible but very different results of a curriculum.

Content

Content is defined as those facts, ideas, concepts, processes, generalizations, attitudes, beliefs, and skills with which students interact as they experience a curriculum. Content is that which teachers and students consider as they engage in the processes of teaching and learning. Content may be derived from humankind's carefully organized and preserved wisdom as represented by the disciplines, or it may be from less traditionally organized fields of human endeavor, such as driver education, human safety, home economics, or physical education.

Materials and Resources

Materials and resources are the objects, places, and people used to facilitate the learning process—the tools used with students to assist learning. They include resource people, textbooks, magazines, computers and software, videotapes, records, games, realia, and the fixtures of schooling such as chalk, chalkboards, crayons, scissors, and special laboratories with their essential equipment. They include the resources typically found in instructional materials centers, school and community libraries, museums, the workplace, and the talents of parents and other community volunteers in the school. Resources should not be thought of as those restricted to the school setting; they also include those available but not often used in the community at large.

Activities

Activities are what students do as they engage in the process of learning. They may be the more passive ones of listening to the teacher and reading books, or they may be more overt and active, such as working at the computer or acting out a story or historical episode. Activities cover a wide range, such as recitation, listening, reading, writing, role-playing, reflecting upon an idea, taking field trips, doing homework, watching television, working at a computer, playing games, and acting out sociodramas and simulations.

Teaching Strategies

Teaching strategies are defined as the role taken by a teacher or a teaching device such as a computer, programmed text, or television set in order to facilitate learning. A teacher (or the teaching source such as a computer) can play a variety of roles. He, she, or it, for example, can question the students, present information, reinforce the responses given, or redirect what the student might do in the learning process. These techniques define the concept of teaching strategies. Teaching strategies are represented by the different models of teaching as identified by Joyce and Weil (1980) and by the more generic behaviors of diagnosis, prescription, presentation, monitoring, and feedback (Denham & Lieberman, 1980).

Although the distinction becomes somewhat blurred in practice, there is a conceptual difference between the activities the students engage in and what the teacher does within the activity to foster learning. For example, within a single activity such as a discussion, the teacher may be a monitor who reinforces right answers and corrects wrong ones to help students develop knowledge of the subject, or the teacher may primarily question the comments of students in order to develop their critical thinking abilities. The teacher's role is not necessarily defined through the use of any particular activity for learning. It must be clarified by making a separate decision about what the teacher is to do within the activity in relation to the learning outcome. Different teaching strategies will help students develop different learning outcomes as they engage in classroom activities.

Evaluation

Evaluation is the procedures for determining what students are learning or have learned. It may include testing, observing, grading papers, analyzing student products, conducting interviews, or administering surveys, and it can occur at any point in time—prior to teaching, ongoing during teaching, at certain points in the curriculum (such as a weekly test or pop quiz), or at the conclusion of the curriculum. These processes can be conducted by any person charged with the responsibility for evaluating student learning, such as administrators, consultants, researchers, teachers, or students themselves. Program evaluation is differentiated from student evaluation in that the former often has a broader focus but may include data about student learning as well as data about personnel, financial resources, and school organization, for example.

Grouping

Grouping is the processes and results of determining the sizes and compositions of clusters of students formed to facilitate the learning process. It includes grouping students in particular grades or classes at the institutional level of decision making and intraclass grouping based on ability levels, interests, self-selection, sociological clusters, and other such bases used by teachers and students in determining the groups in which students will learn. Classroom groupings range from total group instruction to individual students learning on their own, including groups of any intermediate size. Groups may be formally organized by the teacher or students, or they may evolve informally as the learning tasks change and student interests shift.

Time

Time is also a fundamental curriculum element about which decisions must be made. It may be allocated on a formal or informal basis, and decisions regarding it often occur at several levels: sometimes through legislative decrees at the societal level, such as by the number of hours for driver education, which may be established as a basis for funding; by state department or district mandates at the formal level, as when the minimum length of the physical education period is determined; at the institutional or school site level, as when the length of class periods is decided; at the instructional level by each teacher as he or she plans how time will be allocated in the classroom; and particularly by the students at the experiential level as they decide how long to remain involved in the processes of learning.

Time as a resource for learning has received considerable attention in recent research. The use of time by teachers and students has been shown to be a powerful determinant of what is learned (see, for example, Denham & Lieberman, 1980).

Space

Space is the design and use of school and classroom physical dimensions. The allocation and use of space can have a significant influence on the curriculum. Inadequate or inflexible space can impede the success of any curriculum. If space is not available for science laboratories or if a classroom is overly crowded, the type of curriculum desired may be impossible to implement. It does little good to plan curricula if the type of space needed is not available. by contrast, sufficient, flexible space can be a great asset to teachers and students as the curriculum is planned and implemented.

Interaction of Variables

These nine variables are the fundamental curriculum elements about which decisions must be made. It is possible, and even very probable, that decisions will be made at several of the different levels that affect any one of these curriculum elements for a particular curriculum. For example, in math, scholars (academic level) may advocate problem-solving capabilities as a goal, and business and industry leaders (societal level) as well as state and district consultants (formal level) also may concur that this is a desirable goal. Textbook developers (formal level) and teachers (instructional level), however, may make decisions which counteract this goal. Textbooks may have very little emphasis on problem solving as a goal or as objectives in their lessons, and teachers may feel inadequately prepared to teach problem solving or be concerned about the increased amount of time required to teach problem solving at the expense of other subjects in the curriculum. These multiple decisions affecting a goal of the curriculum emphasize the complexity of curriculum decision making and the importance of a comprehensive framework for analyzing and improving curriculum development such as the one presented in this chapter.

The Framework in Perspective

The curriculum decision-making framework is both comprehensive and complex. The preceding discussion identified the broad parameters of curriculum decision making and defined the important elements of curriculum. The framework needs further discussion, however, in three broader aspects: the assumptions inherent within it, its potential role in curriculum development, and the complexity of the concept of curriculum.

Inherent Assumptions

Although the framework is not prescriptive, it is, at the same time, not value free. By identifying the possible participants in and the elements of curriculum decision making, it assumes that curriculum development is a rational, complex, deliberate, preplanned process, at least in part. There are some curriculum scholars who reject aspects of this position and who choose to view curriculum from very different perspectives. For example, some scholars would not accept the elements of this conceptual framework as defining the parameters of decision making, and they view curriculum development as a much more spontaneous, emergent process which should be restricted primarily to the teacher and students in the classroom (see, for example, Pinar, 1988; Sears & Marshall, 1990). The framework discussed here presents a particular view of curriculum based upon a value position which affected how it was formulated. If this value position about curriculum is adopted, only then can the framework be seen as descriptive, not prescriptive of who ought to make curriculum decisions.

The framework also reflects an assumption regarding the traditional view of curriculum versus instruction. A dominant role has been assigned to curriculum in relation to instruction, and the separation of curriculum and instruction as different spheres of activity has been rejected as an artificial and simplistic dichotomy. Curriculum is viewed broadly as a cluster of nine elements, with instruction identified as only one element of curriculum decision making—that of teaching strategies. What form of instruction—that is, which teaching strategy to use, is an important decision; but in this framework it is not given the prominence that some scholars place upon it when they make a clear conceptual differentiation between curriculum as the what of schooling and teaching as the how (see, for example, Beauchamp, 1981).

Within this framework, the what and how are considered as distinctly different but highly interactive elements—the what of the curriculum (content) can be dramatically affected by decisions about the how (teaching strategies), and decisions about each of these two elements can be made at various levels. For example, carefully planned science content which is taught by the lecture method will have a different impact on students than the same content taught through an inquiry or discovery method. Such interaction of the different curriculum elements is recognized in this framework.

The framework further suggests that as curriculum decisions are made at one level, they can be mediated by decisions made at other levels, thus changing the curriculum as other decisions are made. The teacher at the instructional level, for example, can significantly alter what the state or district expects the curriculum to be. Instruction or the teaching strategy chosen by the teacher can have a significant impact on the content the state may expect to be taught, the way the adopted textbooks (materials) are used, the willingness of students to engage in learning activities, and the time allocation recommended by the district. Thus, to assume that once the curriculum, the what, is planned at one or more levels, that then the processes of instruction, the how, will implement the curriculum in the classroom is a simplistic and even a distorted view of what often occurs when curriculum decisions are analyzed using the framework. A decision about instruction cannot be made without significant interaction with decisions about the other curriculum elements.

Based upon this framework, then, it would be exceedingly naive to believe that a single act such as the adoption of a new textbook by the state, the curriculum decision of selecting materials at the formal level of decision making, would be powerful enough to have much of an impact on the education of students. Yet this is a strategy often adopted to effect curriculum change. The framework identifies the many other decisions which are likely to significantly affect that single, though very important, decision. Other participants in the process may lobby to get different kinds of curriculum materials and resources into the curriculum; thus, the decision of what materials will be used also becomes one of political power and influence.

The impact of the textbook may also be mediated by decisions made about the general goals desired by the parents and the specific objectives communicated by district administrators, the content considered important enough by the teacher to be "covered" or omitted from the text, how time is apportioned by the teacher to other subjects, the content included in state or district tests, and concepts which need to be supplemented beyond what is included in the text before students can learn what is expected. A single decision such as adopting a text at the state level, then, can be altered in very significant ways by what participants at other levels want as materials and resources and by the decisions made regarding the other curriculum elements. This illustration suggests the complexity of curriculum decision making, which is only beginning to be recognized and documented, and the importance of a comprehensive framework which points out the possibilities.

Role in Curriculum Development

It was noted earlier that the framework is descriptive, not prescriptive. It does not prescribe who *should* make what type of decision; that can be done only by imposing a particular value position on the framework. It is, however, an important tool for curriculum developers. The framework allows one to identify what decisions must be made and to analyze those which are actually made at the various levels about the different curriculum elements. Thus, gaps and duplications in curriculum decision making can be identified more easily. It will also assist curriculum developers in sorting out the confusion and contradiction in decision making by identifying incompatible decisions made at the different levels about the same curriculum element and incompatible decisions made about the different elements within any given curriculum. The framework can serve as an important tool by making curriculum decision making more informed and consistent, thus increasing the potential impact of the curriculum upon the students.

Complexity of Curriculum

Another aspect about curriculum decision making which the framework clearly demonstrates is the complexity of curriculum. The two-dimensional figure indicates that not only are there seven levels and nine curriculum elements involved in decision making, but these two dimensions intersect to account for the myriad decisions which ultimately might be made by someone, regardless of who else might be making the decision. (Some of the cells in the framework could, of course, be null; that is, decisions might not be made at a particular level about an element of curriculum.) The framework, through its complexity, more realistically reflects the political context of schooling, the complexities of teaching and learning, classroom interactions and dynamics, and the processes of planning and implementing curricula.

The framework will undoubtedly be criticized for being unnecessarily complex. To reduce it to fewer dimensions, however, is to less adequately reflect the realities and complexities of the processes of curriculum development. There are many individuals and groups who are and who would like to be involved in curriculum development. There are basic decisions which must be made by someone or some group if a curriculum is to be offered to and experienced by students. No apologies should be necessary that the array of decisions and how they get made are very complex phenomena. Those who expect to study and understand the field of curriculum, work within its parameters, and develop better curricula in order to improve the schooling of young people must deal with the complexity. Unless the complex dimensions of curriculum decision making are recognized, simplistic solutions will continue to be developed to resolve the difficult problems in curriculum development.

This framework reflects one view of and a particular value position about curriculum. There is no general agreement by curriculum scholars as to what a framework for curriculum decision making should include. Some suggest fewer curriculum elements—such as only goals, content, activities, and evaluation—in combination with the view that instruction should be considered as a different, but related realm of decision making (see, for example, Beauchamp, 1981). Others insist that only the teachers at the instructional level should have responsibility for global curriculum development without articulating the specific decisions to be made, and yet others believe the curriculum should evolve only through the cooperative planning of teachers and students with all other participants eliminated from the decision-making process. Whatever conceptual framework is used, it is of tremendous importance to curriculum leaders because it will identify the tasks to be engaged in and will suggest some possible answers to the fundamental issue of who makes what type of curriculum decision. The making of curriculum decisions must be systematically studied and clarified so that the curriculum will be more likely to have the desired impact upon the students—the major purpose of schooling.

References

Beauchamp, George A. (1981). *Curriculum theory.* Itasca, IL: F. E. Peacock.

Denham, Carolyn, & Lieberman, Ann (Eds.). (1980). *Time to learn.* Washington, DC: National Institute of Education.

Eisner, Elliot W. (1985). *The educational imagination: On the design and evaluation of school programs.* New York: Macmillan.

———. (December 1987/January 1988). On discipline-based art education: A conversation with Elliot Eisner. *Educational Leadership,* 45 (4), 6–9.

Goodlad, John I. (1979). Coda: The conceptual system for curriculum revisited. Chapter 14 in John I. Goodlad & Associates, *Curriculum inquiry: The study of curriculum practice,* (pp. 343–364). New York: McGraw-Hill.

———. (1984). *A place called school.* New York, McGraw-Hill.

Goodlad, John I., and Associates. (1979). *Curriculum inquiry: The study of curriculum practice.* New York: McGraw-Hill.

Goodlad, John, I., Klein, M. Frances, & Tye, Kenneth A. (1979). "The domains of curriculum and their study. Chapter 2 in John I. Goodlad & Associates, *Curriculum inquiry: The study of curriculum practice* (pp. 43–76). New York: McGraw-Hill.

Goodlad, John I., von Stoephasius, Renata & Klein, Frances. (1966). *The changing school curriculum*. New York: Fund for the Advancement of Education.

Griffin, Gary A. (1979). Levels of curricular decision-making. Chapter 3 in John I. Goodlad & Associates, *Curriculum inquiry: The study of curriculum practice* (pp. 77–100). New York: McGraw-Hill.

Hass, Glenn. (1987). Who should plan the curriculum? In Section 6 of Glenn Haas (Ed.), *Curriculum planning: A new approach* (5th ed.). Boston: Allyn & Bacon.

Hirsch, E. D., Jr. (1987). *Cultural literacy: What every American needs to know.* Boston: Houghton Mifflin.

Jackson, Phillip W. (1966). The way teaching is. Chapter 1 in *The way teaching is: Report of the seminar on teaching* (pp. 7–27). Washington, DC: Association for Supervision and Curriculum Development and National Education Association.

Joyce, Bruce, & Weil, Marsha. (1980). *Models of teaching* (2nd ed.). Englewood Cliffs, NJ: Prentice-Hall.

Klein, M. Frances. (1989). *Elementary school curriculum reform: Creating your own agenda.* New York: Teachers College Press.

McLaughlin, Milbrey W., & Marsh, David D. (1978). Staff development and school change. *Teachers College Record, 80* (1), 69–94.

Pinar, William F. (Ed.). (1988). *Contemporary curriculum discourses.* Scottsdale, AZ: Gorsuch Scarisbrick.

Sears, James T., & Marshall, J. Dan (Eds.). (1990). *Teaching and thinking about curriculum: Empowering educators through curriculum studies.* New York: Teachers College Press.

3 Two Visions of Federalism and the Control of the Curriculum

Tyll van Geel

There already exists an extensive literature on the history of the federal government's influence upon the curriculum of the public schools. Much of this literature deals with such milestones as the National Defense Education Act (1958), and federal legislation directed toward improving the schooling of the educationally disadvantaged and the handicapped (Schaffarzick & Sykes, 1979; Thomas, 1983; Broudy, 1983; Graham, 1984; Kaestle & Smith, 1982). Especially controversial and a topic of many other articles has been federal involvement in the funding of new curriculum materials and the federal government's policy regarding the education of non-English-speaking pupils (Orfield, 1986; Short, 1983; Ravitch, 1985; Atkin, 1981; Sykes, 1981; Gideonse, 1981; Goodlad, 1981). In addition, the federal judiciary's decisions affecting the curriculum are reviewed in several books (van Geel, 1976, 1987).

Beyond recounting the history of the federal government's involvement in curriculum formation and regulation, commentators have examined the implications of this ever-changeable federal role for the future of local control of education and the assurance of equal educational opportunity nationwide (Kirst, 1988; Knapp, 1987; Chubb, 1985; Doyle & Finn, 1984; van Geel, 1976). Some analysts have looked at the impact of these federal efforts on the programs delivered to pupils at the local level (Knapp, Stearns, Turnbull, David, & Peterson, 1983;

Elmore & McLaughlin, 1983; Kuriloff & Kirp, 1979; Weatherly, 1979; Dolbeare & Hammond, 1971; Way, 1968; Johnson, 1967). Different writers have examined the question of what *ought* to be the federal role in shaping the curriculum, and, in doing so, have announced their own version of what that role should be (Hawley, 1983; Goodlad, 1981; Minter, 1982; Finn, 1982). And an occasional commentator has reviewed educational policy as an aspect of the larger debate between liberals and conservatives (Pincus, 1985; Lee, 1965).

I want to carry further the latter analysis by demonstrating that the struggle over the federal role in education has involved a conflict between two different visions regarding federalism and the role of public schools in a democracy. The first two sections of this chapter describe the two visions, traditionalism and liberalism, using nonlegal materials. The next section briefly discusses federal legislation affecting the curriculum. The next two sections provide evidence that the liberal and traditionalist visions have shaped the legal debate among the justices on the Supreme Court over constitutional law and education. The summary and conclusion section provides a final scorecard and looks at the implications of the conflict between the visions for several issues that have not yet been resolved by the Supreme Court.

Before proceeding I want to say a word about the notion of 'a vision'. A vision, as the term is used here, is neither a wholly internally coherent theory about how society in fact works nor a wholly internally consistent set of prescriptions about how it should work. It does embody an intuitive sense of what people are like and how they behave, a diagnosis of the ills or the body politic mixed with some general prescriptions about what morally ought to be. A vision combines a hope of what ought to be with fears of what could happen and an explanation of, for example, the causes of tyranny and totalitarianism. A vision combines a sense of how social life works with a set of values which enables citizens to determine what they prefer and do not prefer. Visions serve as the starting point for the formulation of more specific social agendas and actions (Sowell, 1987).

Finally, three notes of caution. First, the representatives of traditionalism and liberalism I cite may not embrace all the tenets of the vision with which I associate them, yet each contribute to a piece of the vision. My descriptions of the visions are deliberately drawn in broad strokes. Second, the nuances in the positions of those who share the same vision are not explored. Finally, proponents of the same vision do not always agree on the same policy prescriptions. These visions are sufficiently general that even adherents of the same vision might reach different conclusions on a specific problem.

The Traditionalist Vision

The traditionalist vision is a subtle and complex affair, but for these purposes I will summarize the vision as embodying the following central propositions:

- Primary control of education should rest with the states and not the federal government (Berger, 1987, p. 74).
- State and local government have a special function to "shape" the children, to bring them into the local community, to socialize and inculcate them in community values, and to make them good citizens (Tussman, 1977; Bell, 1976).
- Moral rules are religiously based, externally imposed restrictions to which people need to acquiesce and conform, and children need to be instructed to conform to these rules (Nash, 1976).
- Traditional authority structures within and without the family deserve respect and support and instruction, and these structures should be part of the curriculum (Harbour, 1982).
- The traditional values of Western civilization should remain at the heart of the educational program (Rossiter, 1962).
- The free market system, laissez-faire capitalism, is both the traditional and the preferable economic system (Rossiter, 1962; Nash, 1976; Hayek, 1960).
- As George Will has written, government has a special duty to "'strengthen the social bonds that are weakened by the dynamism of a restless society of atomized individuals preoccupied with getting and gaining'" (Pincus, 1985, p. 335).

Twin fears seem to animate the traditionalists—a fear of chaos and simultaneously a fear of tyranny. The fear of tyranny pushes the traditionalists toward a federal system of government composed of strong state governments and a federal government with limited powers (Bailyn, 1967; Rossiter, 1962; Wood, 1969; Harbour, 1982). The states are to serve as a buffer against the threat of the central government armed with the material and men that could be turned from national defense to internal dictatorship (Nisbet, 1986; Harbour, 1982). The traditionalist seeks to limit the federal government's power and to enhance the power of those branches of government nearest to the people.

The fear of chaos pushes the traditionalists to embrace tradition, to a passing on of community values as a means of checking or restraining the potentially extreme behavior of people (Harbour, 1982; Will, 1983; Nisbet, 1986). It is the local community, operating within a loose federal system, which is to serve as the "keeper of the flame." Furthermore, because humans have a "dark side" as well as a capacity to learn habits to bring out their better selves, certain educational efforts are needed in order to make the child safe for the society (Rossiter, 1953). Traditionalists argue that for a democratic society to survive, its citizens must be imbued with "virtue," that is, the disposition to sacrifice self-interest for the public good. Popularly elected leaders can only be effective if the populace is public-spirited, self-sacrificing, and moral (Wood, 1969; Koch, 1943; Rossiter, 1962; Nash, 1976).

The effects of free market capitalism on society point to an additional function for education. The free market is itself so dynamic and disrespectful of tradition and habits that it poses a threat to social stability built upon bonds rooted in a continuing culture. It is in part the threat of the destructive effects of the market that lead traditionalists to place great weight upon education as the way to shore up and defend tradition (Will, 1983). Education is to serve as a kind of immunization; education is the way to walk a middle road between an authoritarian regime which uses coercion to force people to be virtuous and the potential chaos of unabated individualism and materialism.

In summary, I will list some of the more specific educational policies traditionalists have embraced. Traditionalists see only a limited education role for the federal government. Whereas some traditionalists would eliminate federal funding of education altogether, others would limit Congress to the role of writing small checks to support local government (Bell, 1972; Nash, 1976). And because Congress should not control local education, these monies should be accompanied by a minimum of regulations. Thus, traditionalists favor the use of the block grant to distribute federal funds (Clark & Amiot, 1983; Pincus, 1985).

The traditionalists would keep the federal courts out of the business of running the public schools' curriculum. The local public school should be left free to instruct pupils in local community values and traditions (Crawford, 1980). Specifically, traditionalists expect the curriculum to stress the importance of the values of Western civilization and to reject critiques of Western civilization as ethnocentrist, racist, sexist, and classridden (Bloom, 1987; Kneller, 1984). They are critical of public schooling today for systematically denying the religious heritage of the country (Vitz, 1986). Traditionalists would have students learn the basic skills, read the "great books," study the lives of great "men," and study classical and modern literature (Kneller, 1984). In one version of a traditionalist world, local public education would dominate the scene free from any significant congressional or federal judicial controls which interfere with the primary function of these schools, the inculcation of students in the values of the community.

As for private education, which could operate to subvert local community values, the traditionalist takes a somewhat contradictory position. Today many traditionalists favor tuition tax credits for parents of children attending private schools (Abram, 1986; Pincus, 1985), but there are traditionalists who fear private schools because they are also capable of providing a radical or alien education (Will, 1983). So strong has been the feeling toward these schools that in the past serious efforts have been made to close them down (Tyack, James, & Benavot, 1987). Nevertheless, most traditionalists today would defend the existence of private schools, especially the private religious school.

The Liberal Vision

The liberal vision is even more complex than the traditionalist vision. Any brief summary will be inadequate; neverthless, here are some of the central propositions of this vision:

- A strong central government is essential to the realization of the liberal agenda (Cohen, 1982; Wood, 1969).
- Individual liberty is to be protected, especially individual conscience, and freedom of expression (Richards, 1986; Berlin, 1969). Government should be neutral regarding different conceptions of lifestyles (Rawls, 1971).
- At the same time government must simultaneously pursue social equality and equality of opportunity (Rae, 1981; Rawls, 1971; Okun, 1975; Girvetz, 1963). Specifically, government should seek to ameliorate and limit the effects of a free market economy on social inequalities.
- The rules, principles, and laws by which people are to live are the product of human rational thought and choice and not merely of externally imposed directives (Spragens, 1976; Rawls, 1971; Benn & Peters, 1959).
- A peaceful society is best achieved by the sovereign people creating a democratic government limited in its powers in certain ways and dedicated to the concept of the rule of law (Spragens, 1976; Wood, 1969; Benn & Peters, 1959).

Education in a society governed by such principles ends up pursuing a particular set of goals by certain means. Although education in the liberal society should introduce students to the basic premises and values of that society, and thus to this extent be an agent of socialization, it must also not neglect the twin values of liberty and equality. Education should expand opportunities, open all roles to potentially all students, liberate the mind, and prepare the student to be an active participant in a robust, wide-open democratic and secular political process (Goodlad, 1984). Education should liberate the child, expand the child's horizons, and assure the child of his or her right to an open future (Feinberg, 1980). Education should also ameliorate the social inequalities that can arise from the market system (Tollett, 1982; Ryan, 1982).

There is in liberalism, however, a significant confusion over whether the effort should be directed toward equality of opportunity or equality of result, and this confusion has led to considerable conflict among liberals (Bell, 1972). But the liberal approach to education is tied not just to the values of liberty and equality, but also to the basic assumptions of the liberal vision itself. The liberal vision assumes that society is created through the voluntary agreement of autonomous individuals. Keeping faith with the notion of the autonomous person shapes the liberal view of education. Thus, the liberal wants education to be capable of evaluating competing conceptions of the good life and good society (Gutmann, 1987). And the liberal finds yet more confirmation of the wisdom of this kind of education program in his or her view of what it means to engage in moral reasoning. To engage in moral reasoning is to get beyond "dogmatic adherence to prevalent ideological fashions, as well as from the dictates of authority," and to "ask for justifications, whether the issue be factual or practical" (Scheffler, 1973, pp. 142, 143). Liberals recognize the risk that liberally educated students may ultimately reject the values of liberty and equality. But the liberal notes that this kind of risk is taken in scientific education, and "it is central to the democratic commitment which holds social policies to be continually open to free and public review. In sum, rationality liberates, but there is no liberty without risk" (Scheffler, 1973, p. 143). There is, thus, at least one obvious tension within liberalism—the tension between belief in the autonomous individual and the belief in the correctness of the principles of liberty and equality.

To sum up, I will simply list some of the specific educational policies liberals embrace. Liberals project an active role for the federal government in reforming education so that education better serves the principle of equality (Hawley, 1983; Tollett, 1982). Thus, liberals support efforts to equalize educational expenditures, to provide compensatory education, to provide special education for the handicapped, and to provide special instruction to non-English-speaking pupils (Educational Visions Seminar, 1985; National Education Association, 1985). At the same time, liberals oppose the uncritical inculcation of pupils in traditional values, especially religious inculcation (Gutmann, 1987). Liberals would use federal power, especially judicial power, to ensure that the public school program does not impose a pall of orthodoxy. In one ideal of a liberal education, schools would introduce students to the fundamental principles of a democratic system of government while also encouraging them to think for themselves, to become critical thinkers.

Finally, like the traditionalists, liberals also tend to be wary of private schooling, but for different reasons. Some liberals see in private schools a threat to social equality (Walzer, 1983; Levin, 1982). Others are concerned that private education will be used to inculcate the child in the parents' preferred way of life, thereby frustrating the child's right to an open future. Yet others are concerned that private education will be used to instruct students in doctrines inimical to liberalism, such as racism and sexism (Feinberg, 1980; Gutmann, 1987). Yet the liberal's commitment to freedom and liberty, especially freedom of expression, makes it difficult to argue in support of legislation to control the curriculum of private schools (van Geel, 1989).

Traditionalism, Liberalism, and Federal Legislation

The traditionlist commitment to a limited central government means that adherents of this view have not as actively pursued extensive congressional control of the curriculum of local public schools as have the liberals. Nevertheless, there have been several pieces of federal legislation that reflect traditionalist ideology. In 1984 conservatives succeeded in amending a federal law providing grants for magnet schools which declared that these funds could not be used "for courses of instruction the substance of which is secular humanism" (Education for Economic Security Act, 1985). After some controversy raised by liberal groups, however, in 1985 Congress dropped this limitation. Another provision, popularly termed the Hatch Amendment after its sponsor, conservative senator Orrin Hatch, requires that all instructional materials used in connection with research or experimentation program be available for inspection by parents of the children involved in the program [20 U.S.C.A. §1232 (h) (Cum. Sup. 1985)]. And again, during the Reagan presidency, Congress adopted the Equal Access Act, which requires federally assisted schools under certain carefully defined circumstances to permit even student religious groups to use school facilities for prayers and Bible discussions (Equal Access Act, 1985). All in all, however, traditionalists have not been successful in using federal power to shape the curriculum of the schools by either excluding "secular humanism" or by introducing religion into the school curriculum. This is underscored by the notable failure of traditionalists to obtain a constitutional amendment permitting voluntary prayer in the public schools.

In contrast, the liberal agenda has met with more success. So familiar is the story of liberal legislation on behalf of racial miniorities, the educationally disadvantaged, the handicapped, and non-English-speaking students that I will not repeat it here (see materials cited in first paragraph of this chapter). I will limit my comments to observing that this body of legislation was at a minimum designed to overcome various kinds of barriers standing in the way of a child obtaining an education capable of making him or her an equal competitor in the race for social and economic well-being. Some proponents of these reform efforts hoped that with federal prodding and federal financial assistance schools would be able to mount educational programs that would end the correlation between, on the one hand, race and social class, and, on the other hand, educational achievement. Although the precise effects of the legislation may remain in some dispute, it does seem to be clear that, for whatever reasons, the liberal legislative efforts have not in fact achieved their loftiest goals; research does not consistently support the conclusion that increased expenditures affect student achievement (Hanushek, 1986). The strong positive correlation between family background and a child's educational achievement remains basically unaffected, posing a severe problem for the liberal vision. Although liberals may deplore the continuing effect of family upon student achievement, the liberal ideology counsels against taking any such drastic steps as removing the most deprived children from the immediate control of their parents. Liberal policy is caught on the horns of a dilemma that pits respect for the autonomy of the family against the desire to eliminate social and economic inequalities (Fishkin, 1983).

Traditionalism in the Supreme Court

The themes of traditionalism flow through many of the Supreme Court's opinions, especially the opinions of Chief Justice William Rehnquist. I begin with traditionalist thinking on federalism as reflected in a specific case, *Board of Education v. Rowley* (1982). There are many places to begin the story of this case, but for the purpose of this discussion its start is to be found in the adoption by Congress of the Education for All Handicapped Children Act of 1975 (EAHCA), a statute authorizing federal grants in support of educational programs for handicapped pupils. This is a complicated law, but in essence it requires, as a condition of receiving federal assistance, that handicapped children be given a "free appropriate public education" (FAPE), which includes "special education" and "related services" (van Geel, 1987). The definitions of "special education" and in "related services" provided in the statute itself and the implementing regulations, are sufficiently general as to open the door to disputes about their meaning and what they require local public school districts to do. The specific dispute which the Supreme Court chose to hear in *Rowley* involved the education of Amy Rowley, who suffered from a significant hearing impairment *(Board of Education v. Rowley*, 1982). It was the position of the school district that Amy, an intelligent and highly motivated youngster, could be adequately educated in a regular classroom if she were provided with a special hearing aid, a tutor who would meet with her on a daily basis, and three hours per week of speech therapy. In fact, under such an arrangement Amy received above-average grades. Nevertheless, Amy's parents argued that Amy could do even better if she were assigned a full-time, in-class interpreter. The dispute went to court, and the federal district court concluded that the EAHCA meant that a handicapped child must be given something *more* than an "adequate" program. EAHCA required, said the court, that Amy be provided a program that would give her an opportunity to achieve her full potential in the same way that such an opportunity is given to nonhandicapped pupils. The second circuit affirmed, but the Supreme Court by a five to four vote reversed the decision. Justice (now Chief Justice) Rehnquist wrote the majority opinion.

Justice Rehnquist is a strong proponent of maintaining the sovereign independence of the states, and hence is wary of extending federal power over state policy. It was with these perspectives on our federal system of government that Justice Rehnquist approached the writing of the majority opinion in *Rowley*. He rejected the conclusion of the federal district and appellate courts that Congress imposed on the states the condition that the education program maximize the potential of handicapped pupils. Justice Rehnquist said he could not find the sort of clear, unambiguous statement of condition necessary to impose such a far-reaching, expensive, and difficult-to-implement requirement on the states. But Justice Rehnquist did find a clear expression of intent from Congress to require that the federally assisted program be one which was "reasonably calculated to enable the child to receive educational benefits" *(Board of Education v. Rowley*, 1982, p. 207). Thus, if, for example, a child like Amy were being educated in a regular classroom, he or she would be deemed to be getting such a program if he or she achieved passing grades and advanced from grade to grade. In this case, Justice Rehnquist concluded, Amy did receive a FAPE.

Sensitivity to federal efforts to reshape curriculum requirements has surfaced in another case dealing with the handicapped, *Southeastern Community College v. Davis* (1979). With surprising unanimity the Court said a federal statue prohibiting discrimination against the handicapped did not require a nursing program to revise its curriculum substantially in order to accommodate a seriously impaired student. The opinion was also significant in that it specifically noted the absence of a "clear expression of legislative intent" to impose an affirmative action obligation on all recipients of federal funds (*Southeastern Community College v. Davis*, 1979, p. 411, n. 11). Thus, even if the Department of Health, Education and Welfare interpreted that statute to impose such an obligation, and even if the Court typically defers to an agency's interpretation of the statute under which it operates, the Court refused to defer in this case.

I turn now from traditionalist views of federalism to traditionalist views of the school curriculum, and specifically the traditionalist view on religion in the classroom. In a variety of cases Chief Justice Rehnquist has attempted to persuade the Court, without success, that the establishment clause of the First Amendment (the clause prohibits "the establishment of religion," U.S. Constitution, First Amendment) was intended to permit government to aid all religions evenhandedly so long as a single state religion was not established (*Wallace v. Jaffree*, 1985). Thus, in *Wallace* Chief Justice Rehnquist argued in his dissenting opinion for the constitutionality of a state statute that authorized opening the school day with a one-minute period of silence "for meditation or voluntary prayer." Similarly, when a majority of the Court said that Kentucky could not require public schools to post copies of the Ten Commandments on the school's walls, Rehnquist dissented (*Stone v. Graham*, 1980). He argued that the history and culture of the country are saturated with religion and that Kentucky only sought to make students aware of this "by demonstrating the secular impact of the Ten Commandments" (*Stone v. Graham*, 1980, p. 46).

The Chief Justice has not been alone in supporting voluntary prayer in the public schools. Justice Stewart dissented from the Supreme Court's famous decisions barring school-opening ceremonies involving a *voluntary* prayer and Bible-reading exercise (*Abington School District v. Schemmp*, 1963; *Engle v. Vitale*, 1962). According to Justice Stewart, not to permit students to join in a voluntary prayer session "is to deny them the opportunity of sharing in the spiritual heritage of our Nation." The prayer sessions merely recognized and followed "the deeply entrenched and highly cherished spiritual traditions of our Nation" (*Engle v. Vitale*, 1962, p. 445). And Justice Scalia has written in a dissenting opinion that public school officials should be permitted to shape the public school curriculum in light of religious concerns so long as there was also a "genuine secular purpose" behind their decision (*Edwards v. Aguillard*, 1987). In that case a majority struck down a Louisiana statute which required any school which taught either evolution or creationism to teach the other theory. The one "religious" victory traditionlist thinking achieved was in *Zorach v. Clauson* (1952), in which a majority of the Court upheld a modest released time program. Specifically, the arrangement approved by the Court involved excusing students from the public school to permit them to attend religious studies programs several times a week held at religious centers near the public school. Those students who did not wish to be excused remained in the public school until the end of the regular school day. The Court held that this arrangement merely involved an accommodation of the public school's schedule, as when the school breaks for Christmas, and not public support for religion.

The traditionalists's interest in inculcating pupils with tradition extends beyond religion to include socialization in patriotism through the study of U.S. history, the celebration of presidents' birthdays, and participation in such ceremonies as the flag salute ceremony. Twice the Supreme Court reviewed the constitutionality of compelling students to participate in a flag salute ceremony. In the first case, *Minersville v. Gobitis* (1940), a majority upheld the use of the compulsory flag saltue. Justice Frankfurter, writing for the majority, sang the praises of such traditional values as the "family relation" and the "authority and independence which give dignity to parenthood" (*Minersville School District v. Gobitis*, 1940, p. 600). The flag salute, he said, was an "educational process for inculcating those almost unconscious feelings which bind men together in a comprehending loyalty" (*Minersville v. Gobitis*, 1940, p. 600). He provided further support for his argument with the claim that the "binding tie of cohesive sentiment" was the "ultimate foundation of a free society" (*Minersville v. Gobitis*, 1940, p. 596). However, a few years later, with new appointments to the Court and several justices having changed their minds, the Court once again took up the issue and reversed itself (*West Virginia State Board of Education v. Barnette*, 1943). Thus, to this day traditionalism does not command a majority on the Court on this issue.

More recently the Supreme Court took up the question of the constitutionality of a school board's removal of some dozen books from its own school libraries, books which the school board had character-ized as "anti-American, anti-Christian, anti-Sem[i]tic, and just plain filthy" (*Board of Education v. Pico*, 1982, p. 857). A majority of five remanded the case back to the lower court for further proceedings. Justice Rehnquist was one of four dissenters who argued that the Constitution should not be interpreted to limit the discretion of school boards to control the content of the school library and school program. He based this conclusion on his view that it was the function of the public schools to inculcate pupils in the "social values" of the community.

Although the traditionalist argument did not prevail in *Pico,* it did prevail in two recent freedom of speech cases. In the first case a student named Fraser nominated another student for a school office with a speech filled with sexual innuendo (*Bethel School District No. 403 v. Fraser,* 1986). Fraser was given a short suspension. In the second case a school principal confiscated an issue of the school's newspaper because he was concerned that several of the student-authorized articles invaded the privacy of certain students and parents (*Hazelwood School District v. Kuhlmeier,* 1988). The student editors of the paper complained that their First Amendment right of freedom of speech had been violated. In both cases a majority of the Court upheld the action of school officials on the grounds that the assembly and school paper were school-sponsored activities, and that the school boards were authorized to pursue their agenda of inculcating in pupils certain values and norms of civilized behavior. In fact, so concerned have some justices been with ensuring that students are inculcated in traditional American values that a majority approved of a New York State rule that denied certification as a public school teacher to any person who was not a citizen of the United States unless that person manifested an intent to apply for citizenship (*Ambach v. Norwick,* 1979). Teachers who did not intend to become citizens simply could not be trusted to teach the correct values.

To conclude, evidence of the traditionalist vision is to be found in a wide range of majority and dissenting opinions. Traditionalist justices seek to limit congressional control of the school program; they refuse to use their own federal judicial power to control that same program; and they voice support of an instructional program in traditional values. Though these positions have only from time to time been held by a majority on the Court, traditionalism will continue to be reflected on the Court so long as people such as President Richard Nixon and Ronald Reagan are elected to the presidency, who are themselves traditionalists and who appoint people to the Court like Chief Justice Rehnquist (Simon, 1973).

Liberalism in the Supreme Court

The struggle between traditionalism and liberalism is well reflected in the conflict between Chief Justice Rehnquist's majority opinion in *Board of Education v. Rowley* (1982) and the concurring and dissenting opinions of that same case. Though Chief Justice Rehnquist was cautious in interpreting the demands Congress had made of states and localities, the concurring and dissenting opinions interpreted EAHCA more boldly, reflecting the liberal position in support of strong congressional authority to control education (van Geel, 1987, pp. 71–72). Justice Blackmun took the position in his concurring opinion that the critical issue was whether Amy's educational program, "viewed as a whole offered her an opportunity to understand and participate in the classroom that was substantially equal to that given her nonhandicapped classmates" (*Board of Education v. Rowley*, 1982, p. 211). He said this equivalent opportunity standard was preferable both to Rehnquist's standard, which focused too much on a handicapped child achieving a certain level of educational outcome (promotion from one grade to the next), and to the lower court's standard, which focused too much on the issue of whether or not Amy received a particular form of service, that is, an interpreter. Nevertheless, Justice Blackmun concurred in the conclusion of the majority that Amy had received a "free appropriate education" because her program, viewed as a whole, did give her an opportunity substantially equivalent to that offered her classmates.

Justice White, writing for himself and Justices Brennan and Marshall, went even further in his dissenting opinion. In his view EAHCA was "intended to eliminate the effects of the handicap, at least to the extent that the child will be given an equal opportunity to learn if that is reasonably possible" (*Board of Education v. Rowley*, 1982, p. 215). Thus these justices concluded that, since providing a sign language interpreter would have effectively equalized Amy's opportunity to learn, one should have been provided.

Though liberalism did not prevail in *Rowley*, it did prevail in the one case the Court took for review dealing with non-English-speaking students (*Lau v. Nichols*, 1974). The majority deferred to the federal agency's interpretation of the statute it was authorized to enforce. The statute in question was Title VI of the Civil Rights Act of 1964, which in simple terms prohibited discrimination on the basis of race in federally assisted programs. The Department of Health, Education and Welfare interpreted this provision to mean that any program which had a discriminatory effect, even an unintended effect, was prohibited. And, more specifically, the department elaborated by saying that the law meant that, if a child cannot effectively participate in an education program because the child cannot speak English, then school districts "must take affirmative steps to rectify the language deficiency in order to open its instructional program to these students" (*Lau v. Nichols*, 1974, p. 568). The Supreme Court's virtually unanimous opinion deferred to this interpretation of the statute. The Court simply noted that when school districts take federal money they contractually agree to comply with Title VI and the regulations issued pursuant to the Title. "The federal government has power to fix terms on which its money allocations to the States shall be dispersed" (*Lau v. Nichols*, 1974, p. 569). It was this decision which opened the door to vigorous federal involvement in reshaping the educational program offered non-English-speaking pupils (van Geel, 1987). This opinion appeared prior to Chief Justice Rehnquist's successful effort to get a majority of the Court to accept his clear expression doctrine. Federal assistance and regulation of the education of educational disadvantaged pupils has, of course, also been extensive (Graham, 1984).

Liberal victories were also realized in the Court cases barring prayer and bible-reading ceremonies in the public schools (*Abington School District v. Schemmp*, 1963; *Engle v. Vitale*, 1962). On the basis of these decisions the Supreme Court and lower federal courts have blocked the teaching of "scientific creationism" (*Edwards v. Aguillard*, 1987; *McLean v. Arkansas Board of Education*, 1982). Second in importance was the Court's decision striking down a Louisiana statute which required any school which taught either evolution or creationism to teach the other theory (*Edwards v. Aguillard*, 1987). In another case a majority prohibited schools from posting even donated copies of the Ten Commandments (*Stone v. Graham*, 1980). A liberal majority struck down a religiously motivated law making it a crime to teach the theory of evolution. Thus the liberals sent a message that they will not tolerate religiously motivated decisions to exclude from the curriculum topics and perspectives offensive to the prevailing religious group (*Epperson v. Arkansas*, 1968). In brief, the liberal vision sees the school curriculum as something other than an instrument of inculcation. Justice Stevens forcefully articulated this vision when he wrote, "Just as the right to speak and the right to refrain from speaking are complementary components of a broader concept of individual freedom of mind, so also the individual's freedom to choose his own creed is the counterpart of his right to refrain from accepting the creed established by the majority... [T]he Court has unambiguously concluded that the individual freedom of conscience protected by the First Amendment embraces the right to select any religious faith or none at all... [R]eligious beliefs worthy of respect are the product of free and voluntary choice by the faithful" (*Wallace v. Jaffree*, 1985, pp. 52–53). These Supreme Court opinions have set the stage for continued battles over scientific creationism, secular humanism, and religion in the schools—a topic I shall return to at the end of the chapter.

When Justice Stevens wrote his comments in the *Jaffree* case, he might well have been thinking of the Court's second flag salute opinion, which struck down the compulsory flag salute as a violation of a student's right of freedom of speech (*West Virginia State Board of Education v. Barnette*, 1943). In that opinion Justice Jackson wrote that, because boards of education were educating the young for citizenship, the Court has "reason for scrupulous protection of Constitutional freedoms of the individual, if we are not to strangle the free mind at its source and teach youth to discount important principles of our government as mere platitudes" (*West Virginia State Board of Education v. Barnette*, 1943, p. 637). Some forty years later Justice Brennan observed that

> the right to receive ideas follows ineluctably from the *sender's* First Amendment right to send them. [More] importantly, the right to receive ideas is a necessary predicate to the *recipient's* meaningful exercise of his own rights of speech, press and political freedom. [Students] too are beneficiaries of this principle. [In] sum, just as access to ideas makes it possible for citizens generally to exercise their rights of free speech and press in a meaningful manner, such access prepares students for active and effective participation in the pluralistic, often contentious society in which they will soon be adult members. (*Board of Education v. Pico*, 1982, p. 867–868)

Based on this premise, Justice Brennan, writing for a plurality of the Court, ordered that the case be sent back to the lower court to determine if the Island Trees school board had removed books from the library because the board intended by its removal to deny students access to ideas with which the board disagreed.

The liberal plurality's effort to keep the library collection broadly inclusive of a wide range of opinions and perspectives parallels the Court's efforts in other cases. In upholding the right of a student to wear a black armband to school in protest against the Vietnam War so long as this did not cause material and substantial disruption of the school, Justice Fortas said that the other students were not "closed-circuit recipients of only that which the State chooses to communicate" (*Tinker v. Des Moines Independent Community School District*, 1969, p. 511). He said that the classroom was peculiarly the "'marketplace of ideas.'" Quoting from yet another opinion, Justice Fortas added that "'the Nation's future depends upon leaders trained through wide exposure to that robust exchange of ideas which discovers truth 'out of a multitude of tongues, [rather] than through any kind of authoritative selection'" (*Tinker v. Des Moines Independent Community School District*, 1969, p. 512). Support of such an open and frank dialogue between school and student was further underscored by liberal Justice Brennan in a dissenting opinion. In it he approved subversion of the school's efforts to inculcate a belief in capitalism by endorsing the right of a student to respond to a teacher's questions by retorting that socialism is good (*Hazelwood School District v. Kuhlmeier,* 1988).

Before concluding this section of the chapter, I want to briefly note that many other liberal Supreme Court opinions have had an indirect effect upon the shaping of the school curriculum. Most important have been the Court's opinions on race, which have made clear that students should not be placed in inferior programs or closed out of superior programs merely because they belong to a racial minority (*Brown v. Board of Education,* 1954). This prohibition has led the lower courts to closely examine tracking and ability grouping systems for racial bias and to skeptically examine for racial or cultural bias I.Q. and other testing requirements which have an adverse impact on minority students (van Geel, 1987). The Supreme Court has even said that curricular reform may be ordered with a view to undoing the harm caused by the segregation *(Milliken v. Bradley,* 1977). The Court has not to date taken a case in which it was asked to review curriculum materials for their racial, cultural, or gender bias.

Liberal justices have also successfully resisted the exclusion of certain people as teachers on the grounds that merely because they were Communists they would subvert the official curriculum (*Keyishian v. Board of Regents,* 1967). The liberal wing of the Court did not prevail, however, in the case mentioned earlier in which the Court upheld the denial of teacher certification to certain people who had not applied for citizenship (*Ambach v. Norwick,* 1979).

To conclude, liberal justices have voiced their support of a school program which avoids the imposition of traditional orthodoxies but instead exposes pupils to a wide range of viewpoints and perspectives. Behind these prescriptions has been a desire to protect the student as a person who is free to choose his or her own creed, his or her own beliefs. So important have these values been to the liberals that they have brushed aside Justice Frankfurter's warning that the Court should not become "the school board for the country" (*Minersville School District v. Gobitis,* 1940).

Summary and Conclusions

How does the scorecard now stand after a long struggle between judicial proponents of traditionalism and liberalism? On the issue of *congressional* power to reshape local education, the liberals have won the day. In one way or another the liberals' support of expansive congressional authority has been triumphant. Since the late 1930s doctrines which support a strong central government in all matters including education have prevailed in the court (van Geel, 1987). Chief Justice Rehnquist has won a majority to his side only on the proposition that Congress may only exercise its control of state and local government through clear and unambiguous conditional grants. This proposition had a notable success in the *Rowley* decision; beyond that, the liberal agenda of not standing in the way of an expanding congressional authority has prevailed. And there are no signs to indicate that Chief Justice Rehnquist will in the next years be able to swing a majority of of the Court to his vision of a more sharply limited federal government.

I turn now to the Court's own power to control the curriculum. The liberals have gone a long way in using the Court's power to shape the school's curriculum. They have banned school-sponsored religious activities as well as the compulsory flag salute. Liberalism managed to command only a plurality of the Court in the book removal case. Liberals have placed constitutional doctrine in opposition to traditional attitudes toward women, minorities, and non-English-speaking pupils. Thus the liberal vision of the school as a marketplace of ideas, as a place where the free mind of all students may grow, has been partially embodied in legal doctrine. (Whether the schools in fact fulfill the ideas expressed in the liberal opinions of the Supreme Court is a different question, which I do not address here.)

These vistories have been accompanied by continuing controversy. Some traditionalists have raised the serious charge that liberal policies have forced the schools to teach and promote the "religion" of secular humanism. Secular humanism is a complex and sophisticated perspective that, in brief, strongly opposes traditional religions and supports the idea that humans are rational truth seekers who can themselves, without devine intervention, forge meaningful moral rules (Kurtz, 1983, 1988). But this charge that the liberals rest their decisions upon and promote secular humanism is incorrect for a number of reasons. Most importantly, liberals have been careful to voice legal objection to any form of an *explicitly* antireligious education program or any program created with the motive of attacking religion. In fact, liberal justices would permit the objective study of religion and the Bible. Yet aspects of the secular humanist perspective may enter the classroom. Schools constitutionally may teach that values are a matter of personal choice; they may teach critical thinking; and they may teach the value and importance of scientific knowledge. Of course, important parts of the traditionalist agenda may also be taught in the schools, such as the traditional values of patriotism and the duty to obey the law. Nevertheless, the tension between the two visions continues, for reasons too complex to explore here.

The possibility of a resurgence of traditionalism is evidenced in the recent victories won by that perspective in the two recent student free speech cases. And Chief Justice Rehnquist continues to hammer away at the liberal position on religion and the schools. But at this point I want to draw an important distinction. Some school-religion cases involve the school board itself seeking to introduce religion into the schools, as when, for example, the school board seeks to have the school open with a prayer. Other cases involve the board resisting the religiously based demands of parents and students. A traditionalist Court may very well react differently to these two types of cases.

In the first type of case the sequence of events is as follows: the school board adopts a policy, for example, of requiring the school day to open with a moment of silence. Then somebody challenges this policy as unconstitutional, and the judiciary is asked to stop the board from continuing its policy. Thus, in this type of case the Court is asked to prevent the board from doing something the board *wants to do*. A traditionalist such as the chief justice would find this kind of case a relatively easy problem. *Not* to order the board to stop would serve two traditionalist concerns: it would limit the authority of one branch of the federal government, namely, the Supreme Court, and by not acting the Court would let go forward an educational policy the traditionalist favors. In fact, the Chief Justice today could probably persuade a majority of the Court to not interfere with a school board's desire to open the day with a moment of silence so long as school officials did not expressly suggest that students ought to pray (*Wallace v. Jaffree,* 1985).

Whereas a traditionalist Supreme Court justice is most comfortable in letting school boards carry forward a traditionalist curriculum, that same justice is in a most awkward position when the school board is resisting traditionalist demands of parents and parents want the Court to use its power to reshape the curriculum in accord with the traditionalist vision. In this case the traditionalist justice is caught on the horns of a dilemma: the traditionalist justice must choose between using federal power (something he or she usually opposes) in the name of policies he or she favors, or letting the school board pursue policies he or shes does not favor. I want to briefly look at some examples posing this dilemma.

First, there are those cases in which parents have argued that the materials to which they object establish a religion of secularism and therefore ought totally to be barred from the public schools (*Smith v. Board of School Commissioners of Mobile County, Alabama,* 1987). It seems unlikely that these suits would succeed in the Supreme Court, just as they generally have not succeeded in the lower courts. Even traditionalist justices, who arguably would be most receptive to such claims, would balk at the thought of the judiciary reviewing the schools' curriculum to determine which materials were too "secular" to be permitted in the schools at all.

Second, there are those cases in which parents seek not to totally bar the use of certain materials but only to obtain an *exemption* for their children from the requirement to use them. Parents who have brought such suits have claimed that the school's materials have been so inconsistent with their own and their children's religious beliefs that the materials undermined the religious convictions of the child, thereby interfering with the child's and the parents' right to the free exercise of religion. The lower court ruled, however, that exposure to offensive views did not cause or create an unconstitutional burden on the free exercise of religion (*Mozert v. Hawkins County Public Schools*, 1987). The court said in effect that the compulsory exposure to materials offensive for religious reasons is not unconstitutional. Despite the lack of success parents have met with in these cases in the lower courts, it is possible that with regard to a certain limited set of materials, such as instruction in the theory of evolution, parents might be able to persuade a majority of the Supreme Court to heed their claim, despite the justices' misgivings about judicial control of the school program. Traditionalists have in the past favored strong parental rights and the granting of religious exemptions, as occurred in *Wisconsin v. Yoder* (1972), but at the same time, in more recent cases (e.g., *Bowen v. Roy*, 1986) the Court has refused to grant free exercise exemptions. Constitutional doctrine in the religion area is in such flux that it is difficult to see exactly where the Court is headed, especially with regard to this kind of case, in which parents would be seeking a special accommodation for their children that would clearly complicate the operations of the public school. The situation is made more complicated by the fact that liberals on the Court have tended to support these claims for religious accommodation. And one prominent liberal scholar seems to have adopted the position that accommodation of the religious interests of the parents should prevail in these cases (Tribe, 1988, p. 1168–1169).

To conclude, neither traditionalists nor liberals are content. Traditionalists have much to be concerned about: legal doctrine today continues to favor congressional and judicial involvement in control of the local school program; federal congressional policy has in fact intruded deeply into the public schools in order to promote equal educational opportunity; religion still has no place in the school; a curriculum may be offered which in its unavoidable implications runs counter to fundamentalist beliefs (students may be taught situational ethics in public schools); evolution may be taught, but the doctrine of scientific creationism may not; and students cannot be compelled to salute the flag. On the other hand, traditionalists may gain some comfort from the fact that they have won two recent student free speech cases, and the principle of local control continues to serve as an important limit on the Supreme Court's own ventures into educational policy. And in the years to come, traditionalists may yet gain the upper hand on the Court and may be able to steer it onto a traditionalist path. Nevertheless, traditionalists still feel that there is much to do, that they have a great challenge to reverse a century's worth of doctrines with which they profoundly disagree.

As for the liberals, although they have seen much of their agenda adopted in constitutional doctrine, they cannot be resting easily. The student free speech cases may be a harbinger of increased traditionalist power on the Court. Many of the liberal victories remain controversial, such as no prayer in the public schools. The liberals may find themselves split over certain issues yet to reach the Court. And if President Bush has the opportunity to make one or more appointments to the Court, he may decisively swing the Court into the traditionalist camp. The country is thus at a moment when the traditionalists, who usually oppose change, are eager and poised for change, and the liberals, who are usually the most vocal proponents of change, are all too fearful that substantial change is but one Supreme Court appointment away.

References

Abington School District v. Schemmp, 374 U.S. 203 (1963).

Abram, M. B. (1986). Is 'strict separation' too strict? *The Public Interest,* No. 82, 81–90.

Ambach v. Norwick, 441 U.S. 68 (1979).

Atkin, J. M. (1981). Federal role in curriculum development, 1950–80. *Education Evaluation and Policy Analysis, 3,* 5–36.

Bailyn, B. (1967). *The ideological origins of the American Revolution.* Cambridge, Mass.: Belknap Press of Harvard University Press.

Bell, D. (1972). On meritocracy and equality. *The Public Interest,* No. 29, 29–68.

Bell, T. H. (1976). Values and morality. In U.S. Department of Health, Education and Welfare, *Education and citizenship.* Washington, D.C.: U.S. Government Printing Office.

———. (1982). The federal role in education. *Harvard Educational Review, 52,* 375–380.

Benn, S. I., & Peters, R. S. (1959). *The principles of political thought.* New York: The Free Press.

Berger, R. (1987). *Federalism: The founders' design.* Norman, OK: University of Oklahoma Press.

Berlin, I. (1969). *Four essays on liberty.* London: Oxford University Press.

Bethel School District No. 403 v. Fraser, 106 S. Ct. 3159 (1986).

Bloom, A. (1987). *The closing of the American mind.* New York: Simon & Schuster.

Board of Education v. Pico, 457 U.S. 853 (1982).

Board of Education v. Rowley, 458 U.S. 176 (1982).

Bowen v. Roy, 476 U.S. 693 (1986).

Broudy, H. S. (1983). Federal intervention in education: Expectations and frustrations. *Education and Urban Society, 15,* 291–308.

Brown v. Board of Education, 347 U.S. 483 (1954).

Chubb, J. E. (1985). Excessive regulation: The case of federal aid to education. *Political Science Quarterly, 100,* 287–311.

Clark, D. L., & Amiot, M. A. (1983). The disassembly of the federal education role. *Education and Urban Society, 15,* 367–387.

Cohen, David. (1982). Policy and organization: The impact of state and educational policy on school governance. *Harvard Educational Review, 52,* 474–499.

Crawford, A. (1980). *Thunder on the right.* New York: Pantheon Books.

Dolbeare, K. M., & Hammond, P. E. (1971). *The school prayer decisions.* Chicago: University of Chicago Press.

Doyle, D., & Finn Jr., C. E. (1984). American schools and the future of local control. *The Public Interest,* No. 77, 77–95.

Education for All Handicapped Children Act of 1975, 20 U.S.C. §1400–61 (1982).

Education for Economic Security Act, Title VII—Magnet Schools Assistance, 20 U.S.C. §4059 (Supp. III 1985).

Educational Visions Seminar. (1985). Progressive federalism: New ideas for distributing money and power in education. In B. and R. Gross (Eds.), *The great school debate.* New York: A Touchstone Book.

Edwards v. Aguillard, 107 S. Ct. 2573 (1987).

Elmore, R. F., & McLaughlin, M. W. (1983). The federal role in education: Learning from experience. *Education and Urban Society, 15,* 309–330.

Engle v. Vitale, 370 U.S. 421 (1962).

Epperson v. Arkansas, 393 U.S. 97 (1968).

Equal Access Act, 20 U.S.C.A. §4071 et. seq. (Supp. 1985).

Feinberg, J. (1980). Child's right to an open future. In W. Aiken, & H. LaFollette (Eds.), *Whose child?* (pp. 124–153). Totowa, NJ: Littlefield, Adams and Company.

Finn, C. (1982). Responses. *Harvard Educational Review, 52,* 529–531.

Fishkin, J. S. (1983). *Justice, equal opportunity, and the family*. New Haven, CT: Yale University Press.

Gideonse, H. D. (1981). What should we mean by curriculum development and did a consensus dissolve? *Educational Evaluation and Policy Analysis, 3*, 41–47.

Girvetz, H. K. (1963). *The evolution of liberalism*. London: Collier Books.

Goodlad, J. I. (1981). Curriculum development beyond 1980. *Educational Evaluation and Policy Analysis, 3*, 49–54.

_____. (1984). *A place called school*. New York: McGraw-Hill.

Graham, H. D. (1984). *The uncertain triumph: Federal education policy in the Kennedy and Johnson years*. Chapel Hill, NC: University of North Carolina Press.

Gutmann, A. (1987). *Democratic education*. Princeton, NJ: Princeton University Press.

Hanushek, E. (1986). Economics of schooling: Production and efficiency in public school. *Journal of Economic Literature, 24*, 1141–1177.

Harbour, William R. (1982). *The foundations of conservative thought*. South Bend, IN: University of Notre Dame Press.

Hatch Amendment, 20 U.S.C.A. §1232(h) (Cum. Supp. 1985).

Hawley, W. (1983). Criteria for determining an appropriate federal role. *Education and Urban Society, 16*, 45–79.

Hayek, F. A. (1960). *The constitution of liberty*. South Bend, IN: Gateway Editions.

Hazelwood School District v. Kuhlmeier, 108 S. Ct. 562 (1988).

Johnson, R. M. (1967). *The dynamics jof compliance*. Evanston, IL: Northwestern University Press.

Kaestle, C. F., & Smith, M. S. (1982). The federal role in elementary and secondary education. *Harvard Educational Review, 52*, 384–408.

Keyishian v. Board of Regents, 385 U.S. 589 (1967).

Kirst, M. (1988). Who should control our schools: Reassessing current policies. (Report No. 88-CERAS-05). Stanford: California Center for Educational Research.

Knapp, M. S. (1987). Educational improvement under the education block grant. *Educational Evaluation and Policy Analysis, 9*, 283–299.

Knapp, M., Stearns, M. S., Turnbull, B. J., David, J. L., & Peterson, S. M. (1983). Cumulative effects at the local level. *Education and Urban Society, 15*, 479–499.

Kneller, G. F. (1984). *Movements of thought in modern education*. New York: John Wiley.

Koch, A. (1943). *The philosophy of Thomas Jefferson*. New York: Columbia University Press.

Kuriloff, R., & Kirp, D. (1979). *When handicapped children go to court: Assessing the impact of the legal reform of special education in Pennsylvania.*

(Project N. Neg.-003-0192). Washington, D.C.: National Institute of Education.

Kurtz, P. (1983). *In defense of secular humanism.* Buffalo, NY: Prometheus Books.

————. (1988). *Forbidden fruit: The ethics of humanism.* Buffalo, NY: Prometheus Books.

Lau v. Nichols, 414 U.S. 563 (1974).

Lee, G. C. (1965). *Education and democratic ideals.* New York: Harcourt, Brace & World.

Levin, H. (1982). Federal grants and educational equity. *Harvard Educational Review, 52,* 444–459.

McLean v. Arkansas Board of Education, 529 F. Supp. 1255 (E.D. Ark. 1982).

Milliken v. Bradley, 433 U.S. 267 (1977).

Milliken v. Bradley, 418 U.S. 717 (1974).

Minersville School District v. Gobitis, 310 U.S. 586 (1940).

Minter, T. K. (1982). The importance of the federal role in improving educational practice: Lessons from a big-city school system. *Harvard Educational Review, 52,* 500–513.

Mozert v. Hawkins County Public Schools, 827, F.2d 1058 (6th Cir. 1987).

Nash, G. H. (1976). *The conservative intellectual movement in America.* New York: Basic Books.

National Education Association (1985). The NEA's plan for school reform. In B. and R. Gross (Eds.), *The great school debate* (pp. 405–418). New York: A Touchstone Book.

Nisbet, R. (1986). *Conservatism.* Minneapolis: University of Minnesota Press.

Okun, A. (1975). *Equality and efficiency: The big tradeoff.* Washington, DC: The Brookings Institute.

Orfield, G. (1986). Hispanics education: Challenges, research and policies. *American Journal of Education, 95,* 1–25.

Pincus, F. L. (1985). From equity to excellence: The rebirth of educational conservatism. In B. and R. Gross (Eds.), *The Great School Debate* (pp. 329–344). New York: A Touchstone Book.

Rae, D. (1981). *Equalities.* Cambridge, MA: Harvard University Press.

Ravitch, D. (1985). Politization and the schools: The case of bilingual education. *Proceedings of the American Philosophical Society, 129,* 121–128.

Rawls, J. (1971). *A theory of justice.* Cambridge, MA: Harvard University Press.

Richards, D. A. J. (1986). *Toleration and the Constitution.* New York: Oxford University Press.

Rossiter, C. (1953). *Seedtime of the Republic.* New York: Harcourt, Brace.

Rossiter, C. (1962). *Conservatism in America: The thankless persuasion* (2nd ed.). New York: Vintage Books.

Ryan, W. (1982). *Equality.* New York: Vintage Books.

Schaffarzick, J., & Gary Sykes, G. (Eds.). (1980). *Value conflicts and curriculum issues.* Berkeley, CA: McCutchan.

Scheffler, I. (1979). Moral education and the democratic ideal. In I. Scheffler, *Reason and teaching* (pp. 136–145). New York: Bobbs-Merrill.

Short, E. C. (1983). Authority and governance in curriculum: A policy analysis in the United States context. *Educational Evaluation and Policy Analysis, 5,* 195–205.

Simon, J. F. (1973). *In his own image: The Supreme Court in Richard Nixon's America.* New York. David McKay.

Smith v. Board of School Commissioners of Mobile County, Alabama, 827 F.2d 684 (11th Cir. 1987).

Southeastern Community College v. Davis, 442 U.S. 397 (1979).

Sowell, T. (1987). *A conflict of visions.* New York: William Morrow.

Spragens, Jr., T. A. (1976). *Understanding political theory.* New York: St. Martin's Press.

Stone v. Graham, 449 U.S. 39 (1980).

Sykes, G. (1981). Reprise: Federal involvement in the school curriculum. *Educational Evaluation and Policy Analysis, 3,* no. 5, 37–40.

Thomas, N. C. (1983). The development of federal activism in education: A contemporary perspective. *Education and Urban Society, 15,* 271–290.

Tinker v. Des Moines Independent Community School District, 393 U.S. 503 (1969).

Tollett, K. S. (1982). The propriety of the federal role in expanding educational opportunity. *Harvard Educational Review, 52,* 431–443.

Tribe, L. (1988). *American constitutional law.* Mineola, NY: The Foundation Press.

Tussman, J. (1977). *Government and the mind.* New York: Oxford University Press.

Tyack, D., James, T., & Benavot, A. (1987). *Law and the shaping of public education 1785–1954.* Madison: University of Wisconsin Press.

van Geel, T. (1976). *Authority to control the school program.* Lexington, MA: Lexington Books.

———. (1987). *The courts and American education policy.* Buffalo, NY: Prometheus Books.

———. (1989). State control of the private school's curriculum: An essay in law, jurisprudence, and political philosophy. In N. E. Devins (Ed.), *Public values, private schools* (pp. 251–273). London: The Falmer Press.

Vitz, P. C. (1986). Religion and traditional values in public school textbooks. *The Public Interest,* No. 84, 79–90.

Wallace v. Jaffree, 472 U.S. 38 (1985).

Walzer, M. (1983). *Spheres of justice.* New York: Basic Books.

Way, Jr., H. F. (1968). Survey research on judicial decisions: The prayer and Bible reading cases. *Western Political Quarterly, 21,* 189–205.

Weatherly, R. (1979). *Reforming special education: Policy implementation from state level to street level.* Cambridge, MA: MIT Press.

West Virginia State Board of Education v. Barnette, 319 U.S. 624 (1943).

Will G. F. (1983). *State craft as soul craft.* New York: Simon & Schuster.

Wisconsin v. Yoder, 406 U.S. 205 (1972).

Wood, G. S. (1969). *The creation of the American republic 1776–1787.* New York: W. W. Norton.

Zorach v. Clauson, 343 U.S. 306 (1952).

4

Centralizing Curriculum at the State Level

Chris Pipho

State authority over education is absolute (Good, 1963, p. 572). Local school districts can be created and abolished, curriculum can be mandated, textbooks prescribed, and the training and certification of teachers specified. In short, states are the central determinant in the federal, state, and local educational governance mix. This textbook description of state authority over education, although generally correct, does not reflect the vast differences among the various states. Not all states adopt textbooks or mandate curriculum. Colorado, for example, in Article IX, Section 16, of the state constitution, mandates "that neither the general assembly nor the state board of education shall have power to prescribe textbooks to be used in the public schools" (Abrahamson, 1962, p. 34). States, in their constitutions and statutes, delegate varying degrees of authority to local school boards. These differences, when combined with local control traditions and political reality, have contributed to a system of public education in this country that resembles a crazy quilt of different degrees of state control.

Foreign delegations making their whirlwind visits to this country usually display a great deal of perplexity over this decentralized system of education. They frequently stop at the Education Commission of the States, assuming they have found the central thread of authority over state education. Their questions are often more revealing than the answers provided. Who controls what the states do? What is the role of the U.S. secretary of education? Why do schools look so similar from one part of the country to the next? Why do states not prescribe the same curriculum? If states have authority over education, what is local control? Why do school districts differ in size? Answering these questions, especially when communication flows through an interpreter, gives one the opportunity to wonder about the wisdom of it all. Viewing the system through the eyes of a foreign visitor who only understands a centralized governance structure either strips away the power of logically defending what is done or increases one's faith in local control. Trying to explain a system that mixes a tradition of state and local control with a little federal categorical support, and then bends all of this through a filter of regional and cultural differences, sets the stage for a discussion of centralizing curriculum at the state level.

State Control over Curriculum

Describing the amount of control over the curriculum that has been kept at the state level and the amount of curriculum control that has been delegated to local school districts is, at best, an imprecise exercise. Certain key events, such as textbook adoption, curriculum guideline mandates or suggestions, and high school graduation requirements, can be used to indicate the amount of state and local control visible within a state. Certain generalizations can be made about the governance structure, the size of the state board (elected versus appointed), and the accountability measures that states have placed back on local districts. All this can be combined with some subjective categorization of states by ranking them from high state control to high local control states, but in the end a certain amount of subjectivity has to be involved in the process. One attempt to categorize these states has used a ranking of decentralized states, moderately decentralized states, and centralized states. This categorization of the states can be found in Table 4.1 (van Geel, 1976). Although the decision to group states in these three categories was based on van Geel's analysis of state law and operation in the mid-1970s, he also admitted it was risky to categorize states in this fashion.

Announcing that state control over the curriculum has increased dramatically because of recent education reform mandates may have been a correct assessment of the state scene in 1988. However, if state controls are on the increase, then there should be a corresponding decrease in the amount of control that is visible over the curriculum at the local school district level or at the classroom level. Although more centralized mandates were a by-product of the major reform legislation in the period of 1983 to 1988, just being able to categorize and detail these legislative pronouncements does not necessarily translate into a decrease in local control.

Textbook Adoption

Perhaps the best single indicator of the degree of state control over curriculum is the textbook adoption process. In 1985 twenty-two states (see Table 4.2) were known as "adoption states." In general, if one were to separate the states into two categories, strong state control versus strong local control, the twenty-two adoption states would be on the strong state control side, and the nonadoption states would probably be on the strong local control side. From the textbook adoption process flows additional state mandates and controls over the curriculum, curriculum guides, and content coverage, which in turn is mirrored in state testing programs. Wide variances of operating style and control can be found, however, within the twenty-two adoption states. Those states that operate book repositories or depositories in which the publishers send textbooks to the states, and the states in turn distribute the textbooks, collect surplus books, rebind books, and generally handle the textbook distribution process tend to have high levels of state control. In other states, where the adoption process identifies a single or a multiple text for local school districts to order on their own, the amount of state control is much less. Generally a textbook adoption committee is appointed by the state board or some other entity. The adoption process concentrates on one or two subject areas each year. Typically the textbook adoption process triggers a budget allocation process from the state with either a per student or a lump sum amount assigned for textbook adoptions. In some states the appropriation varies from year to year and occasionally cycles of adoption are skipped, but in general local school districts are not in control of finding the latest or most up-to-date science or history textbooks. Recently in Alabama this issue was dramatized by a textbook read-in on the state capitol steps where schoolchildren from various districts participated by reading out of their history books. The press and media highlighted the fact that students were reading from history books in which the last President covered in the book was Richard Nixon. Local school districts in this case had little control over the content aspect of the curriculum.

The number of "adoption states" has not changed significantly in recent years, and, in fact, has been reduced by Indiana removing itself from the state adoption list a few years back. If textbook adoption were the only indication of state control, little change would be evident. However, within the last decade a concept known as 'learner verification' has been adopted by five states (California State Department of Education, 1984). Textbook manufacturers have to verify that the textbooks and instructional materials being supplied for the adoption process have been actually tried out with a specified number of students in real schools. Publishers are concerned that this will drive up the cost of producing a textbook and slow the development process down an additional one or two years. Thus, although the number of states adopting textbooks at the state level has decreased, the process probably has become more rigorous. Demands that minority-group topics be included in textbooks as well as demands from right-wing pressure groups for teaching scientific creationism and other controversial subjects have all increased the number of groups watching and attempting to influence the adoption process. for the most part this does not appear to change the degree of state control, but it does add more complexity to the process.

Testing

State testing of student achievement is on the increase. Well before the beginning of the reform movement, perhaps as early as the 1970s at the beginning of the accountability movement, the call for better student test data started to materialize. Management by objectives (MBO), program planning budgeting systems (PPBS), and a host of other management tools set the stage for a new kind of student achievement test data. Norm-referenced tests, which compared grade levels on a national basis, did not seem to meet the needs of the new state accountability legislation. Approximately at the same time, technology and advances in test construction pushed the advantages of a criterion-referenced test over a norm-referenced test. These changes, along with use of National Assessment of Educational Progress test data, set the stage for over thirty states to move into the state assessment arena (Education Commission of the States, 1985).

Another outgrowth of the accountability movement was the call for minimum standards for high school graduation. As early as 1974 and 1975, California and Colorado initiated such legislation. It was quickly picked up in another twenty states in the next two years. By 1978 this number had increased to well over thirty states, and currently forty-two states have some form of minimum competency testing. Twenty of these states include mandates for high school graduation. The debate over minimum competency testing standards driving the curriculum is an emotional issue. Most district-level curriculum directors probably would agree that these tests influence the average or below-average students the most. Students failing the test consistently as they move toward high school graduation are usually scheduled into a heavy load of remediation classes in their eleventh- and twelfth-grade years. In one sense the state is completely mandating the curriculum for these students. State testing officials, however, would answer that the

criterion-referenced goals and objectives for these minimum competency tests were developed with the assistance of local school district
officials, and that the process, although initially state mandated, is as
much locally controlled as it is state controlled.

Education Indicators

Public interest in comparative education data seemingly is on the rise.
Former education secretary Terrel Bell's "wall chart" of 1984 has fueled
the media appetite for more of this kind of data (U.S. Department of
Education, 1984). States have responded by adopting, in varying
degrees, lists of education indicators for school district reporting. In
some instances, school districts issue their own "stockholders' reports"
or "report cards." In other instances states have mandated that each
local school building issue a yearly report card to its patrons on a
specified list of indicators.

This indicator movement offers an opportunity for individual state
policy makers to sharpen their focus on education goals. Without this
focus, the states, and in turn, local districts, could gather and
disseminate reams of information that would prove of little use in
drawing district-by-district comparisons. A potential side effect of this
movement, however, is the prospect of engendering too much central
control through state or national goals and objectives. Such a mono-
lithic national school system would see the cherished local "lighthouse" school district concept vanish from the landscape of American
education.

If the use of education indicators in status reports to the public, in
assisting educators with management decisions, and as policy-relevant
data for state legislators and state board members seems familiar, it
may well be part of a continually reoccurring accountability theme.
Currently more than two dozen states require some form of district or
building report card.

Although this body of data could yield more relevant state decisions
for education and provide the evidence needed to muster public
support, the indicators push will also leave local school districts with
unequal resources. The pool of available administrators, teachers,
parents, and students, coupled with a local property tax base, provides
some of the most variable of variables. Turning the media spotlight on a
host of outcome variables without alerting everyone to the differences
at the starting gate will undoubtedly cause problems at the local level.
How state policy makers use these indicators for resource allocation
over the next few years will determine their appropriate role as a
decision-making tool. The improper use of indicators will surely bring a

series of charges that schools are teaching for the test, manipulating data to improve their public image, or worse, bringing a new round of court cases related to equity and finance. Clearly, education indicators could be a tool for improvement, but the tool could also tip the scales to the state control side.

Academic Bankruptcy

Theoretically it has always been possible for a state to intervene and take over a local school district. In isolated instances, in Florida and New York City, for example, this has occurred in the last twenty years. Usually the management of the district is not called into question, and very seldom is the curriculum or instructional side of the school program an influence in a state takeover. Growing out of the educational reform movement has been a call for states to strengthen their takeover procedures through a process called "academic bankruptcy." The issue is the failure of a school district over a long period of time to adequately serve the needs of students. When it can be documented that the operation of the school district is harming students and their academic achievement levels, the proponents of this movement argue that a state should have the power to take over a school district and improve the curriculum and instructional quality.

Generally states have always had control over the fiscal side of a school district operation. Program deficiencies is a new addition. The power of the local school board is called into question by this process, and various national and state school board associations have registered opposition to this movement. Eight states in the last few years have enacted academic bankruptcy laws (see Table 4.3). Academic bankruptcy laws usually call for some process for identifying program deficiencies; some level of warning in which a district is given a chance to correct its deficiencies; and in the final state, some degree of takeover, including unseating the local board, calling for new board election, increasing or decreasing state aid, and elaborating a process for the district to move off from state control.

High School Graduation Requirements

Since 1980, at least forty-five states and the District of Columbia have altered high school graduation requirements. Generally mathematics and science courses have led the increase, but more than forty states also have increased the total number of units required for graduation. Quite often the increase in academic courses has been achieved by decreasing the number of elective course credits students are permitted to earn or by just increasing the total. In 1980, 17 units of credit, on the average, were required for graduation. In 1987 this had moved to an average of 19.7 units of credit. Florida was the first to raise the total to 24 units of credit (*Florida Statutes*, 1983) for all students, followed by Missouri for its college-bound students in 1985.

One of the more significant changes between 1980 and 1987 was the increase in the number of states thatprovided for a dual-track diploma, that is, a college-bound or vocational and technical diploma in addition to the standard diploma. In 1980 only the District of Columbia and New York had this requirement, but in 1987 this had increased to fifteen states. California is moving toward an advanced diploma with a "suggested model" for college-bound students; the District of Columbia uses a "comprehensive" and a "career/vocational" diploma. In Florida, the top diploma is labeled "academic scholars"; Georgia, "advanced"; Indiana, "academic honors"; Kentucky, "commonwealth diploma"; Michigan, "college preparatory"; Missouri, "college preparatory studies certificate"; New York, "regents diploma"; North Carolina, "scholars program"; Oklahoma "college preparatory", South Carolina, "academic achievement honors"; Texas, "advanced high school honors program"; and Virginia, "advanced studies."

In three states, a three-level diploma has been established: Louisiana uses "standard," "scholars program," and "regents scholar"; Rhode Island, "basic," "career bound," and "college bound"; and Tennessee labels them "standard," "honors-general," and "honors-vocational education." Typically, the college or academic diplomas require additional courses in math, science, language arts, and social studies, and often require or encourage foreign language courses. In two states, Arkansas and Vermont, the curriculum requirements were modified to give flexibility in the math and science areas. The chief reasoning for the action was a need to address the needs of the vocational track students. State-by-state changes in the high school graduation require-ments for 1980, 1985, and 1987 can be found in Table 4.4 (Education Commission of the States, 1989).

Vocational Education

The contrast between traditional views of vocational education and the emerging approaches being explored in vocational education is striking. A mixture of the plummeting pupil enrollment, the demand for an educated and skilled work force for the future, and the congressional focus on a competitive work force in the future inter-national market evidenced in the Carl Perkins Act has changed the face of vocational education and will affect school programs for years to come. Across the nation vocational educators are reviewing and revamping the curriculum offerings of vocational programs to ensure that vocational students have both a broad grasp of the traditional basic skills and the chosen vocational path. The states are articulating the vocational track into the traditional curriculum to prepare students for the workplace from middle school until the completion of their education.

As evidenced in the 1989 report commissioned by the government assessing vocational education, the schools which rank at the bottom in terms of student achievement and poverty have less access to specialized vocational courses, less access to advanced-level vocational courses, and less access to supervised work study programs. Given the rising costs of a college education, more and more students will be pursuing the vocational areas in the future. More federal and state funds and more alignment of the curriculum is key to the economic stability of the nation (*PSBA bulletin,* 1989; Minnesota Department of Education, 1989; *USA Today,* June 27, 1989, p. 9A).

Trends

Since the beginning of the education reform movement in 1983, state control over education has increased. In the eighteen months following the release of *A Nation at Risk* (National Commission on Excellence in Education, 1983), more than 250 state level commissions and task forces were appointed to make recommendations to state policy makers. The result was mega-reform legislation enacted in more than fifteen states and either legislative or state board action taken in all of the remaining states to raise academic standards for students, to make changes in the preparation and certification of teachers, and to reward and hold teachers in the profession.

The cumulative effect of these recommendations and resulting state actions can only be interpreted as a swing to more state control. Local school boards, teachers, and administrators, however, were also caught up in the public mood for more reform, and their support of some of the state-level changes made this something less than a one-sided grab for power. In fact, in some instances states took their cue for reform mandates from a few lighthouse school districts who were already mandating stiffer graduation requirements and stronger testing programs. In some instances states led the call for reform over the objections of local school districts. No-pass no-play regulations calling for higher academic standards for participation in extracurricular activities is one example. (For further discussion of this regulation, see Chapter 8.) In Texas various education groups opposed this mandate openly, and it became an issue in the re-election campaign of Governor Mark White. Although the no-pass no-play rules that are being implemented in nine states do not always directly raise curriculum standards, their second-order effect may be much more important. In Texas and other states students will often scale down their academic course load during the sport season in which they want to achieve eligibility. This has an immediate effect on the sequence of courses that students are taking, and probably also has an impact on the quality and content of some of these courses in school districts where football ranks higher in importance than do math and science.

Another example of state mandates enacted over the objection of local school districts is the academic bankruptcy area. In most states where this proposal was put forward, the local school boards and state school board associations were often joined by administrative groups and others in opposing the concept mainly because it was viewed as a grab for power or an effort to reduce the power of local school boards. While these groups kept the focus on governance and control, the states usually were forced to emphasize the point that some school districts have never taken seriously the academic and program side of school district management. Efforts to establish state control over the public school curriculum are often viewed as legislatively driven, even when occasionally the call for change comes from the state board of education or the governor's office. In other instances, however, noneducation branches of state government, including juvenile courts, drivers license bureaus, welfare agencies, and a host of others, are all taking steps to establish more direct connections with school instructional affairs. Recently states have moved to add high school graduation as a requirement for getting off welfare. These welfare reforms mandate a new student body, but they also force more state controls since the welfare budget will, in part, be an education budget. Recent moves by state legislatures, with the support of traffic and law enforcement agencies, to make the driver's license a feature in preventing or reducing dropouts is also going to have a second-order impact on the curriculum. A recent ruling by a judge in Hammond, Indiana, sentencing a seventeen-year-old youth to serve forty-eight days in a windowless jail for failing to keep his grades above a C average as required by a probation sentence growing out of a driving offense, and a West Virginia court upholding the no-pass no-drive law are examples of a new level of state control over grades and academic affairs. In 1989 fifteen states introduced legislation calling for a student's drivers license to be revoked if the student dropped out of school, or to award a drivers license based on grade point averages or other academic achievement. This concept is gathering more favor on the part of legislators. Florida, Louisiana, Texas, and Virginia enacted such laws in 1989.

Increased use of test data by legislative oversight committees will also be another movement to watch as control over the curriculum comes from different directions. Idaho's attempt to mandate stronger minimum grade point average for graduation from high school is also an indication that grades tied to certain academic courses will result in more state control. The use of test scores in the academic bankruptcy area, the use of certain advanced test scores for the award of incentive money to local school districts, the use of advanced placement scores for raising additional school revenues, and the awarding of a special academic diploma all are putting more emphasis on the academic curriculum. The next wave of state interest in this arena will most likely come from legislative oversight. In some states these committees are worried that school districts have met the letter of the law for increasing high school graduation requirements but that the content of some of the courses in the advanced math and science areas may not be equal from district to district. If legislative oversight hearings turn up evidence of wide differences, it could be expected that the legislature will have to counter with stronger mandates that will detail course content rather than just course title. In at least three states the science requirement has been changed to specify that a portion of the class must be spent in laboratories rather than science textbook activities. This type of ruling will likely have a different impact on rural and small districts than on large urban school districts. The symbiotic relationship of all of these reform standards and others that are being added by other state and government agencies points the way to even more state control and centralization over the curriculum.

Table 4.1
CATEGORIZATION OF STATES BY AMOUNT OF STATE CONTROL

Decentralized States

Alaska	Maryland	Ohio
Colorado	Massachusetts	Pennsylvania
Connecticut	Michigan	Rhode Island
Delaware	Minnesota	Vermont
Idaho	Montana	Washington
Illinois	Missouri	Wisconsin
Iowa	Nebraska	Wyoming
Kansas	New Hampshire	

Moderately Decentralized States

Maine	New York	Oregon
New Jersey	North Dakota	South Dakota

Centralized States

Alabama	Indiana	Oklahoma
Arizona	Kentucky	South Carolina
Arkansas	Louisiana	Tennessee
California	Mississippi	Texas
Florida	Nevada	Utah
Georgia	New Mexico	Virginia
Hawaii	North Carolina	West Virginia

Source: *Authority to Control the School Program,* (van Geel, 1976).

Table 4.2
STATES ADOPTING TEXTBOOKS AT THE STATE LEVEL

Alabama	Kentucky	South Carolina
Arizona	Louisiana	Tennessee
Arkansas	Mississippi	Texas
California	Nevada	Utah
Florida	New Mexico	Virginia
Georgia	North Carolina	West Virginia
Idaho	Oklahoma	
Illinois	Oregon	

Source: Education Commission of the States (1985). Clearinghouse Notes. List of members, National Association of Textbook Administrators, Denver, Colorado.

Table 4.3
STATES WITH ENACTED ACADEMIC BANKRUPTCY PROVISIONS

The term academic bankruptcy takes on a variety of meanings. For example, not all of the states call for the unseating of local boards or the state takeover of a school district. Most of the regulations have several levels of warning for school districts. The first warning often includes some form of targeted technical assistance from the state agency to the school district. In most cases this includes extra financial aid. School districts usually have several years to free themselves from state sanction. The debate quite often focuses on the takeover provisions and fails to point out the extra state resources which will be brought in to correct problems. Many of the states with academic bankruptcy provisions have or are working on incentive programs. The following is a look at the academic bankruptcy provisions in the nine states with provisions on record.

ARKANSAS
Citation—Act 89 of 1983, Competency Based Education Act of 1983, effective 2/9/84.

Purpose—To ensure that all public school students, to the extent of their individual mental, physical and emotional capacities, master the basic skills necessary to succeed in their educational experiences throughout life.

Measurement Instrument—The state basic skills competency test, which is given in grades 3, 6 and 8, will be used. This test will provide diagnostic information needed to identify the strengths and weaknesses of the district's instructional program, assist local districts in planning educational programs and help the state assess the overall performance of all schools and school districts.

Process—The process has several stages. Any school district or school in which less than 85 percent of students achieve specified levels of mastery of the basic skills are to participate in a school improvement program administered by the State Department of Education. This process is to help the districts develop a plan for improving instruction under the department's supervision and assistance.

Final State Action—Districts that fail all stages of the process eventually would lose accreditation and, in a later stage, could be forced to consolidate. Several districts are under suspended order of consolidation and have until 1989 to correct the situation.

GEORGIA
Citation—Quality Basic Education Act, Part 12, Sections 20-2-282 and 20-2-283, effective 7/1/86.

Purpose—To develop and conduct a comprehensive evaluation of each public school, school system and regional education service agency at least once every five years. It provides for assisting districts to develop a strategic plan for curriculum instruction and a sequenced core curriculum. Other areas cover evaluation, student count and fiscal procedures and public awareness of education programs.

Measurement Instrument—The primary measurement tool will be the student evaluation system, which is under development by the Department of Education.

Process—The program also has several stages. The first warning designates a school district as nonstandard with a corrective plan to be submitted to the state agency. The state is to give technical assistance if the district requests it. At that point, the state board would review the progress every six months, followed by a comprehensive evaluation within two years after the corrective plan has been approved by the state and put into place. If necessary, the state board could authorize increased state aid to help the district correct the identified deficiencies.

Final State Action—The state board is authorized to file civil action in the superior court of the county in which the school district is located to determine if any board member or administrator has delayed the implementation process. The court would have the power to appoint a trustee to make sure the court order is carried out, and school officials could be removed from office and replaced by the courts if deemed necessary.

KENTUCKY
Citation—SB 202, KRS Chapter 158, Educationally Deficient School Districts, effective 7/15/84.

Purpose—To establish program and service standards for school districts and minimum performance levels for students in the basic skills.

Measurement Instrument—The state testing program is to be used to measure student academic progress.

Process—This also is a "staged" program, with the state agency identifying educationally deficient school districts and giving technical assistance and other aid to help correct the deficiencies. The Superintendent of Public Instruction, with the approval of the state board, may require an annual reallocation of some of the state aid funds to address specific program deficiencies.

Final State Action—Failure to implement the education improvement plan shall constitute grounds for removing boards or administration from office. A disclaimer states that the act shall not be deemed to create a statutory cause of action for educational malpractice by students, parents or guardians.

NEW JERSEY
Citation—NJ 1987, Ch. 398 and 399.

Purpose—To implement a comprehensive monitoring process that will ensure that all New Jersey students receive the educational opportunities guaranteed by law.

Measurement Instrument—The State Department of Education's compliance unit will systematically review the district's educational programs, governance, management and fiscal operations. Student testing was not mentioned in the law but is presumed to be included in "rules and regulations" approved by the state board.

Process—The law calls for a staged program moving from a self-correcting stage to varying degrees of state control by a monitor general team.

Final State Action—State officials can take complete control of a district for up to 5 years. School board members and top administrators can be dismissed.

NEW MEXICO

Citation—Public School Code, New Mexico Statutes Annotated 1978, Sec. 22-2-2 (W), enacted in 1969.

Purpose—To empower the State Board of Education with the responsibility of providing for management and other necessary personnel to operate any public school or school district which has failed to meet requirements of law, state board standards or state board regulations.

Measurement Instrument—The state accreditation process.

Process—State Board of Education is to provide for management and other necessary personnel to operate any public school or school district which has failed to meet requirements of law, state board standards or state board regulations; provided that the operation of the public school or school district shall not include any consolidation or reorganization without the approval of the local board of that school district.

Final State Action—Until such time as requirements of law, standards or regulations have been met and compliance is assured, the powers and duties of the local school board shall be suspended by the State Board of Education.

OHIO

Citation—SB 140, 1989, Sections 3302.01–3302.06, effective 1990-91 academic year.

Purpose—To adopt rules that include standards defining indicators for establishing levels of school district and school building performance for determining whether any school district or school building is educationally deficient.

Measurement Instrument—Performance indicators shall be measurable and may include such indicators as graduation rates, attendance rates, dropout rates and academic achievement levels as assessed under Sections 3301 of the school code.

Process—The State Board of Education is to annually identify each school district or school building that is educationally deficient under the adopted standards and notify the board of education of each identified school district and the board of education operating each identified school building of the fact and nature of the educational deficiency. The district board has 90 days to submit a corrective action plan. The state board is to approve or disapprove the plan in accordance with the standards. If the plan is not approved, the state board, with consent of the district board, shall assign one or more educational experts to the district to assist in developing a corrective action plan that meets state board standards. If the affected district or building is not solving the educational deficiency through the approved plan, the State Board can disapprove the existing plan and assign one or more educational experts to the district to aid in developing another corrective action plan designed to enable the district board to make satisfactory progress to eliminate the deficiencies.

Final State Action—If the district board fails to consent to the assignment of one or more educational experts or fails to develop and submit an approved corrective action plan, the state board, on recommendation of the Superintendent of Public Instruction, may issue an order requiring the school board to be placed under monitoring by the state superintendent and with the appointment of a state monitor to act on his behalf to ensure that an approved corrective action play is developed and implemented, and that the district board makes satisfactory progress toward eliminating the deficiencies. The monitoring is eliminated by written order from the state board releasing the district or school building. No mention is made of unseating either the board or the superintendent.

SOUTH CAROLINA
Citation—Education Improvement Act of 1984, Subdivision E, Sub-part 4, effective 1/85.
Purpose—To give the state board and state Superintendent of Education a process to assure quality education programs in each local school district.
Measurement Instrument—The state board has been charged to develop an evaluation plan for local districts using the California Test of Basic Skills to measure student progress. Other factors will include the district dropout rate and the failure rate on the state high school exit exam.
Process—Program stages range from advisements and warnings to the assignment of monitors and masters to help run the school district.
Final State Action—The state Superintendent of Education, with the approval of the board, has several options. (1) He or she may declare a state of emergency in the school district. This requires a joint meeting of the senate and house education committees, which must concur in the findings and may, at that point, put state funds going to the school district in escrow to be released only as the program is corrected. (2) The superintendent may provide technical assistance and advice in implementing state board recommendations. (3) He or she may recommend to the governor that the district superintendent's office be declared vacant with a replacement to be named by the state superintendent until the vacancy can be filled by the local board.

TEXAS
Citation—HB 72, Article V (school districts), Part A (accreditation), effective 1984-85 school year.
Purpose—To establish a set of standards for school district accreditation and state monitoring.
Measurement Instrument—The state accreditation process mandates that districts have a plan for establishing goals and objectives for the district and a process to ensure that all statutory requirements imposed by the state board are met. The quality of learning in each building will be based on achievement test scores. Other indicators will be based on teacher performance, administrator performance, principal effectiveness, fulfillment or curriculum requirements, correlation between student grades and performance on standardized tests, quality of teacher inservice training, paperwork reduction efforts, and training of local boards.
Process—This is a "staged" program whereby the state Commissioner of Education and state board can notify districts of deficiencies and then provide

them with plans for improvement and technical assistance. The program ranges from public notification of the deficiency and appointment of a monitor to help evaluate district progress in correcting deficiencies to appointment of a master to oversee district operation.

Final State Action—If a district fails on all stages, the State Board of Education can revoke the district's accreditation and may withhold state funds from the district.

WEST VIRGINIA

Citation—SB 114, 1988, Section 18–2E–5 Performance Based Accreditation, effective 7/1/89.

Purpose—To provide assurances that a thorough and efficient system of education is being provided for all public school students on an equal educational opportunity basis and that the high quality standards are being adopted in the areas of curriculum, finance, transportation, special education, facilities, administrative practices, training of school district board members and administrators, personnel qualifications, professional development and evaluation, student and school performance and other such areas as determined by the State Board of Education.

Measurement Instrument—Annual state accreditation process measuring the performance of each school on measures of student and school performance for: student performance by grade level on state testing, attendance rate, dropout rate, percent of students promoted to next grade, graduation rate, average class size, pupil-teacher ratio, number of exceptions requested to the ratio, number of split-grade classrooms, pupil-administrator ratio and the operating expenditure per pupil. School accreditation classifications of full accreditation status or probationary accreditation status are issued. The state may issue accreditation levels to each school district board of education of full approval, probationary or nonapproval.

Process—To assist the state board in accreditation status determination, the state board shall from time to time appoint an educational standards compliance review team to make unannounced on-site reviews of the educational programs in any school or school district to assess compliance of the school or district with the adopted state board standards including, but not limited to, facilities, administrative procedures, transportation, food services and all matters relating to school finance, budgeting and administration. The compliance team reports findings to the State Board of Education for inclusion in the determination of accreditation or approval status. The state board is to make accreditation information available to the legislature, the governor, the general public and any individual who requests such information.

Final State Action—Whenever a school is given probationary status or determined to be seriously impaired and fails to improve status within one year, any student attending such school may transfer only once to the nearest fully-accredited school, subject to approval of the receiving school and at the expense of the school on probationary status. Whenever nonapproval status is given, the State Board of Education shall declare a state of emergency in the district and may intervene in the operation of the district to (1) limit the authority of the district superintendent and district board as to the expenditure of funds, employment and dismissal of personnel, establishment and operation of school calendar, establishment of instructional programs and policies and such other areas as may be designated by the state board by rule; (2) take such direct action as may be necessary to correct the impairment; and (3) declare the office of the district superintendent vacant.

Compiled by ECS Clearinghouse
Education Commission of the States

Table 4.4

MINIMUM HIGH SCHOOL GRADUATION REQUIREMENTS BETWEEN 1980 AND 1989: STANDARD DIPLOMAS

September 1989

STATE	YEAR	ENGLISH/LANG ARTS	SOCIAL STUDIES	MATH	SCIENCE	PHYS EDUC/HEALTH	ELECTIVES	OTHER	TOTAL UNITS	ADOPTED BY	DATE ENACTED	EFFECTIVE DATE	GEN REF NOTE #
AL	1980	4	3	1	1	4	7		20				
	1985	4	3	2	1	3.5	6.5		20	SBE*	5/80	1985	
	1987	4	3	2	2	1.5	9	.5 home/personal mgmt	22	SBE	1985	1989	01
	1989	4	3	2	2	1.5	9.5		22	SBE	1988	1989	
AK	1980	1	1	1	1	1		Local board determines	19			1978	
	1985	4	3	2	2	1	9		21	SBE	4/84	1985	
	1987	4	3	2	2	1	9		21				
	1989	4	3	2	2	1	9		21				
AZ	1980	3	2	1	1		8.5		16				
	1985	4	2	2	2		9.5	.5 free enterprise	20	SBE	2/83	1987	
	1987	4	3	2	2		9	.5 free enterprise	20	SBE	1986	1991	02
	1989	4	2.5	2	2		9	.5 free enterprise	20	SBE	1986	1991	
AR	1980	4	1	1	1	1	10		16				
	1985	4	3	...5...	1	1	6.5	.5 fine arts	20	SBE	2/84	1988	03
	1987	4	3	...5...	1	1	6.5	.5 fine arts	20	SBE	2/84	1988	
	1989	4	3	2	1	1	6.5	.5 fine arts	20	SBE	2/84	1988	

Table 4.4 (con't)

State	Year	Units required	State permits local board to set minimum academic standard	Total	Authority	Date	Date	Note
CA	1980							
	1985	3, 2, 2	1 fine arts or foreign lang.	13	Leg*	1983	1987	04
	1987	3, 2, 2	See note	13	Leg	1983	1987	04A
	1989	3, 2, 2	1 fine arts or foreign lang.	13				
CO	1980		1 fine arts or foreign lang.					05
	1985							
	1987							
	1989							
CT	1980	Local board determines						
	1985	4, 3, 3, 2, 1, 6	1 arts or voc. ed.	20	Leg	1984	1988	
	1987	4, 3, 3, 2, 1, 6	1 arts or voc. ed.	20	Leg	1984	1988	
	1989	4, 3, 3, 2, 1, 6	1 arts or voc. ed.	20	Leg	1984	1988	
DE	1980	4, 3, 1, 1, 1.5, 7.5		18				
	1985	4, 3, 2, 2, 1.5, 6.5		19	SBE	7/83	1987	
	1987	4, 2, 2, 2, 1.5, 6.5		19	SBE	7/83	1987	
	1989	4, 3, 2, 2, 1.5, 6.5		19	SBE	7/83	1987	06
DC	1980	4, 1.5, 1, 1, 1.5, 8		18				
	1985	4, 2, 2, 1, 1.5, 8	1 foreign language	20.5	BE	1980	1985	07
	1987	4, 2, 2, 1, 1.5, 8	1 foreign language	20.5	BE	1980	1985	07A
	1989	4, 2, 2, 1, 1.5, 7	1 foreign lang., 1 life skills	20.5	BE	1984	1985	
FL	1980	Local board determines						
	1985	4, 3, 3, 1, 9	.5 practical/.5 fine arts	24	Leg	1983	1987	08
	1987	4, 3, 3, 1, 9	.5 practical/exploratory voc.ed., 5 performing art or speech/debate	24	Leg	1987	1989	08A
	1989	4, 3, 3, .5, 9	.5 practical/exploratory voc. ed, .5 performing arts or speech & debate, .5 life management skills	24	Leg	1987	1989	

Table 4.4 (con't)

		1	1	2/3	10	3 1/3						
GA	1980	3	3	1	1	1	2/3	10	3 1/3	20			
	1985	4	3	2	2	1	1	8	1	21	SBE	11/83	1988	09
	1987	4	3	2	2	1	1	8	1	21	SBE	4/87	1988	09A
	1989	4	3	2	2	1	1	8	1 computer tech. and/or fine arts and/or voc. ed, and/or junior ROTC	21	SBE			
HI	1980	4	4	3	3	3	1.5	6	.5 guidance	20	SBE	1978		
	1985	4	3	2	2	2	1.5	6	.5 guidance	20	SBE	1978	1983	
	1987	4	4	2	2	2	1.5	6	.5 guidance	20	SBE	1978	1983	
	1989	4	4	2	2	2	1.5	6	.5 guidance	20	SBE	1978	1983	
ID	1980	3.5	2	1	1		1.5	8		18				
	1985	4	2	2	2	2	1.5	6	2.5 (see note)	21	SBE	1984	1988	10
	1987	4	2	2	2	2	1.5	5	3.5 (see note)	21	SBE	1984	1989	10A
	1989	4	2	2	2	2	1.5	6	3.5 (see note)	21	SBE	1988	1989	11
IL	1980	3	1	1		Local board determines remaining				16				
	1985	3	2	2	2	1	4.5	2.25	1.25	16	Leg	5/83	1988	
	1987	3	2	2	2	1	4.5	2.25	1.25	16	Leg	5/83	1988	
	1989	3	2	2	2	1	4.5	2.25	1.25	16	Leg	5/83	1988	
IN	1980	3	2	1	1	1	.5	.5	8	16				
	1985	4	2	2	2	2	1.5	8	8	19.5	SBE	9/83	1989	12
	1987	4	2	2	2	2	1.5	8	8	19.5	SBE	9/83	1989	12A
	1989	4	2	2	2	2	1.5	8	8	19.5	SBE	9/83	1989	
IA	1980		1.5	1	1									
	1985		1.5	1	1						Leg.			13
	1987		1.5	1	1							1988		13A
	1989		1	1	1						Leg.	1988	1989	13B

Table 4.4 (con't)

KS	1980	4	2	1	1	8		17				
	1985	4	3	2	1	8	1 local bd. determines	21	SBE	1983	1989	14
	1987	4	3	2	1	8	1 local bd. determines	21	SBE	1983	1989	
	1989	4	3	2	1	9		21	SBE	1983	1989	14A
KY	1980	3	2	2	1	8		18				
	1985	4	2	3	1	7	1 (see note)	20	SBE	1982	1987	
	1987	4	2	3	1	7	1 (see note)	20	SBE	1982	1987	
	1989	4	2	3	1	7	1 (see note)	20	SBE	1982	1987	
LA	1980	3	2	2	2	8.5	.5	20				
	1985	4	3	3	2	7.5	.5 computer literacy	23	SBE	4/84	1989	15
	1987	4	3	3	2	7.5	.5 computer literacy	23	SBE	6/88	1989	
	1989	4	3	3	2	7.5	.5 computer literacy	23	SBE	6/88	1989	
ME	1980	4					Local board determines remaining with American History required	16				
	1985	4	2	2	1.5	3.5	1 fine arts	16		9/84	1989	16
	1987	4	2	2	1.5	3.5	1 fine arts	16		9/84	1989	
	1989	4	2	2	1.5	3.5	1 fine arts	16		9/84	1989	
MD	1980	4	3	2	1	8		20				
	1985	4	3	2	1	5	1 fine, 1 practical arts	20	SBE	6/85	1989	17
	1987	4	3	2	1	5	1 fine, 1 practical arts	20	SBE	6/85	1989	
	1989	4	3	2	1	5	1 fine arts, 1 industrial arts/technology ed., home ec., voc. ed. or computer studies	20	SBE	6/85	1989	17A
MA	1980	Local board determines										
	1985	1				4						
	1987	1				4						
	1989	1				4						18
MI	1980	.5	Local board determines remaining									
	1985	.5							Leg			19
	1987	.5										
	1989	.5										19A

Table 4.4 (con't)

	Year						Local board determines remaining	Total				
MN	1980	3	2 (gr. 10, 11, 12)	1	1		Local board determines remaining	15				
	1985	4	3	1	1.5		9.5	20	SBE	1982	1982	20
	1987	4	3	1	1.5		9.5	20	SBE	1982	1982	20A
	1989	4	3	1	1.5		9.5	20	SBE	1982	1982	
MS	1980	3	2.5	1	1.5		8.5	16		1970		
	1985	3	2.5	1	1.5		8.5	16	SBE	1985	1989	21
	1987	4	2	2	1		8	18	SBE	1985	1989	21A
	1989	4	2	2	1		8	18				
MO	1980	1	1	1	1	4	11	20				
	1985	3	2	2	2	1 fine, 1 practical arts	10	22	SBE	3/84	1988	22
	1987	3	2	2	2	1 fine, 1 practical arts	10	22	SBE	3/84	1988	
	1989	3	2	2	2	1 fine, 1 practical arts	10	22	SBE	3/84	1988	
MT	1980	4	1.5	1	1		4	16				
	1985	4	1.5 or 2	1	1		10.5 or 10	20	SBE	1984	1986	23
	1987	4	1.5 or 2	1	1		10.5 or 10	20	SBE	1984	1986	23A
	1989	4	1.5	1	1		10.5	20	SBE	1988	1989	
NB	1980	Local board determines										
	1985	Local board determines							Leg	4/84	1991	24
	1987	Local board determines							Leg	4/84	1991	
	1989	Local board determines							Leg	4/84	1991	
NV	1980	3	2	1	2.5		9.5	19				
	1985	3	2	2	2.5		9.5	20	SBE	7/83	1986	
	1987	4	2	2	2.5	1 arts/hum., .5 computer lit.	8.5	22.5	SBE	11/86	1992	25
	1989	4	2	2	2.5	1 arts/hum., .5 computer lit.	8.5	22.5	SBE	11/86	1992	
NH	1980	4	2	1	1.25		8	16				
	1985	4	2.5	2	1.25	4 (see note)	4	19.75	SBE	7/84	1989	26
	1987	4	2.5	2	1.25	4 (see note)	4	19.75	SBE	7/84	1989	26A
	1989	4	2.5	2	1.25	4 (see note)	4	19.75	SBE	7/84	1989	

Table 4.4 (con't)

State	Year							Notes	Total	Authority	Date	Year	Ref.
NJ	1980	4	2	2	1	4	4						
	1985	4	2	2	1	4	4	1.5 (see note)	18.5	SBE	12/79	1985	27
	1987	4	2	3	2	4	4	2.5 (see note)	21.5	SBE	12/86	1988	27A
	1989	4	3	3	2	4	4	1.5 (see note)	21.5	SBE	09/87	1990	
NM	1980	4	2	2	1	1	7	2 practical/1 fine arts	20				
	1985	4	2	2	2	1	9	1 practical or fine arts	21	SBE	4/83	1987	28
	1987	4	3	3	2	1	9	1 communication skills	23	SBE	1986	1990	28A
	1989	4	3	3	2	1	9	1 communication skills	23	SBE	1986	1990	
NY	1980	4	3	1	1	.5	6.5		16				
	1985	4	4	2	2	.5	(see note)	(see note)	18.5	Reg.	1984	1989	29
	1987	4	4	2	2	.5	(see note)	(see note)	18.5	Reg.	1984	1989	29A
	1989	4	4	2	2	.5	(see note)	(see note)	18.5	Reg.	1984	1989	
NC	1980	4	2	1	2	1	6		16				
	1985	4	2	2	2	1	9		20	SBE	1/83	1987	30
	1987	4	2	2	2	1	9		20	SBE	1/83	1987	
	1989	4	2	2	2	1	9		20	SBE	1/83	1987	
ND	1980	3	3	1	2	1	7		17				
	1985	4	3	2	2	1	5		17	Supt.	8/83	1984	31
	1987	4	3	2	2	1	5		17	Supt.	8/83	1984	
	1989	4	3	2	2	1	5		17	Supt.	8/83	1984	
OH	1980	3	2	1	1	1	9		17				
	1985	3	2	2	1	1	9		18	SBE	1983	1988	32
	1987	3	2	2	1	1	9		18	SBE	1983	1988	
	1989	3	2	2	1	1	9		18	SBE	1983	1988	
OK	1980	4	1.5	1	1	1			10.5				
	1985	4	2	2	2		10		20	SBE	1982	1987	33
	1987	4	2	2	2		10		20	SBE	1982	1987	
	1989	4	2	2	2		10		20	SBE	1982	1987	

Table 4.4 (con't)

State	Year								#	Agency	Adopt	Impl	Note
OR	1980	3	3.3	1	1	2	9	1.5	21				
	1985	3	3.5	2	2	2	8	1.5 (see note)	22	SBE	4/84	1988	34
	1987	3	3.5	2	2	2	8	1.5	22	SBE	4/84	1988	34A
	1989	3	3.5	2	2	2	8	1.5	22	SBE	4/84	1988	
PA	1980	3	2	1	1	1			13				
	1985	4	3	3	3	1	5	2 arts/humanities	21	SBE	1983	1989	35
	1987	4	3	3	3	1	5	2 arts/humanities	21	SBE	12/83	1989	35A
	1989	4	3	3	3		9	2 arts/humanities	21	SBE	12/83	1989	
RI	1980	4	1	1	1				16				
	1985	4	2	2	2		6		16	Bd. of	1/85	1989	
	1987	4	2	2	2		6		16	Reg.	1/85	1989	
	1989	4	2	2	2		6		16		1/85	1989	36
SC	1980	4	3	2	2	1	7		18				
	1985	4	3	3	3	1	7		20	SBE	7/84	1987	37
	1987	4	3	3	3	1	7		20	SBE	7/84	1987	
	1989	4	3	3	3	1	7		20	SBE	7/84	1987	37A
SD	1980	4	2	1	1		8		16				
	1985	4	3	2	2		8	.5 computer, .5 fine arts	20	SBE	2/84	1989	38
	1987	4	3	2	2		8	.5 computer, .5 fine arts	20	SBE	2/84	1989	
	1989	4	3	2	2		8	.5 computer, .5 fine arts	20	SBE	2/84	1989	38A
TN	1980	4	1.5	1	1	1.5	9		18				
	1985	4	1.5	2	2	1.5	9		20	SBE	8/83	1987	
	1987	4	1.5	2	2	1.5	9		20	SBE	8/83	1987	39
	1989	4	1	2	2	1.5	9	.5 economics	20	SBE	1988	1989	39A
TX	1980	3	2.5	2	2	1.5/5	6.5		18				
	1985	4	2.5	3	2	1.5/5	7	.5 economics/free enterprise	21	SBE	9/84	1988	40
	1987	4	2.5	3	2	1.5/5	7	.5 economics/free enterprise	21	SBE	9/84	1988	
	1989	4	2.5	3	2	1.5/5	7	.5 economics/free enterprise	21	SBE	9/84	1988	40A

Table 4.4 (con't)

UT	1980	3	2	1	1	1.5/5	6.5		15				
	1985	3	3	2	2	1.5/5	9	3 (see note)	24	SBE	1/84	1988	41
	1987	3	3	2	2	2	9.5	2.5 (see note)	24	SBE	11/85	1988	41A
	1989	3	3	2	2	2	9.5	2.5	24	SBE	11/85	1988	
VT	1980												
	1985	4	3	3	3	1.5		1 arts	15.5	SBE	8/84	1989	42
	1987	4	4	. . . 5 . . .		1.5		1 arts	14.5	SBE&	1986	1989	42A
	1989	4	4	. . . 5 . . .		1.5		1 arts	14.5	Leg.	1986	1989	
VA	1980	4	3	1	1	2	7		18				
	1985	4	3	2	2	2	6	1 addl. math or science	20	SBE	7/83	1988	43
	1987	4	3	2	2	2	6	1 addl. math or science, 1 fine or practical arts	21	SBE	6/87	1989	43A
	1989	4	3	2	2	2	6	1 addl. math or science, 1 fine or practical arts	21	SBE	6/87	1989	
WA	1980	6	5	3	2	2		3 occupational education					
	1985	3	2.5	2	2	2	5.5	1 occupational education	18	SBE	1983	1989	44
	1987	3	2.5	2	2	2	5.5	1 occup. ed., 1 fine/visual or performing arts	19	SBE	1985	1991	
	1989	3	2.5	2	2	2	5.5	1 occup. ed., 1 fine/visual or performing arts	19	SBE	1985	1991	
WV	1980	4	3	1	1	2	7		19				
	1985	4	3	2	2	2	7	1 (see note)	21	SBE	1985	1989	45
	1987	4	3	2	2	2	7	1 (see note)	21	SBE	1985	1989	45A
	1989	4	3	2	2	2	7	1 (see note)	21	SBE	1988	1989	
WI	1980	Local board determines requirements											
	1985	4	3	2	2	2			13	Leg.	1984	1989	46
	1987	4	3	2	2	2			13	Leg.	1984	1989	
	1989	4	3	2	2	2			13	Leg.	1984	1989	
WY	1980		1	Local board determines remaining					18				
	1985		1	Local board determines remaining					18				
	1987		1	Local board determines remaining					18				47
	1989		1	Local board determines remaining					18				47A

*SBE = State Board of Education Leg. = Legislature

NOTES

01 AL—Students must become computer literate through related course work. A minimum competency test is required for graduation.** With modified academic coursework, students may earn a college bound diploma.

02 AZ—Passage of a minimum competency test is required for graduation.

03 AR—Social studies options—3 units or 2 units social studies and 1 practical arts.

04 CA—State board has published "Model Graduation Requirements" to be used as a guide by local districts. These include specifics in core subjects plus computer studies and foreign language.

04ACA—Dept. of Education has test and cut-off standards for early exit, with parental approval. Passage of a minimum competency test is required for graduation. State has a suggested model of curriculum to guide local districts advising students on requirements for college entry.

05 CO—Local boards determine requirements. State has constitutional prohibition against state requirements. School accreditation requirements are a total of 30 units, appropriately covering language arts, social studies, science, math, foreign language, fine/vocational/practical arts, health/safety and physical education.

06 DE—Passing the minimum competency test is required for graduation.

07 DC—Electives must include life skills seminar or students may pass a test in lieu of the seminar.

07ADC—With modified academic coursework, students may earn a college-bound diploma.

08 FL—Two of the science units must be in a lab. Beginning with the class of 1989, students must have a 1.5 grade point average to graduate. Vocational students may substitute certain sequences of vocational courses to satisfy up to 2 of the requires credits in each of the areas of English, math and science. The state's junior and senior class students may receive dual credits for college courses. The state does require passage of a minimum competency test for graduation.

09 GA—"Other" column: 1 fine arts, vocational education or computer technology.

09AGA—ROTC was added to the list within the "Other" column. Students who successfully complete 4 units in voc. ed. courses in addition to requirements receive a formal seal of endorsement by the SBE. Passage of a minimum competency test is required for graduation. With modified coursework, students may earn a college-bound diploma.

10 ID—"Other" column: .5 each, reading, speech and consumer education and 1 humanities. Humanities will increse to 2 units after 1988 with a total of 21 units. Practical arts may substitute for the 1 unit of humanities at this time.

10AID—Humanities increased to 2 units within the "Other" column; total requirement remains the same with electives decreasing. SBE requires either a C average, demonstrated competency in core curriculum on a junior class competency test, or adherence to local district's achievement plan for graduation. State has available a competency test for optional usage by districts. If students pass the test they receive a special proficiency endorsement on their diploma.

11 IL—"Other" column: .25 consumer education, 1 art, foreign language, music or vocational education. One year of math may be computer technology; 1 year of social studies must be U.S. History or half U.S. History and half American Government. Beginning in 1985-86 the school boards were allowed to excuse pupils in 11-12th

**A more detailed analysis of state minimum competency testing is available from the Education Commission of the State's Clearinghouse.

grades from physical education to: 1) participation in interscholastic athletics or 2) enroll in academic class required for admission to college or in order to graduate from high school. Beginning in 1986-87, pupils in 9-12th grades may elect to take a SBE developed consumer education proficiency test; if passed, they will be excused from requirement.

12 IN—The state board regulations were approved and signed by the governor in September 1983.

12AIN—The state does not use standard Carnegie units. With modified academic coursework, students may participate in the Academic Honors Program.

13 IA—Legislative requirements in effect for many years. Local districts determine remaining requirements.

13AIA—State allows students in junior and senior classes to receive dual credits for college coursework.

13BIA—SBE decided to drop the 1.5 credit hour requirement for social studies; the legislature accepted dropping the requirement as long as the curriculum covered the social studies topics.

14 KY—"Other" column: 1 additional math, science, social studies or vocational education. Additional core subject credit is a legislative requirement passed in 1984 and approved by the state board to be effective for graduates in 1985. Graduates in 1985 and 1986 needed 18 units to graduate.

14AKY—Minimum competency test passage is required for graduation. With modified academic coursework a student may earn a college-bound diploma.

15 LA—Graduates in 1988 needed 22 units.

15ALA—With an ACT score of 29 or above, 3.5 GPA with no semester grade lower than a B, no unexcused absences and no suspensions students receive a Scholar Program seal on diploma. With modified academic coursework, a student may earn a college-bound diploma. Minimum competency test passage is required for graduation.

16 ME-Enacted by legislature and approved by state board. American History is required. All students must pass computer proficiency standards. One of the science units must include lab study.

17 MD—Four credits must be earned after Grade 11. Students can now earn statewide certificate of merit with fulfillment of additional requirements. Special education certificates are available for students unable to meet requirements but who complete a special education program.

17AMD—Minimum competency test is required for graduation, as is a writing test and passage of a quiz on citizenship.

18 MA—Legislative requirements in effect for many years. American History is required. Local boards determine additional requirements.

19 MI—Legislative requirements in effect for many years. Local boards determine additional requirements. The state board, in January 1984, published graduation requirement guidelines which local districts are urged to incorporate.

19AMI—Included in the recomendations are a minimum of 15.5 units, which includes an option of 2 units picked from foreign language/fine or performing arts/vocational education and .5 computer education. Recommendations include modified academic coursework for students who are college-bound.

20 MN—Requirements took effect immediately for all students.

20AMN—Students in junior and senior classes may receive dual credits for college coursework.

21 MS—In May 1985, the state board adopted new requirements which were to be field-tested for one year.

21AMS—At least one of the science units must include lab. Minimum competency test passage is required for graduation.

22 MO—The college preparation diploma became available to qualifying graduates in 1985. For college preparation, specific core subjects must be taken.

23 MT—Core requirements in effect for several years. State board raised the total—1985 graduates needed 19 units; 1986 graduates needed 20. Social studies requirement has 2 alternatives.

23AMT—Effective 7/92 requirements will be changed to 2 units of social studies, 2 units of science, 1 unit of fine arts and 1 unit of vocational/practical arts.

24 NB—For graduation, 200 credit hours are required, with at least 80% in core curriculum courses. The state board is conducting hearings to define core courses.

25 NV—Computer literacy may be waived by demonstration of competency. Minimum competency test passage is required for graduation.

26 NH—"Other" column: .5 arts; .5 computer science; 3 from 2 of the following—arts, foreign language, practical arts, vocational education.

26ANH—The usage of minimum competency test passage for high school graduation is an option of the local districts.

27 NJ—"Other" column: 1 fine, practical or performing arts; .5 career exploration. 92 credit hours are required for graduation. The state does not use standard Carnegie units.

27ANJ—State does not use graduating class as the base for changes but uses the terminology of "the students entering ninth grade class". Consequently the increased math requirements becomes effective for the ninth grade class entering in the 1990-91 academic year. Minimum competency test passage is required for graduation.

28 NM—In 6/84 the state board approved requiring all students achieve computer literacy prior to graduation.

28ANM—In 1989 the legislature approved a bill allowing languages other than English to satisfy the communication skills requirement which emphasizes the areas of writing and speaking. Students preparing for college have an advanced curriculum. A state level minimum competency test is available and the districts have the option of usage. If a student passes the test a special proficiency endorsement is included on their diploma.

29 NY—Electives vary for the local (regular) and the Regents' (college-bound) diploma. "Other" column: 1 art and/or music for local; 3 to 5 from a sequence of specific courses must be chosen by Regents' diploma students and is an additional requirement for local. The local diploma notes .5 for health only, 2 noncredit units of physical education beyond the total are required. For all students, comprehensive tests are required. By 1991, areas covered will include reading, writing, math, American History and government, and science/global studies. For a Regents' diploma comprehensive exams are required in most subjects.

29ANY—Minimum competency test passage is a graduation requirement for all students.

30 NC—One science class must include lab. With modified coursework, students may earn a college-bound diploma. Minimum competency test passage is required for graduation.

31 ND—One unit of higher level foreign language may be substituted for the 4th unit of English; 1 unit of math may be business math. Although 17 units are required the local education agencies are urged to establish requirements at a minimum of 20 units.

32 OH—Passage of a minimum competency test is a graduation requirement by 1990.

33 OK—"Other" column: For college preparation diploma—choice of foreign language, computer science, economics, English, geography, government, math, history, sociology, science, speech and psychology. There are slight variations between 2-and 4-year and junior colleges. If foreign language is elected, student must take 2 years of

same language. Although total hour requirement is less for college prep. path, curriculum is more rigorous and restrictive.

34   OR—"Other" column: .5 career development, 1 applied arts, fine arts or foreign language.

34AOR—Minimum competency test passage will be required for graduating class of 1992. "Honors Degree" diplomas were available for students graduating in 1988 and subsequent years who maintain at least a 3.5 GPA. Recipients will have an honors seal on the diploma.

35   PA—Local boards determine the remaining 5 units.

35APA—Computer science can be option instead of arts and humanities. State has prescribed learning objectives and curriculum guidelines for 12 goals of quality education.

36   RI—College-bound students are required to complete 2 units of foreign language, .5 arts and .5 computer literacy and have a total unit requirement of 18.

37   SC—Enacted by the state board of education and passed by the legislature.

37ASC—If approved by the state department of education, students may count one unit of computer science for a math requirement. Students who earn 1 unit in science and 6 or more in a specific occupational service area will fulfill the science requirements. State allows students in the junior and senior classes to receive dual credits for college coursework. With modified coursework, students may earn a college-bound diploma. Beginning with the graduating class of 1990, students mut pass an exit exam of minimum competency.

38   SD—Increased total number of requirements was phased in—16 through 1986; 18 in 1987; 19 in 1988.

38ASD—Beginning in 1990 the requirements will be raised to 3 in science and the electives will drop to 7.

39   TN—With modified coursework, a student may earn a college-bound diploma or an honors vocational education diploma. Minimum competency test passage is a requirement for graduation.

39ATN—Students may meet the economics requirement by: 1 semester in economics, out-of-school experiences through Junior Achievement, or marketing education.

40   TX—"Other" column: For college preparation—.5 economics/free enterprise, 2 foreign language, 1 computer science, 1 fine arts, 1.5 units of physical education and .5 of health are required for either regular or college prep. program.

40ATX—Junior and senior students are allowed to receive dual credit for college courses. Minimum competency test passage is a requirement for graduation.

41   UT—"Other" column: 1.5 arts, 1 vocational ed., .5 computer science. The state board makes specific course recommendations for college entry, vocational, etc.

41AUT—If computer literacy isn't obtained in related coursework, .5 of the electives must be devoted to computer science.

42   VT—Enacted by state board and approved by the legislature.

42AVT—To allow more flexibility to both vocational education students and smaller or more rural districts, the previous math and science requirement of 3 units in each was modified to a combination of 5 units which may be 2 of one and 3 of the other.

43   VA—Advanced studies diploma available beginning with the 1985 graduates.

43AVA—Additional math or science requirement included in the "Other" column may be fulfilled by an appropriate ;vocational education class or ROTC. Grade average of "B" or better earns a SBE seal on the diploma. With modified coursework, a student may earn a college-bound diploma. Students in junior and senior classes are allowed to receive dual credits for college coursework. Minimum competency test passage is required for graduation.

44   WA—45 hours required for graduation beginning in 1980. 1985 legislature passed

addition of a credit for students graduating in 1991. This may be in fine, visual or performing arts or any of the subject areas currently required.

45 WV—"Other" column: 1 of student's electives must be for choice of applied arts, fine or performing arts or a foreign language.

45AWV—State has approved, and policies reflect, an advanced studies certificate, Certificate of Academic Excellence, which has not yet been implemented.

46 WI—Electives are the option of the local school district. The state recommends that districts require a total of 22 units. State recommendations emphasize vocational education, foreign language and fine arts to make up the difference between the 13 mandated and 22 recommended units. State requires that all students in Grades 7-12 be participating in a class or a board approved activity each period of the day. Local districts have the option of using minimum competency test passage as a requirement for graduation.

47 WY—Requirements in effect a number of years.

47AWY—Accreditation standards indicate 4 units of English/language arts, 3 of social studies and 2 each of math and science.

The National Reform Report Recommendations

The National Commission on Excellence in Education's *A Nation at Risk*, recommended the following guidelines for high school graduation requirements: 4 years of English; 3 years each of mathematics, science and social studies; 2 years of foreign language and a half year of computer science.

The National Science Board, in *Educating Americans for the 21st Century*, recommended 3 years for each of math, science and technology, including one year of algebra and one semester of computer science. They also recommended all secondary schools offer advanced mathematics and science courses.

In *Making the Grade* the Twentieth Century Fund recommended a core curriculum of reading, writing, calculating, computers, science, foreign languages and civics.

Ernest Boyer stressed needed changes to make mastery of language the first priority and writing as most important. His recommended core curriculum reported in *High School* was literature, arts, foreign language, history, science, mathematics, technology and one semester of speech.

John Goodlad's *A Place Called School* urged a change from core curriculum as a common set of topics to a common set of concepts, principals, skills and ways of knowing. He felt there was not enough discussing, writing, problem-solving, analysis, etc.—the concepts associated with higher-order skills.

The Education Commission of the States' *Action for Excellence* recommended strengthening the curriculum from K-12 not only in math and science but in all disciplines; providing richer substance and greater motivational program and eliminating the "soft" or nonessential courses.

Compiled by: ECS Clearinghouse
9/89

References

Abrahamson, S. S. (1962). *Constitutions of the United States, National and State* (Vol. 1). Published for Legislative Drafting Research Fund of Columbia University by Oceana Publications, Inc., Dobbs Ferry, NY. *Colorado,* Article IX, Sec. 16, p. 34.

California State Department of Education. (1984). *Survey of Textbook Evaluation and Adoption Processes.* Sacramento, CA: Author.

Education Commission of the States. (1985, November). State Activity—Minimum Competency Testing. Education Commission of the States, Denver, CO. In *Clearinghouse Notes.*

_____. (1989, September). Minimum high school graduation requirements between 1980 and 1989: Standard diplomas. In *Clearinghouse Notes.*

Florida Statutes. (1983). Senate Bill 6B, Part I, Section 1, amending Sec. 1, Section 232.246.

Good, H. B. (1963). *A History of American Education* (2nd ed.). New York: McMillan Company.

Minnesota Department of Education. (1989, September). *Education Update, 24* (1), 2.

National Commission on Excellence in Education. (1983). *A Nation at Risk.*

PSBA bulletin. (1989, August). New Cumberland, PA: Pennsylvania School Boards Association, vol. 53, no. 4.

U.S. Department of Education, Office of Planning, Budget, and Evaluation, Planning and Evaluation Service. (1984, January). *State Education Performance Chart.*

van Geel, T. (1976). *Authority to Control the School Program.* Lexington, MA: D. C. Heath.

5

Historical Perspective on Centralizing Curriculum

William H. Schubert

*T*oday curriculum is controlled at the state level more than ever before in American history. It is therefore timely to reflect on the history of centralized and decentralized curriculum efforts. Since curriculum became a formal area of study in the late nineteenth century, the tide of influence has ebbed and flowed on the issue of local- versus state-developed curriculum.

Numerous questions emerge about the relative desirability of mandated curriculum versus curriculum developed at the local level. Most prominent is the following question: Which is more desirable, that which is mandated or that which is developed at the grassroots? Should this question be answered with an either-or response? This would present a choice of either grassroots or a more removed level as the center from which curriculum should emanate. Or, should it be assumed that the problem is much more complex and situational than this? For instance, should it be assumed that neither a grassroots approach nor a top-down mandate for curriculum works best in all circumstances? To assume otherwise may be to oversimplify. What is needed, some argue, is the careful and ongoing exercise of judgment in an effort to determine what blend of external and internal expertise is most appropriate for each situation faced by curriculum developers in the practical flow of situations.

To conclude that this is the best stance in principle is probably a good decision, but it is extraordinarily difficult to carry out in practice. Clearly, it is nearly impossible and politically unwise to discard a mandate from the school board, the state, or a funding agency in light of a momentary decision that situational decision making would make more sense. Similarly, in the course of grassroots curriculum development, questions often arise about the relationship of local decisions to decisions elsewhere. How important, local decision makers often ask, is it to provide consistent and noncontradictory learning experiences for students throughout a larger locale, state, region, nation, or even world?

Historically, since the establishment of universal schooling as a goal, these questions have been raised often and in many different ways. Moreover, ways of asking and answering such questions invoke fundamentally different belief systems, philosophies, and ideologies on the part of educators. To address the fundamental curriculum question (What knowledge and experience are most worthwhile?) invokes even more pervasive philosophical and cultural questions, such as the following: What does it mean to grow as a person? What kind of learning contributes to a more just society? What should be the social and individual purposes of schooling?

Level of Control

A fundamental question for the topic of this book, centralizing and mandating curriculum, is one of level of control. What is meant by external control? From the perspective of teachers and students, the school board might represent a large and oppressive external force—especially in large urban school systems. On the contrary, from the vantage point of state education officials, the granting of significant discretionary decision making for curriculum development to the local boards of education and school district leaders may be perceived as a major move in the direction of local control. Likewise, school board members and central office administrators may view the decentralization of certain curriculum decisions to teachers as the ultimate evidence of local control; however, students may see teachers in much the same way as school district officials perceive the state—as external control.

The question of where control ought to reside obviously should be contingent upon who has greatest expertise about which aspects of curriculum. Drawing upon John Dewey, Harold Rugg, and others, Ralph Tyler (1949) pointed out that curriculum should be based upon authority found in subject matter, social needs, and needs of learners as individuals. Those who have expertise in each of these bases for curriculum development, depending on a particular problem in a particular place, might be state officials, funding agents, school board members, central office administrators, parents, teacher educators, researchers in the disciplines, educational theorists and researchers, principals, teachers, students, or others. The balancing act of providing for relative degrees of control from these curriculum decision makers according to their expertise in a given set of circumstances is a difficult task indeed; yet it is one that must be addressed anew by each generation amidst their unique set of circumstances. Despite the uniqueness of circumstances in each generation, however, enough similarity exists with earlier generations to benefit from a historical perspective.

A Historical Perspective

Issues pertaining to the centralization of curriculum began to emerge in full force as universal schooling gained ascendance in America. Moves toward centralization were often powerful, with or without the accompaniment of mandates or legislation. Major statements by scholarly and professional associations addressed the question of that which is most worth knowing and how it might be made available to children and youth. Certain traditional voices in curriculum emerged to call for centralization and sometimes for state mandates as well. Providing counterpoint, those immersed in particular educational settings (and their advocates among curriculum scholars and educational leaders) issued frequent calls for greater involvement of teachers, parents, students, and grassroots curriculum leaders in determining what is worthwhile to know and experience.

Nineteenth Century

Throughout the latter three-quarters of the nineteenth century, educators hailed the Yale Report of 1828, published in the prestigious *American Journal of Science and Arts* (Yale, 1829), which promoted faculty psychology. When applied to curriculum and methods of teaching, faculty psychology likened the mind to muscles to be trained, and designated certain subjects as justified curriculum inclusions because they trained the faculties of reason, imagination, and other such human characteristics. Faculty psychology as a basis for liberal education carried much weight in curriculum development even though it was not made official through legislation. Although the Yale Report was not made a legal requirement, it markedly influenced numerous policy documents, particularly in colleges and secondary schools. In the late nineteenth century the assumptions behind faculty psychology as a basis for curriculum were challenged by the research of pragmatist William James, who believed that the value of propositions (e.g., faculty psychology) lies in consequences. Later, his former student, E. L. Thorndike, continued empirical study that demonstrated that the medieval *trivium* (grammar, rhetoric, and logic) and *quadrivium* (arithmetic, astronomy, geometry, and music) had no monopoly on the development of the mind when compared with topics for study that might be selected for their relevance to particular needs and interests (Schubert, 1980, 1986). Such studies provided justification for local curriculum decision makers to pull away from exclusive adherence to the seven liberal arts which had been taken for granted as the mainstay of sound curriculum that would train the faculties of the mind. Moreover, it gave increased confidence to these curriculum leaders to listen to their own insights about the needs and interests of the increased numbers of children and youth entering school during the expansion of the universal education promise. With universal schooling came new kinds of students with different backgrounds than those who received the liberal arts curriculum from the old world.

Universal Schooling

Universal schooling, ironically, was at once an example of mandated and local curriculum. It can be argued that the desirability of universal schooling emerged as local publics decided they needed a more educated populace. Thus, universal schooling became mandatory—legislated and centralized. With legislation of universal schooling came questions of what should be obtained from it by all engaged. As far back as 1839, Henry Barnard's first annual report as secretary to the Board of Commissioners of Common Schools in Connecticut (Barnard, 1839) raised the question of what the common school curriculum should be. In the second half of the nineteenth century William T. Harris was a dominant force in keeping alive the liberal arts tradition as the centralized curriculum. As U.S. commissioner of education, superintendent of the St. Louis Schools, and a highly regarded Hegelian philosopher, Harris spoke strongly in favor of the "five windows on the soul" (mathematics, biology, art and literature, grammar, history), his version of the liberal arts (Schubert, 1986; Kliebard, 1986). Remarkable in debate, Harris led educational reform efforts through deliberations of the National Education Association (NEA) in the 1890s (Committee of Ten, 1893; Committee of Fifteen, 1895). He and President Charles Eliot of Harvard led the influential Committee of Ten of the NEA as it focused on what secondary school studies should include. The emergent American Herbartianism and its advocates (Charles DeGarmo, Frank McMurry, Charles McMurry, and others) tried to challenge the dominant view. They, along with psychologist G. Stanley Hall, argued for a developmental approach to curriculum and method—a position that asserted that the development of the individual recapitulates the evolution of the human race. These developmentalists called for curriculum development which correlated with the developmental level of the learner. The developmentalists were accorded some concessions, such as more emphasis on modern sciences and elective subjects, but they were dissatisfied that the resulting report of 1893 failed to give sufficient emphasis to human development. Therefore they called for another committee, the Committee of Fifteen, to address the problem of correlation.

Francis Parker was the major force to succeed in establishing the Committee of Fifteen, but Harris was appointed as its chair. This led to a traditional liberal arts image of curriculum in the report of the Committee of Fifteen in 1895. An interesting counterpoint to the contending parties is implicit in Parker's role. Neither a doctrinaire Herbartian nor an advocate of the traditional liberal arts, Parker seemed to assume that the ideas of development and correlation of the Herbartians held greater potential for fundamental reform. Both the intellectual traditionalists (e.g., Harris and Eliot) and the Herbartians sought control with what seemed to be a desire to centralize the curriculum. In contrast, Parker saw in the images of development and correlation a deeper meaning that had potential for grassroots curriculum improvement. According to reflections by Herbartian Frank McMurry as late as 1927, Parker had something quite different in mind—something that reflected the essence of the local control of curriculum: "As I look back on it now, he (Parker) was searching for the problem or project of work, where you find your starting point for both curriculum and method within the child rather than within some branch of knowledge. In that tendency he was a long way in advance of the rest of us." (McMurry, 1927, p. 331). Parker perceived that the answer to Herbert Spencer's 1861 question, frequently taken to be the basic curriculum question (What knowledge is of most worth?), can only be answered in the context of a situation in which a particular person is striving to learn. Although this does not rule out highly centralized knowledge as a basis for curriculum development, it asserts that students and their teachers must be an integral part of the process. Thus, Parker illustrated an alternative to centralized and mandated curriculum in his day and in current times as well. He proposed that the child should be the center of curriculum reform. In other words, the child's own growth, not a subject or external topic, should be the focus of curriculum. To make this the focus of curriculum requires an orientation that reconstructs conditions for growth in every situation. The process of reconstruction becomes the curriculum itself. Such a curriculum requires the steadfast participation of teacher and student throughout.

Influence of John Dewey

Lingering quietly on the sidelines of curriculum debates of the 1890s was a young philosopher named John Dewey. He was formulating a philosophy that could be a theoretical structure for the sentiments promoted so ardently by Parker. In the early 1890s, Dewey began to realize that philosophy and psychology needed to be wedded in experience if these disciplines were to inform the growth of individuals in a democracy. Dewey saw the testing ground of this psychology and philosophy of democracy located in the practice of pedagogy. Thus, when invited to an appointment at the University of Chicago in 1894, he insisted on chairing a department of philosophy, psychology, and pedagogy. Moreover, he requested a laboratory school wherein ideas could be tested and developed. Dewey's resultant philosophy of education (see Dewey, 1900, 1902, 1916, 1938) became the best comprehensive rationale for grassroots democracy thus far developed. It likewise became an elegant argument against the centralized, standardized, and mandated curriculum.

Four hallmarks of Deweyan philosophy of education pertain to curriculum: (1) comprehensive philosophy, (2) integration of dualisms, (3) science as intelligence in everyday problem solving, and (4) democracy as conjoint and associated living. A comprehensive philosophy deals with metaphysics, epistemology, axiology, ethics, aesthetics, politics, logic, and theology. I have argued elsewhere (Schubert, 1987) that Dewey was not only one of the few comprehensive philosophers of the twentieth century to treat all of these areas, but significantly for curriculum perspectives, he brought them all to bear on education. Under this large umbrella of philosophy, Dewey transformed his other hallmarks of integration, science, and democracy into a theory of pedagogy grounded in experience. Out of the wealth of individual experiences of learners and teachers in any educational setting emerge interests and concerns about which group members feel strongly.

At first the interests and concerns of individuals seem disconnected from one another, as do the individuals in the group themselves. As the perceptive teacher leads the group in dialogue, however, these concerns and interests are shared. When shared, they can be seen as connected, that is, as being manifestations of perennial human concerns (love, justice, freedom, death, tradition, and anxiety, for example). Thus, the concerns of different individuals can be seen as integrated in much the same way as Dewey sought to unite dualisms mind and body, means and ends, individual and social, action and inquiry) in his philosophic work. The process of achieving integration is dialogue, which leads to democracy. Further, the democratic pursuit of resolutions to problems implicit in concerns and interests is an everyday notion of science, which Dewey often referred to as the "method of intelligence." This is a method that draws upon the funded knowledge of the human race (disciplines of knowledge) as it fits situations. It posits that acquaintance with centralized knowledge must derive from situational concern in interdisciplinary fashion, not by delivering already analyzed bits of knowledge to students who have no experiential repertoire to relate to them. The disciplines of knowledge and knowledge personally created as learners resolve problems are part of the same continuum. Both serve the inquiring individual and group in search of increased meaning, direction, personal growth, and social justice.

This Deweyan ideal of curriculum, created locally by teachers and learners who pursue genuine interests and concerns, realize that those concerns and interests symbolize perennial human interests, and draw upon extant knowledge, has had an uphill battle since its inception. There seems to be a perpetual tendency to prefer the centralization and standardization it brings. Harry Broudy (1979) once humorously referred to this tendency toward standardization as the search for answers that cause the least cognitive strain. Moreover, the majority of curricularists have sought certainty, which Dewey claimed was an illusion (Dewey, 1929). They also search for control, which they seek from external sources (standardization, policy, or mandate), whereas Dewey asserted that the guiding force must be self-control and the responsibility of those most closely influenced by a given problem in life. Even when the Progressive Education Association (PEA) was formed in 1919 to further Deweyan ideals, some claimed that institutionalization (a form of centralization) marked the death of the movement. Overstated though this criticism may be, it says the same thing that a friend of mine said when asked if he thought a book he praised should be made required reading. His response was that to do so would be likely to destroy interest that might otherwise emerge.

At least two questions evolve from the local curriculum development alternative provided by the work of Parker and Dewey and their criticisms of centralized and generic curriculum mandates. Why was so much resistance mounted against Dewey and Deweyan progressive education? Why is there such a propensity in favor of centralization? Might the propensity to centralize be caused by a lack of faith in human beings to act reasonably and toward good virtuous ends? Might the resistance to the Deweyan emphasis on local curriculum development be due, as well, to the fact that Dewey and kindred spirits held a wholehearted faith in human beings to pursue the good with little external control? Perhaps such faith gives nightmares to those who do not share it. One point, however, seems certain—Dewey's perspective represents a distinct alternative to the prevailing tendency to centralize and mandate curriculum. He added a powerful perspective to the ebb and flow of curriculum history between the centralized and the localized.

Tensions between the Centralized and the Localized: Past Examples

It is said by many that the birthdate of the curriculum field is 1918. In that year Franklin Bobbitt wrote *The Curriculum* and perpetuated the method of curriculum development by "activity analysis." Activity analysis consisted of empirical study of what successful adults do in a society or locality as a basis for formulating objectives which lead to learning activities that enable the young to become successful adults. Ostensibly an approach that focuses on local situations, uncritical use of activity analysis can easily find itself on the centralization side of the ledger. If the ways of living and values of the dominant socioeconomic classes are taken for granted as being most successful, and if the society is rather homogeneous, differences by locale would be diminished considerably and curriculum goals would be centralized by default. This is likewise the case with W. W. Charters's variation on activity analysis, which seeks to discover the ideals of the society as a basis for objectives and learning activities (Charters, 1923).

The second major move toward centralization in 1918 was the approval and publication by the NEA of a publication entitled *Cardinal Principles of Secondary Education,* produced by the Commission on the Reorganization of Secondary Education appointed five years earlier. Under the leadership of Clarence Kingsley, the commission stated seven broad aims of secondary education that moved far afield from the traditional subject curriculum. These aims were health, command of fundamental processes, worthy home membership, worthy use of leisure time, citizenship, vocation, and ethical character. Each was characterized in a way that would be difficult, indeed, to oppose. Apart from this, one of the most significant commission recommendations was the call for universal secondary education for all normal youth. This broadening of the purposes of education was a forbearer of deliberation over curriculum constants and variables that infused debate on issues throughout the remainder of the century. What should be permanent in the comprehensive school and provided for all, what should be designated for particular groups (college preparatory, vocational, etc.), and what should be selected by students? These issues were part of the issue of general education, that is, that which is good for all and therefore should be centralized, and that which would be of value only for particular groups and situations.

The two moves to centralize curriculum noted above were not officially mandated, but particularly in the case of the *Cardinal Principles*, the influence of the NEA rivaled the power of mandates. Mandates however, were a clear part of the curriculum scene in the first quarter of the century, following the Smith-Hughes Act for Vocational Education of 1917. In 1918 all states had submitted plans of compliance through developing vocational aspects in the curriculum (Krug, 1966). From that point onward such subjects as agriculture, home economics, and trade and industrial studies were a major part of the curriculum. Passage of amendments and related legislation such as the George-Deen Act of 1934 provided for distributive education and extended vocational curriculum into the service areas. It was assumed by many that the addition of vocational curriculum helped to balance offerings so that schooling could serve more fully its goal of being universal. With vocational education, provision was made for those more interested in work that could be learned by training rather than by scholarly pursuits. This emphasis was augmented considerably when Lyndon Johnson signed the Vocational Education Act of 1963. It supported nearly all kinds of jobs with unprecedented funding, except those which required professional training or college degrees.

Building upon the legislated curriculum of vocational education was a popular movement called "life adjustment education." Initiated in the summer of 1945 under the leadership of Charles Prosser, the call for life adjustment was based on an argument that approximately 10 percent of the student population had their needs met by college preparatory secondary school curricula and that another 20 percent were served by vocational education. This left a gaping 60 percent of the students with unmet needs. The concern was to provide curricula that enabled "all American youth to live democratically with satisfaction to themselves and profit to the society as home members, workers, and citizens" (Second Commission on Life Adjustment Education, 1954, p. 1). Although life adjustment did not have formal legalistic power, it was first developed at a conference sponsored by the United States Office of Education and throughout the second half of the 1940s, the 1950s, and even into the 1960s carried a similar weight and thrust as had the *Cardinal Principles* in decades before.

In addition to Smith-Hughes, Bobbitt, and the *Cardinal Principles*, the year 1918 marked the publication of *The Project Method* authored by William H. Kilpatrick. As professor of education at Teachers College at Columbia University, Kilpatrick, known for attracting huge audiences of practitioners and scholars alike to his lectures, was a widely regarded interpreter of the philosophy of John Dewey. The "project," a method of curriculum organization, was perhaps his most influential contribution. The project (sometimes later referred to as the "unit") grew out of student interests and concerns. It was pursued in small groups or as whole-class experiences. Knowledge from the disciplines would be brought to bear on the project when it was perceived as relevant. The essence of the project required that teachers and students develop the idea together. The project concretely illustrated Dewey's progressive organization of subject matter. If students were all fascinated by zoos, for instance, all subjects (traditional and modern) could be related to a deepened understanding of zoos. The project represents a grassroots approach that is clearly different from centralized and mandated curricula; students and teachers in the project method are granted greater expertise than outside authorities in determining curriculum. They are deemed in the best position to understand the personal and contextual seedbed from which a meaningful and relevant curriculum can grow.

After the writing of Dewey's *Democracy and Education* in 1916, followed by Kilpatrick's *The Project Method* (1918), teachers (many of whom became members of the Progressive Education Association) in various parts of the United States and elsewhere tried to interpret progressive education ideals in practice. Many of them believed that this new philosophy and its methods were a major step forward; however, they were often discouraged by empirically oriented critics who demanded concrete evidence to support their assertions of success. Teachers and scholars addressed this problem at PEA meetings in the late 1920s, and by 1931 they embarked on what many consider the most important educational research project of the first half of the twentieth century—the Eight Year Study. Directed by Wilford Aikin, the study compared progressively educated students (experimental group) with traditionally educated counterparts (control group) as they moved through the eight years of high school and college. The results were succinctly and eloquently summarized by Aikin (1942) in *The Story of the Eight Year Study,* and were elaborated upon in four additional volumes dealing with the curriculum, evaluation, success in college, and stories from each of the thirty experimental schools. Traditional college entrance requirements were dropped for experimental schools (which represented a wide array of backgrounds and locales), and approximately 1,500 matched pairs of students (one control and one experimental) were followed through college. Instruments designed to assess a wide range of characteristics of success in college (academic, attitudinal, social, and psychological) revealed that on almost all measures (except foreign language study) progressively educated students did better or as well as traditionally educated students. Noting that most of the colleges had traditional curricula themselves, it is all the more impressive that students who could select projects according to their interests would do better than their counterparts, who ostensibly were directly prepared for success in traditional college curricula. What is more, the six most experimetnal of the schools in the experimental group were compared with the control group, and results indicated that students from these six schools were far more successful in college on the measures.

Progressives hailed the Eight Year Study as evidence of the importance of learning to learn; that is, the process of learning was seen as much more important than a product to be acquired. Critics cited the Hawthorne effect, but progressives countered that if it makes a positive difference to know you are participating in a study, if it makes you feel special and thus perform better, then the reasonable conclusion is to always strive to enable learners to feel special. Critics also argued that the study would be impossible to replicate because there was no operational definition or set of criteria that defined progressive education. Progressives countered this criticism by claiming that freedom to determine one's own learning within the community of students and teachers found in the local situation was, in fact, the definition.*

Here again one can see a Deweyan commitment that is at considerable odds with the mandated or centralized curriculum. As further illustration from the Eight Year Study, participating teachers were invited to take part in summer workshops to reflectively develop curriculum for subsequent teaching in the study. Moderately innovative teachers actually devised materials and projects to bring to classrooms from these workshops, and those who grasped the spirit of Deweyan progressive education most fully returned with a method of democratic intelligence that inspired students to work with them to learn about matters of shared interest. This kind of in-service education inspired work in the 1940s and 1950s by Earl C. Kelley, which he described in *The Workshop Way of Learning* (Kelley, 1951). According to Cremin (1961, p. 333), Dewey responded with praise to this kind of workshop, saying, "It supplies the missing and much needed factor in development of the theory of progressive education."

The Eight Year Study, persuasive though it was in educational discourse, was no competition with World War II in getting headlines in 1942. Moreover, the control-prone policies usually associated with

---

*I thank Mary Gauthier for helping to clarify this observation on the Eight Year Study in one of my courses, Foundations of Curriculum and Program Design.

periods of war and other national threats quickly emerged after World War II, as they had after World War I. Centralization was the hallmark of the day, sometimes based on newly devised mechanisms and at other times derived from the development of new powers for old agencies. An example of the latter was the steady emergence of accrediting agencies through both world wars. As early as 1895 the Association of Colleges and Preparatory Schools of the Southern States was founded, and shortly thereafter in 1901 the larger North Central Association emerged. Both organizations, though designed ostensibly to be helpful to the process of continuous evaluation of schools and colleges, were seen as quasi-legal inspectors who centralized standards with which compliance was deemed mandatory. Even today, the much-tempered purport of accrediting agencies as facilitators of "self-study" raises the problem of whether they enable mainly grassroots or centralized curriculum development. Generic categories of assessment, for instance, even when developed by teams of "peers" from neighboring institutions, often seem a far cry from situationally specific considerations of good teachers and their students as they continuously ask about the value of the consequences of their decision and action. Proponents of centralization might well share the conviction that evaluation from within the classroom group is best, but they believe groups who do this are rare exceptions and that most are not to be trusted without external monitoring. Such an argument is reminiscent of a conclusion reached by Joseph Mayer Rice (1893) during investigations of schools at the end of the nineteenth century. A young pediatrician who was genuinely interested in the growth and welfare of children in schools, Rice set out to find schools that were exemplars. Finding only a few, his writings in *Forum* became an exposé on the ineptitude of most schools he visited. Having begun with a progressive hope to find grassroots excellence, Rice (1913) concluded with a call for management in schools of a factorylike efficiency. Such arguments are indeed not foreign to mandated packages in many state reform efforts today.

Throughout the century a major mechanism of centralization has been the emergence of standardized testing. Like accrediting agencies, testing agencies and corporations pushed images of success in school in the direction of test scores. Beginning with the establishment of the College Entrance Examination Board in 1900, the influence of college entrance examinations proliferated in ways that could not have been anticipated, leading to today's powerful creators of tests that some claim drive the curriculum. (See also discussion in Chapter 8.) Others, more sympathetic to the power of the testing industry today, call for the "alignment" of curriculum with major tests used to evaluate students and schools alike. John Dewey, irritated by the puerile assumptions of the burgeoning testing industry, sometimes drew an analogy between standardized testing and the way in which hogs are weighed in some quarters. He explained that the process began by catching a hog, no mean feat in the first place, and tying it to one end of a board. The board was then placed on a large rock which served as a fulcrum. Then the measurement expert would run all around the countryside bringing back rocks that might equally balance with the hog. When, after much trial and error, the expert found a rock that equally balanced with the hog, he or she would promptly guess the weight of the rock, and move on to the next project!" (See Flesch, 1966.) It was disconcerting to many that tests, if based on such shaky ground, would become so central to curriculum and evaluation mandates in reform movements.

Even among progressives, however, there were tendencies to want centralization. One example is found in the teachers who prespecified curriculum for their classroom in the workshops of the Eight Year Study. Obviously a small-scale centralization, this was nevertheless an imposition on what advocates of grassroots progressivism would consider students' rights to be involved in the deliberation of what is worthwhile to know and experience. On a much broader scale, the Progressive Education Association began to split into two contrasting factions in the 1930s, a state of affairs that led to its deterioration by the end of that decade. George Counts and others, often referred to as "social reconstructionists," were sufficiently distraught by human and political conditions in the world that they called for education to reconstruct the social order (Counts, 1932). Theodore Brameld (1956) continued to develop this line of thinking well into the 1950s, arguing that conditions necessary for world peace, democracy, personal growth, and human welfare could not wait for each generation to discover them anew. Proponents of such ideas were sometimes accused of centralizing a worldview in ways that smacked of indoctrination. Within the Progressive Education Association the reconstructionists differed markedly with advocates of child study. The latter called for curriculum starting with the genuine concerns of children (e.g., Kilpatrick, 1918, and Hopkins, 1941) rather than from an adult-conceived image of what is good for the world, as advocated by Theodore Brameld, George S. Counts, and other reconstructionists. Boyd Bode (1938), Paul Hanna, and a few others tried with too little success to help contending parties see that a Deweyan position integrated dualisms of the individual (represented by child interest) and society (represented by adult constructions of knowledge). Many members of the PEA argued that these were opposite organizing centers from which curriculum development could proceed. Clearly,

Dewey saw the individual and society as correlative and complementary, asserting that the genuine development of one enhances the
other (Dewey, 1948).

Contemporary Tensions between the Centralized and the Localized

Today, the conflict between the centralized and the decentralized
continues. Having a strong bearing on today's school reform is the call
for a return to "basics" that seems perennially to accompany wars and
other impending disasters. Following World War II, Arthur Bestor
(1953), Albert Lynd (1953), and Hyman Rickover (1959) were among
those who challenged progressive education. Interestingly, in doing so
they mixed together life adjustment curriculum and the varieties of
progressive education (Deweyan or not) as the enemy, the culprit
whose lenience caused the lack of political or economic readiness of
America to meet necessary challenges. Clearly, today's polemics of
Allan Bloom (1987), E. D. Hirsch (1987), and Diane Ravitch and Chester
Finn (1987) resonate positively with the back-to-basics movement of
the 1950s, and that movement possessed distinct similarity to calls by
William Bagley (1907) and others for a return to essential knowledge
passed on by the human race, an admonition that continued during
and following World War I. Although not necessarily saying it
explicitly, these essentialist calls for "basics" in the curriculum
constitute a position that experts should determine curriculum that is
good for all students regardless of class, race, ethnicity, gender, place,
and situation. This is not far from advocacy of a national curriculum;
surely, it favors centralization. Today, when the driving force behind *A
Nation at Risk* (National Commission on Excellence in Education, 1983)
is to regain a competitive edge in the world market with nations that do
have a national curriculum, it does not seem too far-fetched to wonder
what is on the horizon in the United States, despite frequent reminders
that educational policy is decentralized to state and local governance.
When, for instance, some two hundred "blue ribbon commissions"
scattered about the land (and the several state legislatures and state
departments of education) all emerge from delibration with strikingly
similar reform proposals, the image of centralized curriculum becomes
increasingly clear. Moreover, it raises serious questions about the
nature of democracy as a grassroots enterprise. Advocates of grassroots
democratic life are seldom satisfied by "blue ribbon" commissions that
include a small number of representatives who engage in deliberation
to produce generic solutions. On the contrary, they call for active
deliberation by those most fully engaged in the situations where
curriculum decision becomes action.

The increasing domination of centralized curriculum is evident in dimensions of curriculum development other than contemporary reform initiatives and their essentialist antecedents. Too many examples exist to provide comprehensive treatment in this chapter. For instance, an array of legal decisions has had considerable bearing on curriculum both directly and indirectly, and these will be noted elsewhere in this book (see Chapter 3 by van Geel). The remainder of this chapter concentrates on two major influences on centralization: (1) published materials that directly influence the daily functioning of life in schools, and (2) direct attempts to formulate educational policy.

Published Materials

Compared with the vast array of books on every conceivable subject in libraries, the textbook industry has produced a relatively narrow and homogeneous range of materials for use in schools. Couple this with research (EPIE, 1979) that points out how textbooks, workbooks, worksheets, and instructional media are the basis of more than 90 percent of instructional time in schools, and it is evident that publishing companies exercise inordinate power in shaping learning opportunities in schools. Further, corporations of many kinds provide free and inexpensive materials to classrooms nationwide, materials not without covert and overt messages that favor the interests of those corporations (see Harty, 1979). Even when not overtly supporting an ideological perspective, publishers try to reach the widest array of purchasers; thus, their products covertly promote values that maintain social and economic hierarchies and relationships supported by dominant socioeconomic classes (Apple, 1986). When textbooks that support grassroots interests and counter those supported by dominant social and economic ideology become popular, action often emerges to crush their use in schools. Perhaps the most telling example of this is the case of Harold Rugg's controversial social studies series (Rugg, 1941). Written to teach critical evaluation of American life, these textbooks presented negative as well as positive episodes in the American past. Students were encouraged to inquire carefully and point out both admirable features and needs for reconstruction. Popular though the texts were, they soon met overwhelming conservative opposition that claimed the books were subversive and detrimental to youth. Thus, it is evident that materials published for classroom use constitute a strong force toward centralization—one quite different from the notion of projects that emerges from groups of teachers and learners. Moreover, the influence of textbook publishers is powerful enough when taken alone, but when combined with the weight of test publishers discussed earlier, the power of centralizing forces is indeed accentuated.

Formulation of Educational Policy

The second major influence on centralization is the more direct attempt of government, foundations, and professional associations to formulate curriculum policy. In 1935 the National Education Association formed the Educational Policies Commission (EPC), which "published 98 major policy statements from 1936 to 1968, with a total distribution of over two and one-half million copies" (Ortenzio, 1983, p. 34). Among its most influential titles were *The Purposes of Education in American Democracy* (1938), *Education for ALL American Youth* (1944, revised in 1952), *Education and the People's Peace* (1943), and *Education and National Security* (1951). Funded with a start-up grant of $250,000 from the General Education Board, the EPC was able to distribute copies widely to schools and lay groups alike. The central message running through the ninety-eight documents was to promote education for democracy. Although this message moved in the direction of grassroots or local curriculum development, the carefully delineated generic guidelines and calls for long-term planning pulled in the direction of centralized curriculum formulated by experts who would do the long-term planning. Nevertheless, this effort in curriculum policy making was clearly in the hands of educators.

Historical phases of centralization that are quite familiar to most of today's educators, phases they have lived through as students or professionals, can be treated more briefly. One such phase occurred in the late 1950s and reached fruition in the early 1960s in response to Conant's call for small school districts to consolidate into large, comprehensive ones. Supported by large grants from the Carnegie Corporation, Conant's (1959) proposals were widely disseminated. A major result of this effort was that a greater array of offerings and less sense of community were found in these larger schools.

The support of educational reform by foundations and federal agencies brought a new, more capitalistic, less educator-oriented, and less locally democratic network of curriculum policy makers to replace the Educational Policies Commission of the NEA. The most obvious illustration of this passing of the policy mantle occurred in post-Sputnik curriculum reform projects supported by the National Science Foundation and an array of private foundations such as Ford and Carnegie. Designed to produce U.S. supremacy in the space race, the National Defense Education Act of 1958 helped import specialists from the disciplines to design curriculum packages in the sciences, mathematics, foreign languages, and technology (see review in Goodlad, von Stoephasius, & Klein, 1966). These packages or projects were often intended to "teacher proof" the curriculum, that is, prevent teachers from miseducating by having them follow prescribed activities.

Investigations of what these teachers actually did in classrooms revealed that only the rhetoric of change was in place, not its practice (Goodlad, Klein, & Associates, 1974). Some argued that this was merely due to technical problems such as the inadequate re-education of teachers to use reform packages accurately or to the lack of formative evaluation to spot-check consistency of use throughout implementation. In contrast, proponents of grassroots democracy in curriculum offered the explanation that the failure was due to the blatant disregard of teachers and students in curriculum decision making. This is especially ironic inasmuch as those who promoted inquiry methods with the young neglected to allow inquiry by teachers and students about matters most fundamental to their growing lives, that is, inquiry about that which is most worthwhile to know and experience.

Building on the shoulders of the National Defense Education Act (NDEA) and its 1964 amendments was the 1965 Elementary and Secondary Education Act (ESEA), which provided unprecedented funding for states to purchase instructional materials. Through the Economic Opportunity Act of 1964, the thrusts of ESEA were accentuated in directions to improve the education of the poor through Headstart and related agencies which provided supplementary education for children and parents of poverty. It also established national educational research centers and regional research and developmental laboratories, and reconstituted the image of vocational education through Job Corps. Together these initiatives brought into bold relief the question of whether categorical funding breeds central control of education.

Although the force of centralization was indeed strong, resistance has persisted. In the works of Paul Goodman, Edgar Friedenberg, and others in the late 1950s and early 1960s, there is a seedbed of counterargument to structures of centralization. Similarly, from the mid-1960s to the present, authors such as John Holt, Sylvia Ashton-Warner, George Dennison, Herb Kohl, Johnathan Kozol, James Herndon, and Eliot Wigginton have promoted educational practices variously labeled as "humanistic," "progressive," "open," and "alternative." Under such interpretations, grassroots curricula have been kept alive. In scholarly curriculum discourse, too, one finds a tide of resistance to centralization. Joseph Schwab's (1970) call for practical inquiry focuses on inquiry that proceeds through interaction with a specific state of affairs in an effort to eclectically tailor knowledge and create alternatives that resolve actual problems and provide better curriculum experiences. Reconceptualist scholars provide critiques of and alternatives to structures of centralized curricula (Pinar, 1975, 1988). They energize a call for teachers and learners to create new public spaces that develop increased personal meaning and move toward greater social justice (Greene, 1988).

Indeed, a range of contemporary efforts to restore grassroots democracy in the lives of teachers and learners represents an extension of Deweyan roots. Though muffled by the propensity toward centralization, the message of these efforts raises a telling qustion about perceptions of human nature. It centers on the degree of trust exhibited in fellow human beings. Those who are convinced that most persons need external control to pursue the good life and the just society often advocate centralized curricula embodying treatment specification, carefully verified implementation, and evaluation tied precisely to treatment goals. A distinct contrast to this is a Deweyan trust, expressed in *A Common Faith* (Dewey, 1934), that human beings will grow individually and socially as they follow their genuine concerns. Thus, at the essence of issues of curriculum centralization and decentralization lies the question of faith in human nature and its potential, and the amount of external or internal control needed for decision and action to be good and just.

Notes

I thank Ann Lynn Lopez Schubert for carefully proofreading this manuscript and for sharing ideas about it, and I am grateful to anonymous reviewers for suggestions and to Sharon Coleman for typing.

References

Aikin, W. (1942). *The story of the Eight Year Study.* New York: Harper & Brothers.

Apple, M. W. (1986). *Teachers and texts.* New York: Routledge & Kegan Paul.

Bagley, W. C. (1907). *Classroom management.* New York: Macmillan.

Barnard, H. (1839). The common school curriculum. From his *First annual report* as secretary to the Board of Commissioners of Common Schools of Connecticut.

Bestor, A. (1953). *Educational wastelands.* Urbana, IL: University of Illinois Press.

Bloom, A. (1987). *The closing of the American mind.* New York: Simon & Schuster.

Bobbitt, F. (1918). *The curriculum.* Boston: Houghton Mifflin.

Bode, B. H. (1938). *Progressive education at the crossroads.* New York: Newson.

Brameld, T. (1956). *Toward a reconstructed philosophy of education.* New York: Holt, Rinehart, & Winston.

Broudy, H. S. (1979). *What do professors of education profess?* Annual DeGarmo Lecture of the Society for Professors of Education, Chicago, February 28, 1979.

Charters, W. W. (1923). *Curriculum construction.* New York: Macmillan.

Commission on the Reorganization of Secondary Education of The National Education Association. (1918). *Cardinal principles of secondary education.* Washington, DC: U.S. Government Printing Office.

Committee of Fifteen. (1895). *The report.* Washington, DC: National Education Association.

Committee of Ten on Secondary School Studies. (1893). *The report.* Washington, DC: National Education Association.

Conant, J. B. (1959). *The American high school today.* New York: McGraw-Hill.

Counts, G. S. (1932). *Dare the school build a new social order?* New York: John Day.

Cremin, L. (1961). *The transformation of the school.* New York: Knopf.

Dewey, J. (1900). *The school and society.* Chicago: University of Chicago Press.

_____. (1902). *The child and the curriculum.* Chicago: University of Chicago Press.

_____. (1916). *Democracy and education.* New York: Macmillan.

_____. (1929). *The quest for certainty.* New York: Minton, Balch.

_____. (1934). *A common faith.* New Haven, CT: Yale University Press.

_____. (1938). *Experience and education.* New York: Macmillan.

_____. (1948). *Reconstruction in philosophy.* New York: Macmillan.

Educational Policies Commission. (1938). *The purposes of education in American democracy.* Washington, DC: National Education Association.

_____. (1943). *Education and the people's peace.* Washington, DC: National Education Association.

_____. (1944). *Education for ALL American youth.* Washington, DC: National Education Association.

_____. (1951). *Education and national security.* Washington, DC: National Education Association.

EPIE (Educational Products Information Exchange). (1979). *Selecting instructional materials* (Part 1, Module 3). Stony Brook, NY: EPIE.

Flesch, R. (1966). *The new book of unusual quotations.* New York: Harper & Row.

Goodlad, J. I., Klein, M. F., & Associates. (1974). *Looking behind the classroom door.* Worthington, OH: Charles A. Jones.

Goodlad, J. I., Von Stoephasius, R., & Klein, M. F. (1966). *The changing school curriculum.* New York: Fund for the Advancement of Education.

Greene, M. (1988). *The dialectic of freedom.* New York: Teachers College Press.

Harty, S. (1979). *Hucksters in the classroom.* Washington, DC: Center for the Study of Responsive Law.

Hirsch, E. E. (1987). *Cultural literacy.* Boston: Houghton Mifflin.

Hopkins, L. T. (1941). *Interaction: The democratic process.* Boston: Heath.

Kelley, E.C. (1951). *The workshop way of learning.* New York: Harper & Brothers.

Kilpatrick, W. H (1918). *The project method.* New York: Teachers College, Columbia University.

Kliebard, H. M. (1986). *The Struggle for the American Curriculum 1893–1958.* Boston, MA: Routledge, & Kegan Paul.

Krug, E. A. (1966). *Salient dates in American education, 1635–1964.* New York: Harper & Row.

Lynd, A. (1953). *Quackery in the public schools.* Boston: Little, Brown.

McMurry, F. M. (1927). Some recollections of the past forty years of education. *Peabody Journal of Education, 4,* 325–332.

National Commission on Excellence in Education. (1983). *A nation at risk.* Washington, DC: U.S. Government Printing Office.

Ortenzio, P. (1983). The problem of purpose in American education: The rise and fall of the Educational Policies Commission. In M. R. Nelson (Ed.), *Papers of The Society for the Study of Curriculum History* (pp. 31–34). DeKalb, IL: The Society.

Pinar, W. F. (Ed.). (1975). *Curriculum theorizing: The reconceptualists.* Berkeley, CA: McCutchan.

———. (1988). *Contemporary curriculum discourses.* Scottsdale, AZ: Gorsuch Scarisbrick.

Ravitch, D., & Finn, C. E. (1987). *What do our 17 year olds know?* New York: Harper & Row.

Rice, J. M. (1893). *The public school system of the United States.* New York: The Century Company.

———. (1913). *Scientific management in education.* New York: Nobel & Eldridge.

Rickover, H. (1959). *Education and freedom.* New York: Dutton.

Rugg, H. O. (1941). *That men may understand.* New York: Doubleday, Doran.

Schubert, W. H. (1980). *Curriculum books; The first eighty years.* Lanham, MD: University Press of America.

———. (1986). *Curriculum: Perspective, paradigm, and possibility.* New York: Macmillan.

———. (1987). Educationally recovering Dewey in curriculum. In C.

Eisele (Ed.), *The teacher and curriculum*. Normal, IL: John Dewey Society and Illinois State University.

Schwab, J. J. (1970). *The practical: A language for curriculum*. Washington, DC: National Education Association.

Second Commission on Life Adjustment Education for Youth. (1954). *A look ahead in secondary education*. Washington, DC: United States Office of Education Bulletin Number 4.

Spencer, H. (1861). *Education: Intellectual, moral, and physical*. New York: D. Appleton.

Tyler, R. W. (1949). *Basic principles of curriculum and instruction*. Chicago: University of Chicago Press.

Yale Report Committee. (1829). Yale report of 1828. *The American Journal of Science and Arts, 25*.

Part II

Perspectives on the Centralization of Curriculum Decision Making

6

Teacher Education and Curriculum Decision Making: The Issue of Teacher Professionalism

Gary A. Griffin

*T*he purpose of this chapter is to examine two competing claims for attention in relation to the role of teachers in schools and the impact of these claims on the preparation and continuing education of teachers. On the one hand, many practitioners, scholars, and policy makers are calling for greater professional status for teachers (Devaney & Sykes, 1988). If teachers truly are professionals, it is argued, the nation's children youth will benefit, larger numbers of well-qualified persons will choose to enter teaching, and teachers will be better regarded and rewarded for their work in schools and classrooms.

On the other hand, over the past ten years or so there has been an increasing tendency of state legislation and local school system policy to limit the decision-making scope of individual teachers, thereby diminishing their professional status (Griffin, 1985a). This phenomenon has been demonstrated in the specification of certain behaviors as acceptable and desirable in new teacher programs, district mandates to follow already developed curriculum and instruction manuals, the continued domination of commercially published text as the sole or main source of curriculum content, and others.

Curiously absent from much of the debate about both teacher professionalism and the apparent move toward a kind of "teaching by the numbers" is the issue of teachers as curriculum workers. With few exceptions (Doyle, 1988; Griffin, 1988a; Zumwalt, 1988), teaching as specialized activity, whether considered from intellectual or technical perspectives, is seldom conceptualized primarily as curriculum decision making. Instead, teaching is viewed almost exclusively as action, as observable behavior, as talk.

The reasons for this preoccupation with teaching as technique are complex and interactive. Instances of teachers who were not academically able led to the installation in several states of basic literacy examinations. The growing complexity of providing educational opportunity to a new generation of students with marked linguistic, cultural, and development differences led to the search for and quick implementation of curriculum and instruction packages aimed at ameliorating these differences. The so-called "effective teaching" research findings were believed to be generic and applicable across student populations, curriculum areas, and school environments, and the findings became the basis for instrumentation used in the initial teacher certification and subsequent evaluation of experienced teachers (Hoffman et al., 1986).

The roots of the movement toward greater professional status for teachers are equally complicated. Concern about the probability that the growing demand for teachers will not be matched by sufficient supply led to the belief that more attractive conditions of work, including professional status, would bring more (and better-qualified) persons into teaching (California Commission on the Teaching Profession, 1985). Many of the nation's finest universities had relegated teacher preparation to a sort of second-class intellectual status but now recognized that they needed to get back into teacher education for intellectual and ethical as well as economic reasons. But these institutions of higher education insisted that the new breed of teacher candidates should aspire to be professionals rather than conventional school workers. They needed to ensure that their newly conceptualized programs would both withstand the rigorous intellectual scrutiny of the academic community *and* respond to the prospective teacher's desires for more of the accoutrements of high regard in the society (The Holmes Group, 1986). Teacher unions and professional organizations recognized the advantages to be gained by their members if they focused their considerable energies on fewer "bread and butter" issues and more working condition issues, including professionalism.

The two competing orientations, teachers as technicians and teachers as professionals, are dramatically incompatible on a number of dimensions, one being the preparation and continuing education of teachers. (See also the discussion of two competing metaphors in Chapter 8.) Each has serious implications for the ways in which teachers either do or do not become curriculum workers in their own classrooms and in the larger settings of the school and school system. Each suggests appropriate curriculum and instructional content for teacher education programs. Each is rooted in a set of assumptions about what is valued teacher activity and what is not. This chapter explores the two orientations, illustrates some of the tensions and dilemmas that emerge from each, and suggests how teacher education can contribute to increasing the professional status of teachers, with particular attention to teachers as curriculum workers.

The Case of Teacher as Paraprofessional

For many teachers in today's schools, it is hard to imagine that teachers in other times had primary, ongoing, and comprehensive control over curriculum decisions in their own classroom settings. Having become accustomed to a more centralized system wherein curriculum content, mode of presentation, and methods of evaluation are decided at the state or district level, they find it difficult to conceive of a set of teaching conditions that would not only condone but also promote the classroom or school as the locus of important decisions about educational purposes, learning opportunities, organization, and evaluation.

As noted earlier, the apparent prevalent attitude toward teachers that places them as the implementers of others' decisions about what is appropriate teaching activity has resulted in a kind of paraprofessional belief and practice system regarding teachers' work. Paraprofessionalism assumes that teaching is something that can be easily learned, efficiently observed, and, if the observation results in a deficiency portrait of teacher activity, readily remediated (Griffin, 1985a). This view of teaching is reflected in many new teacher programs, in large numbers of teacher evaluation systems, and in the ways that teachers are viewed in the hierarchy of educational organizations.

In fact, the paraprofessional orientation to teaching fits neatly with the ways that most schools in the United States are organized. These organizational patterns assume that school administrators are "management" and that schoolteachers are "workers." Clearly, if this perspective prevails, the workers do the bidding of the managers, and the intellectual investment, in terms of requisite knowledge that is most relevant for the organization, is held by the administrative cadre. The teachers are to learn from the administrators what is to be done, and then provide evidence that they know how to do that work (Darling-Hammond, 1988).

In terms of curriculum making, this orientation supports the practice of giving teachers curriculum materials and accompanying manuals for use that are developed at some distance from where the teachers meet with students. Teachers, after all, are the implementers of decisions made by persons who, by virtue of place in the organizations, are believed to be better able to make wise choices from multiple options (Griffin & Barnes, 1986). And, following this logic, because the weightiest curriculum decisions are made by state and district officers, these officers are rewarded more generously and assume greater status in educational and lay circles than teachers.

This overly simplified picture of how teachers "fit" the larger educational system, unfortunately, is *not* overly generalized. Survey and observational research, multiple anecdotes, and informal conversation all confirm this view as broadly representative of practice. What are some of the consequences of this prevailing condition of teaching?

Teaching is Not Seen as a Complex Intellectual Activity

As critical decisions about teaching and schooling are made farther and farther from the places where they take place, the intellectual dimensions of teaching are ignored and undervalued. If teaching is conceptualized as following directions, implementing mandates, and moving through predetermined activities, teaching becomes automatonlike and teacher's intellectual authority diminishes.

Yet, it is a great certainty that outstanding teaching is truly and deeply intellectual in nature. Teaching is thinking about and bringing about changes in students' habits of thinking, feeling, and acting. Good teaching is decision making, determining from a variety of options what is best for this student (or these students) in this curriculum area in this group situation (Shulman, 1988). Good teachers engage in this decision making by using their reflective and analytic skills, by putting to curriculum and instructional use their understandings of theories and past experiences, and by weaving together what they already know and what they suspect to be so. Good teachers are disposed to act in certain ways and not others because they have sufficient appropriate knowledge and well-developed interactive skills from which they can draw to make multiple split-second decisions.

Good teaching is also something considerably broader in scope than only meeting with students. Excellent teachers engage in thorough planning, drawing upon their own and others' intellectual resources so that they are prepared to move students through complicated and often unfamiliar terrains of the mind. They reflect upon their practice, testing out their theories in use against their hypotheses about learning possibilities. They know in advance much of what might happen in a given learning situation and have ways of explaining what happened, and why, after that situation has passed and the next is approaching (Schon, 1983).

This intellectual activity probably is most obvious, though, when teachers interact with students. Teaching and learning are extraordinarily complex, especially when they take place in classrooms populated by twenty-five or more students who bring different perspectives, cultural characteristics, and expectations to the interactions. Although children's play and some adult stereotypes seem rooted in a model of teaching that is linear, predictable, and uncomplicated, it is obvious to the thoughtful observer of life in classrooms that teaching is considerably more complex (Good, 1981). Good teaching is timing events, making intellectual connections, engaging in thoughtful questioning, knowing when to praise and when to remain silent, capturing students' attention and engaging their minds and their creativity, selecting appropriate instructional materials, maintaining order, and much more. This complicated amalgam of thought and action simply cannot be mandated from central source of authority and responsibility; it must be the consequence of serious study and understanding and a subsequent disposition to act in reasoned and thoughtful ways. And it must take place in an environment characterized by multiple activities, crosscurrents of thought and emotion, and unpredictable individual and group actions and events.

All Classrooms Are Believed to be Alike

The research of the past two decades into ongoing classrooms and schools has contributed a number of important understandings. Among them, one of the least attended to and most important, is that classrooms and schools differ from one another in significant and influential ways (Lieberman, 1988). Classrooms, for example, differ in terms of students in them: students who are reluctant or eager to learn, well or malnourished, capable in English or struggling to learn a new tongue, characterized by creature comforts or by abject poverty, influenced by parents with high expectations or hopelessness. The physical properties of classrooms also differ: well supplied or impoverished, well lighted and cheerful or dim and gloomy, technologically rich or equipment poor, linked to other school areas and resources or isolated from human and material services.

Importantly, teachers are not all alike either. Some are veterans who have continued to learn to teach and who are expert. Others have the same years of experience but have learned less about becoming expert than about surviving in the system. Some are newcomers who bring rich intellectual and practical resources as a consequence of their participation in outstanding preparation programs. Others are publicly declared "short-timers" who enter teaching on provisional or emergency credentials and who have little or no intention of making teaching a career.

The point to be made is that the conditions of teaching and learning differ from classroom to classroom, and a system of curriculum or instructional decision making that assumes a sameness across settings is foolhardy at best and pernicious at worst. Expecting that the students in an inner-city impoverished environment will bring to the instructional moment the same human characteristics and disposition to learn as another student from an upper-middle-class suburb denies the importance of student variables as an influence upon learning. In the same way, to require from experienced teachers who have invested in their professional development over a number or years the same teaching behavior as one might accept from a novice teacher is to ignore the developmental nature of teacher growth (Sprinthall & Thiess-Sprinthall, 1983). Insisting that the same instructional materials have equal power across varying student groups and in the hands of large numbers of very different teachers is rooted in assumptions about schools, students, and teachers that are just plain wrong.

Yet it is increasingly obvious to the thoughtful observer that large scale curriculum projects most often make just such assumptions. What is expected to work for John and Mary is expected to work for Juan and Maria. What first-year teacher Mr. Smith is expected to do is also expected of respected teacher leader and veteran Ms. Jones. And the same lock-step progression through steps of "teacher-proof" lessons is expected to bring large numbers of students "up to grade level" at about the same point in time. There is ample evidence of the variability of human groups in schools. There is also ample evidence that such variability is largely ignored by centralized curriculum and instructional mandates in terms of expectations for students, teachers, and learning outcomes.

The consequences of these conditions are sadly predictable. Some students become bored because expectations for them are too low, and others give up because they cannot keep up. Some teachers are dismayed because they are denied the authority to use their own knowledge of teaching and of their particular students in making critical curriculum and instructional decisions. Other teachers learn to accept the minimum competence expectation and, indeed, come to believe that it is the standard that should prevail throughout their teaching work lives. Very few students and teachers are well served by centrally determined, relatively invariate intentions about how teaching and learning should take place.

Teacher's Sense of Efficacy is Diminished

The findings of a small-scale study of teachers engaged in teaching a mastery model of reading also suggested that teachers who must follow directions instead of making many of their own decisions about curriculum and instruction suffered a decreased self-estimate of their own professional worth (Griffin, 1986). The teachers in the study were expected to follow very specific steps in teaching a series of predetermined reading lessons. The lessons were augmented by prepackaged student worksheets, flipcharts, and the like. It is important to know that these materials were not designated to be resources for teachers to draw upon for their work with students; they were designed to be used by all teachers with all students and were not to be supplemented or supplanted by other materials.

Observations of instruction in the inner-city classrooms where this district-determined curriculum was in place illustrated a fairly high level of fidelity to the intentions of the curriculum. The teachers, for the most part, did what the curriculum instructions told them to do. The observations also revealed, however, that students were often off task, that the student level of interest in the lessons was low, that student activity was located at a minimum level of intellectual expectation, that the learning that (presumably) took place was almost exclusively private activity, and that the routines of the lessons seemed to be more important than their content or predicted learning processes. In effect, these classrooms demonstrated dramatically many of the recent conclusions about the dull and stultifying nature of much classroom life in this country (Goodlad, 1984).

What was not revealed by the observations but became sharply apparent in interviews with teachers was the impact the packaged curriculum had on teacher imagination, creativity, enthusiasm, and sense of efficacy. Teachers reported that they "did" the curriculum because they were expected to, even though they had many misgivings about its effectiveness. They observed that they had some intuitive hunches that they could do better for their students if freed from the rigid procedures of the curriculum. They drew upon their own experiences as learners and upon their histories as teachers to suggest, haltingly, some alternate ways of teaching young children to read and to help those students learn about and experience the satisfactions associated with being proficient readers.

A major problem surfaced when the veteran teachers were asked why they did not try out their hunches, test out with students their beliefs about bringing about learning. Along with the expected "I can't because the curriculum doesn't allow it," were comments suggesting that their experience with "the curriculum" had left them unsure about their own professional power and authority. They appeared to have developed a mindset that told them that they were not as knowledgeable as they once thought they were. Also, over the five years of implementing the in-place curriculum, they had forgotten (or deliberately set aside) how to be inventive, how to step outside the easily understood and efficiently prescribed way of "doing reading." They had come to the conclusion that they had little control over their in-school behavior and were uncertain about their potential effectiveness if they crossed over the predetermined boundaries.

The conclusions of this study do not stand alone. Self-descriptions of teacher's professional lives abound with similar illustrations of how teachers come to believe that they are silent partners in educational decision making or, worse, victims of uncaring and mindless bureaucracies. Unfortunately, the response to these illustrations more often focuses on greater centralization of control, often as "reforms" to ensure minimum compliance with low standards for teaching behavior rather than as altered conditions of teaching leading to the realization of teacher control over instruction, participation in school decision making, or increased professional authority.

Students Have Limited Options for Learning

The intellectual history of teaching and schooling is rich with pleas for attending to what was once called "the whole child." This theoretical position and some practical applications suggest that the broader the array of opportunities for learning and the greater the number of stimuli to capture student interest in learning, the more probable it will be that learning will occur. Students experiencing instruction aimed at understanding the westward development of the United States, for example, will be more likely to internalize important related knowledge if they have the opportunity to read about it, talk about it, act it out, sing about it, and paint about it (Tyler, 1949).

At the same time that these multiple opportunities to learn are offered to students, the theoretical proposition also requires that students' developmental levels be taken into account. Therefore, the reading materials would present essentially the same content at varying levels of reading difficulty, the options for artistic expression would vary across student groups, the storytelling would focus on interests of subgroups in the class, and the writings and reporting requirements of the instruction would be different for students with different compositional skills and predilections.

The point to be made is that theoreticians, researchers, and expert practitioners agree that there is great value in providing students with as many options for learning as is possible and feasible. With remarkably few exceptions, however, centrally determined curriculum neither provides such options nor encourages teachers to formulate them as additional resources for student learning. Although curriculum materials may be written at different levels of difficulty, this is typically the only attention given to providing variation of content presentation. In the study noted earlier, some of the teachers believed that their students would benefit by more sustained exposure to text in the forms of trade books, newspapers, magazines, and other representative reading materials. The curriculum, as presented to the teachers, implicitly denied them this opportunity because of the time students were required to spend with the centrally determined worksheets, reading series, and such already developed materials (Griffin, 1986).

As curricula have focused more on the development of low-level intellectual skills, too many teachers have taken on the role of being a conduit of instructional strategy rather than inventors and creators of learning opportunities. Of course, the imaginative and resourceful teacher will find multiple ways of connecting students with important knowledge and skill, will develop instructional materials that capture student's creativity, will vary presentation of content according to students' developmental stages, and will orchestrate numbers of activities aimed at increasing the power of instruction over time and at the same time. Unfortunately, school contexts are influenced so pervasively by the perspective that there is "one right way" of teaching that even these skilled teachers often succumb to the daily routine of drill and practice.

Resources For Problem Solving Are Decreased

In her study of effective schools, Rosenholtz (1989) used the terms *learning enriched* and *learning impoverished* schools. She paints dramatic pictures of how teachers come to think of themselves and their work as a consequence of whether or not the school environment in which they work exhibit one or the other of the sets of characteristics exemplified by her category designations.

A critical issue for teachers in today's schools is the degree to which the intellectual and practical resources to solve the growing number of school-related problems are at hand. In a learning-enriched school, one would find multiple opportunities for teachers to share their practices, discuss their problems, invent new solutions, gather relevant information, link it to expert opinion, and generally focus on continuing to learn to teach well. In a learning-impoverished school, one would see teachers isolated from one another and depending upon external decision makers for acceptable instructional practices, receiving wisdom rather than inventing or discovering it, engaging in safe rather than risk-taking practice, and playing out pretty much the same activity year after year after year.

Clearly, in a learning-impoverished school it is unlikely that the tensions and dilemmas of providing rich learning opportunities for students *and* for teachers can be overcome as a consequence of using the school as a source of ideas for improvement. In such a school, where there is typically the one best way to teach and to make curricula accessible to students, it is probable that the same mistakes are repeated year after year until a new best way is substituted for the old one. (The student-level analogy, of course, is found in the case of the student who repeats a grade or subject and, after not succeeding under the instructional conditions the first time, experiences the same conditions again. More of the same is almost always ineffective in causing student learning to occur.)

It can be argued that centralized curriculum decision making, particularly in the typical "one best way" mode, contributes to the development of a learning-impoverished school in that it decreases the variety of curriculum and instructional thought and activity. Because decisions about what and how to teach are already made, inventiveness is blunted. And, when inventiveness and multiple modes of curriculum activity are in short supply, so are opportunities to share intellectual and practical resources across groups of teachers. In short, a unidimensional instructional program cannot, almost by definition, provide options for alternate activities that can be tested for their problem-solving possibilities.

Of course, the learning-impoverished school is explained in some measure by the phenomena already presented in this section. The next section presents an alternate view, the case for teachers as professionals and for curriculum work as a central fact of a teacher's professional life.

The Case of Professional Status for Teachers

Much of the argument for professional status for teachers rests on assumptions about why high-calibre individuals will or would choose teaching over other occupations as a career (Griffin, 1985b). This is underscored by the projected need for one and one-half million teachers in the United States over the next decade. Obviously, it will not be possible to attract such large numbers of persons to teaching if it is viewed as a low-status, low-reward occupation. Equally obviously, the magnitude of the need (and, indeed, of the national teaching force itself) suggests that only a modest proportion of the next generation of teachers will come from "the best and the brightest" group of our citizens. But, it is argued, it is imperative that a fair share of these highly capable people be captured if schools are to accomplish the growing demands placed upon them by the public at large, policy makers, and business and industry (The Holmes Group, 1986).

Professional status and the definitional features of a profession are seen as ways to capture the imagination and intellect of the kinds of teachers wanted in classrooms and to keep them there. There has been considerable discussion about the working conditions of teaching, but the talk has focused on the dramatic issues of salary, violence in schools, deteriorating physical structures, and the like. But, it is clear that conditions of work in teaching encompass a much broader set of concerns about how teachers go about their business, how they are supported by society and school systems, and how they are encouraged or not encouraged to remain in teaching. These conditions of work are directly relevant to the issue of professionalizing teaching. Several are presented here, with particular attention given to their relation to curriculum work.

Members of a Profession Possess Specialized Knowledge and Skill

The primary intellectual distinction between a professional and a lay person is the professional's specialized knowledge (Etzioni, 1969). Although there are still those who believe that anyone who cares deeply about children is well qualified to be a teacher, it is increasingly clear that the best teachers draw upon knowledge, exhibit skill, and have ways of thinking about teaching that distinguish them from people who are not teachers. This set of knowledge and skill ranges from techniques such as differentiating between lower and higher-order questions through grouping students for instruction by interests and abilities to acting upon well-developed philosophical and conceptual perspectives on how learning can and should occur in educational situations. It is unlikely, for example, that persons outside of teaching could draw upon Piagetian principles of child growth and development as a means to determine an appropriate instructional sequence in science for a particular group of eight-year-olds, or could make informed decisions about how best to arrange a stimulating inquiry environment that would lead learning disabled students to higher-than-predicted achievement levels in written composition.

Certainly, curriculum theory and development constitute a specialized body of knowledge that should be a part of every professional teacher's repertoire. Knowledge of theoretical perspectives about curriculum and the various conceptions of curriculum planning is of extraordinary value to the enterprise of providing educational opportunity. And yet, two current conditions often deny this premise. First, teacher preparation programs (and many professional development programs for experienced teachers) do not include any significant attention to curriculum, either from the perspective of theory or in terms of the various approaches to curriculum planning (Griffin, 1988a). (The latter issue receives some attention at the level of lesson planning, but seldom do prospective teachers have experiences that prepare them for long-term planning.) Second, curriculum decisions as noted above, more and more frequently are made at a distance from the teacher and the teaching-learning situation. By default, then, large numbers of teachers do not engage in curriculum planning beyond some tinkering around the edges of what already appears in textbooks and district curriculum guides.

Obviously, then, there is some tension between aspirations for professional status for teachers and at least one central body of specialized knowledge that would buttress those aspirations. The unfortunate fact is that the issue of specialized knowledge for teachers has focused relatively narrowly on teaching techniques as revealed by the research on teaching findings in the past two decades. Although it is important for teachers to have these techniques at hand, exclusive reliance upon them to differentiate between those who are professional teachers and those who are not contributes less to true professionalism than it may to a more sophisticated form of paraprofessionalism as discussed earlier in this chapter.

Professional Work is Carried Forward in a Collegium

Members of a professional group work together toward the advancement of their knowledge and the improvement of their practice (Lanier, 1986). This work is carried forward in organizations such as hospitals and in learned and professional societies. Under the best of circumstances, when individual members of the profession encounter intellectual and practical problems, they consult systematically with their colleagues about how to ameliorate them. The collegium is also supportive of contributing to the knowledge base from which members of the profession draw their experise (see below).

Consider the case of typical teachers in typical schools. Although the teachers are working in the schools, they most often do their work alone in separated classrooms and, in fact, are isolated from other teachers for all or most days of the school year except for infrequent and short-lived social breaks from teaching schedules (Sarason, 1971). When teachers do come together in some sanctioned ways, it is most often at the behest of someone outside the teaching ranks, a principal, for instance, and the interactions during these meetings focus almost exclusively on how to implement decisions or act upon problems that are thrust upon them. Typical examples are faculty meetings about introducing new textbooks, dealing with an attendance policy formulated at a district office, or receiving results of standardized test scores. It is very infrequently that teachers gather together to work interactively on problems of their own identification and even more infrequently that teachers are called upon to take responsibility for knowledge generation about teaching practice or effects. (A dramatic departure from this norm, Interactive Research and Development, demonstrated in a number of school settings the positive effects of introducing into schools a more professionally oriented notion of the collegium as a professional development and school/teaching problem solving strategy [Tikunoff, Ward, & Griffin, 1979]).

What is more central to the work of teaching than the important decisions about curriculum content, instructional approach, materials for learning, sequence of learning opportunities, and the like? In short, could not curriculum work be a major focus of a collegium of professional teachers? As long as teachers are grouped in schools for the purpose of offering instruction, it seems reasonable that some coherent approach to providing an articulated and cumulative curriculum for students should be the work of the teacher group. This work, based upon specialized curriculum knowledge as discussed above, would contribute both to the advancement of teaching as a profession and to the formulation of more appropriate curricula for students in the schools. (See also the discussion in Chapter 10). This approach, obviously, is in marked contrast to the creeping centralization of curriculum decision making that is thrust upon teachers across numbers of schools, even when the institutional characters of those schools are markedly different and therefore, almost by definition, demanding of different ways of thinking about curriculum issues. (Of course, there are instances of teacher participation on district curriculum committees whose work is expected to influence instruction across schools in a district. Unfortunately, with few exceptions, this work involves very few teachers, is directed by persons who are not teachers, and gives little attention to the extreme differences across the schools that are meant to use the work.)

Members of a Profession Contribute to the Knowledge Bases that Guide Their Work and That of Other Colleges

Mature professions have as a basic hallmark the expectation that members are regular contributors to the ways in which the profession does its work. Although there is some dependence upon external knowledge generation sources (the basic sciences in relation to medicine, for example), the professionals determine the problems to be attacked and plan ways to deal with them. In law, it is members of the legal profession who tackle the difficult issues of constitutional interpretation and application. In medicine, it is the physicians who develop the experiments necessary to ensuring that a medical practice is both safe and salutory.

Teachers, in contrast, are seldom responsible for studying and proposing solutions to longstanding or emerging problems of practice. Most often, the description, inquiry, and experimentation required to better understand and improve teaching practice are carried forward by members of the higher education or research and development communities. Although some, by no means all or even a majority, of the members of these nonteacher groups may have had teaching experience in elementary or secondary schools, typically they are not practicing teachers in the lower schools. This divorce of the inquiry and practice of teaching has had serious consequences for teaching as a profession and for the relevance of educational inquiry to education practice (Schon, 1983).

Teachers are expected to make little investment in systematic knowledge production, either individually or collectively. They are more often than not chided for not "using" the research findings of higher education in their work, even though the research findings may or may not have direct meaning for their work. They are criticized for not making significant changes in their practice, based upon new knowledge, even though the new knowledge is presented in what they believe to be arcane and esoteric language. They are accused of not doing their homework about the results of systematic inquiry when those results are presented in publications and forums that are not accessible to them.

At the same time, educational researchers have not been sensitive to what teachers believe to be the most central concerns of providing quality education. Many of these researchers approach the problems of teaching from the outside and have no direct experiential basis from which to formulate their hypotheses or support their conclusions. The research findings are often only the verification of what large numbers of teachers already know to be so, as in a large part of the classroom management research literature, and, therefore, are seen by teachers, rightly or wrongly, as demonstrations of unnecessary or wasted effort (Tikunoff, Ward, & Griffin, 1979).

If teaching is to be a profession, it can be argued that teachers must become more directly involved in generating knowledge about teaching. In the Interactive Research and Development (IR &D) strategy cited earlier, this was the case. (Historically, the action research movement was another example of teacher-directed inquiry, although at more of a situation-specific problem solving level than IR & D [Corey, 1953]). The benefits of this involvement for teachers are broad and deep. Teachers develop more of a disposition toward reflection and analysis of practice. They experience the positive consequences of inquiring collegially into commonly perceived problems. They generate knowledge that has direct meaning and application possibilities for other teachers. They become thoughtful critics of knowledge about teaching. They develop a common language about teaching, a language that has shared meaning rather than only idiosyncratic meaning. In short, the teachers who participate in IR & D develop and act upon specialized knowledge, work together in a collegium, and engage in knowledge production about their important work. Curriculum inquiry could become a major focus for knowledge generation by teachers and, thereby, satisfy one of the essential requirements of a profession of teaching.

A Profession is Characterized by a Career Orientation

Teaching, as currently practiced in most schools, is more of a job than a career (Griffin, 1985b). That is, teachers do pretty much the same things year after year, with some modest alterations of practice over time. The demands of the job, as noted earlier, most often reflect a labor rather than a management perspective; therefore, even the modest changes that are required of teachers arise out of expectations held by school officers who are not teachers.

A career, on the other hand, offers men and women who choose it a set of options over time. These options range from staying at one stage to investing in acquiring the knowledge and skill that would advance the participant in terms of authority, responsibility, and reward (The Holmes Group, 1986). In medicine, for example, physicians in a teaching hospital can choose to maintain roles with clinical functions, can move to the more theoretically driven functions, or can assume research roles. The point to be made is that the physician has such options open to him or her and that choosing a career-oriented option does not take him or her out of the basic business of providing health care. The collegium of physicians, in other words, is made up of a number of functions that become opportunities for participants' career decisions over time.

Consider teaching in these terms. The teacher who decides to make a career change must opt out of teaching and move into school administration. Even though teaching may be extraordinarily rewarding in many ways, the desire for authority, responsibility, and reward in the educational system can only be satisfied by leaving teaching. (It can be argued that these changes are career directed, but the career is an educational, not a *teaching* career). It is not uncommon for teachers to say that they love to teach but that they want more challenges and greater extrinsic rewards and, therefore, choose to become principals or central office officials.

For teaching to become a career, it is necessary for teachers to have opportunities to exercise leadership and authority and still spend substantial amounts of their time and energy in working with children and youth. One way to accommodate this is to match this requirement of a profession with what is known to be necessary for schools to be effective (Rosenholtz, 1989). Schools, especially the complex schools of today, need a number of intellectual resources. They need expertise in the development, use, and interpretation of tests and measurement techniques, especially in light of the pervasive cry for educational accountablilty. They need knowledge and skill related to home-community-school relationships, particularly as traditional neighborhood and family structures change. They need in-place resources to deal with the growing numbers of linguistic-and cultural-minority members in the student population. The list could go on, but the issue is that the myth of the principal as the all-knowing and pervasively skillful leader simply will not suffice as schools meet the challenges that face them. And the persistence of the belief that the teacher force is there, in its entirety, to follow the directions of the principal also will no longer withstand rigorous scrutiny.

In light of the growing complexity of schools as educational organizations and using curriculum work as an example, it is reasonable to propose that teachers assume leadership for some of the specialized knowledge and skills that are central to predicting school success (Griffin, 1988b). One or more teachers in each school could provide the necessary intellectual and practical knowledge and skill to come to grips with the curriculum dilemmas. These teacher leaders, through their own investments in advanced professional education and the investments of school districts in providing the leadership necessary for school effectiveness, could work with their colleagues on curriculum development, curriculum assessment articulation, preparation and testing of instructional materials, the creative use of existing text and other media, inquiry focused on the outcomes associated with the use of various curricula, and integration of content across conventional academic subject matter. These teachers would also remain in contact with students for a substantial part of their time in schools, whether that contact be part of each day, one week with students and one week in curriculum work, or some other arrangement. (In the recent attention to "reform" of teaching and teacher education, the Carnegie Forum [1986] refers to such teachers as "lead teachers," and the Holmes Group [1986] refers to them as "career professional teachers.")

In short, these teacher leaders would have had the opportunity to choose greater responsibility and reward, remain in teaching, and act upon curriculum dilemmas and problems. This matching of one of the central features of a profession with one of the persistent needs of schools will not be served in a situation where curriculum planning is seen as centralized activity and where teachers have little control over either their own career development or over the substance of their teaching.

Members of a Profession Have Considerable Autonomy Regarding the Exercise of their Professional Knowledge and Skill

A significant feature of professional status is the autonomy that professionals have as they go about their work. Because members of the more mature professions such as medicine and law have gained control over the licensure procedures which regulate who enters the professions, there is some certainty that new members of the profession will exercise that autonomy with considerable skill. New doctors and lawyers are expected to practice at or above the level of acceptability, and the profession, through its control over entry standards, guarantees safe practice at least and best practice at most.

This collegial control over licensure and certification is not currently characteristic of teaching, although there is a strong movement to put it in place (Carnegie Forum, 1986). That point will not be argued here. Instead, the issue of autonomy of teacher decision making and practice is discussed with particular attention to autonomy in relation to curriculum and instructional decisions.

As the theme of this book suggests, teachers appear to be losing control over curriculum decisions as more and more of those decisions are centralized in states or school systems. When it is argued that teachers should exercise more professional behavior, in this instance curriculum decision making, the counterargument is often that teaching most often takes place in public institutions, and that therefore a good deal of regulation of practice must be in place to protect the public. Certainly, this position is partly understandable in that there must be public policy to guide public work, but it is not reasonable when it translates to prescriptions for what might be called micropractice: that is, it is oxymoronic to see teaching as complex activity, dependent for success on the orchestration of multiple events and systems of knowledge, while, at the same time, requiring that teaching be prescribed in lock-step fashion, independent of the immediate setting in which it moves forward.

It is seldom acknowledged that the public arena argument also applies to physicians in hospitals, if not in private practice, and to lawyers in such governmental agencies as district attorneys' offices. These professionals are expected to exercise their judgments and do so with considerable autonomy, given broadly stated guidelines for practice. It is possible to think of teachers in schools, public or private, in the same way. A state or a school system, indeed, has the responsibility to provide guidelines for practice and boundaries for decision making. These guidelines and boundaries may be philosophical ("education is designed to equip students to be active participants in a democratic society"), psychological ("our students construct knowledge as a consequence of meaningful experience"), curricular ("the curriculum should help students move from concrete to abstract understandings"), or some combination of these or other perspectives. But within these public policy guidelines, the professional teacher is expected to decide and act upon decisions that emerge out of the blending of an understanding of the guidelines and the knowledge and skill they bring to the acts of teaching.

If one accepts most or all of this orientation to the feature of autonomy in teaching as professional activity, the movement toward centralizing curriculum decision making and prescribing teaching practice in detail is not acceptable. What *is* acceptable and necessary is that teachers, as individuals and as members of a collegium, take considerable responsibility for curriculum work; they, in fact, become curriculum workers.

Teachers as curriculum workers is an important but deceptively simple conception. On the one hand, it requires that teachers take primary responsibility for decision about content, learning opportunities, sequence and organization, selection of instructional materials, evaluation, and other curriculum-specific tasks in relation to particular groups of students in classrooms or other educational settings. On the other hand, it requires that teachers be primary participants *as a collective* in setting the guidelines within which such situation-specific decisions are made. In this conception, teachers would be ongoing rather than sporadic contributors to the discourse about the goals and means of curriculum instruction, the decision criteria which would lead individual curriculum decisions in one direction rather than another, and the array of instructional materials from which particular instances could be selected, for example.

This perspective on teachers' roles in curriculum work satisfies the two conditions noted earlier. It allows for the establishment of guidelines and boundaries as a way to ensure safe practice as required in public institutions, *and* it provides for a high level of individual teacher decision making within those boundaries as a way to satisfy the professional feature of autonomous practice. It also satisfies the expressed desire of both prospective and practicing teachers for more responsible participation in district- and school-level decision making, a variable that is consistently related to school success and teacher satisfaction and morale.

Teacher Education and Professional Status for Teachers

A persistent dilemma for teacher educators has been whether to prepare teachers to somehow "fit" the system or to provide opportunities for teacher candidates that may lead toward empowering them to alter business as usual. The consequences of taking one or the other position as the dominant one are significant in terms of the intentions and the activities of teacher education programs.

Take, for example, the typical complaint of new teachers that their teacher education programs are not helpful as they begin their important work (Hoffman et al., 1986). Usually, the new teachers talk about the university's preoccupation with "theory" and how it doesn't fit the "real world" of schools and classrooms. One way to interpret this, of course, is to take the comments at face value and admit that there is a reality gap between the two settings. Another is to go further and acknowledge that college and university teacher educators simply do not understand what schools are really like.

Notwithstanding the possibility that these two responses may be appropriate in some or many instances, it is also possible to hypothesize that teacher educators have a vision or vision about what teaching should be like and that they act on this view in the hope that their teacher education students will be empowered to move into schools and bring about change. Some curriculum examples of this include the continuing calls for the integration of subjects (versus the school practice of isolated subjects), the strong belief that learning is enhanced by students' encounters with multiple stimuli (versus the textbook as the only instructional resource), the concern for dealing with all developmental aspects of children and youth (versus a unidimensional focus on cognition), and the theoretically powerful relationship between well-articulated curriculum and evaluation systems (versus dependence upon standardized tests). The point to be made is that there continues to be a dichotomous relationship between what colleges and schools of education think it is important to know and do as a teacher and what teachers believe to be the primary features of their work.

Part of the problem surely lies in the already mentioned perceived distance ascribed to the incompatability of theory and practice, although most thoughtful persons would agree that good theory and good practice go hand in hand. Much of the problem, however, lies more directly in the relative absence of strong intellectual and organizational linkages between higher education and the lower schools (Ward, 1987). Recently this problem has been recognized in the teacher education community, and serious work has begun to address it. It became clear early in the debate about teacher education reform that it was impossible to think about major improvement in teacher education or about attracting more capable persons to teaching without also thinking about the conditions of schools in which future teachers would engage in their practice (The Holmes Group, 1986). This recognition led to the development of two complementary ways of engaging in the improvment of teacher education programs. The first focuses on strengthening the intellectual dimensions (and require-ments) of teacher education programs. The second focuses on re-creating the relationships between colleges and elementary and secondary schools toward the goal of school improvement, formulating and testing new ways of going about providing educational oppor-tunity. The assumption, of course, is that each complements the other, that better-prepared teachers will not only be more eager to work in schools that are receptive to their ways of thinking about and doing teaching, but that schools with certain organizational and intellectually appealing characteristics will welcome the new brand of novice teacher.

Central to this simultaneous attention to improving teacher edu-cation and creating more effective schools is the notion of teacher professionalism. It is only the professional teacher who will succeed in effective schools, and it is only the effective school that will welcome the truly professional teacher as characterized in this chapter and in other recent educational literature. The teacher who is prepared to simply accept others' decisions about how he or she should teach will not be a welcome addition to the faculty of a collegially organized, intellectually focused school. The teacher who is prepared to exercise considerable professional judgment, to seek advice and counsel from peers, and to provide leadership about important school issues will be very dissatisfied in a school that runs by the numbers.

As teacher education programs become more direct students of and participants in elementary and secondary schools, perhaps through the institution of "professional development schools," "clinical schools", or "professional practice schools," it is obvious that alterations in the conventions of preparing teachers are necessary. These illustrations are ones that are directly related to professional teachers' curriculum work. (Discussion of the structures of teacher education programs such as fifth-year, postbaccalaureate, and others is omitted here but, obviously, these illustrations of the content and intentions of teacher education programs, if taken seriously, would influence such issues.)

Short-term versus Long-term Curriculum Planning

There is some evidence that teacher education programs prepare new teachers to do lesson planning but do not give attention to curriculum planning that spans the conventional elementary and secondary school semesters and school years. That is, novice teachers may be skilled in thinking about and implementing a plan for this lesson in this subject at this time but are not prepared to think about the "ongoing-ness" of instruction over the time that the students will be with them (Hoffman et al., 1986).

The distinctions between planning an hour's lesson and planning for learning and teaching over time are many. If a teacher has little disposition to think about curriculum enactment as a long-term enterprise, it is likely that he or she will be caught up in staying with the text, giving little systematic attention to issues of organization and sequence, and responding to the apparent needs of the moment without being thoughtful about how the moment fits into the larger scheme of instruction. In short, the teacher whose curriculum planning skills are limited by lack of attention to the scope of a school semester, for example, is a likely subject for becoming a passive recipient of centralized curriculum decisions.

If preparing professional teachers is to be a serious endeavor, teacher education programs must be altered toward purposes that take the long view of curriculum planning into consideration. Teacher education programs must be concerned with providing more powerful and more numerous opportunities for prospective teachers to see how learning is cumulative and how curriculum and instructional activities support that cumulative view. This perspective not only provides new teachers with the disposition to think of schooling as a long-term investment in learning but also contributes to the likelihood that they will be equipped to work with others on conceptualizing curriculum for a school rather than a classroom.

Unfortunately, curriculum planning of the sort briefly described here is typically reserved for advanced degree programs. It is seldom that the initial professional degree in education, whether at baccalaureate or master's levels, attends to issues of scope and sequence and the like. Perhaps because of the belief noted above that teachers need not have broad influence on curriculum beyond following some centralized dictum, specialized curriculum planning knowledge and skill are usually only expected of the person who is preparing for leadership roles in school system. The result of this lack of attention is that teachers are not empowered intellectually to plan curriculum over time or, indeed, to work together toward that end. Central supervisors do have the knowledge but may use it to prescribe broadly for a district, notwithstanding the probable inappropriateness of the plans for all students in all schools. Because curriculum work is at the heart of the educational enterprise and rests upon a critical body of knowledge and skills for professional teachers, teacher education programs should include opportunities for teacher candidates to develop the habits of mind about and dispositions toward curriculum planning, implementation, and evaluation as a long-term versus just a lesson-length activity.

Learning to Teach as Collegial versus Independent Activity

As noted earlier, a key feature of professionalism is the presence of a collegium, the joining together of members of the profession around important intellectual, organizational, and practical issues (Etzioni, 1969). It is the collegium that provides the mechanism for problems to be identified solutions to be tested, and professional growth to take place. Key to the central propositions of this professional feature is the opportunity, indeed, the mandate, for members to interact systematically and consistently over time and across settings.

It is increasingly clear that teaching has been and continues to be activity engaged in by individuals in isolation from others with the same interests, concerns, problems, and expectations. In fact, one can liken teaching to a modern-day cottage industry in which practitioners do pretty much the same thing day after day in different spaces with little or no interaction with peers. It is this collegial distance that has brought about the common phrase "teaching is a lonely profession." The persistence of this intellectual and practical isolation of teachers from one another is a major barrier to teacher professionalism, and it appears from the research literature on school improvement that effective schools are consistently characterized by sustained collegial dialogue, goal setting, and problem solving (Rosenholtz, 1989).

Teacher education programs can act upon this barrier to teacher professionalism in at least two ways. First, they can organize their programs of curriculum and instruction so that prospective teachers are organized into cohorts that move through the program as collegial groups. This cohort arrangement can contribute to the disposition to work cooperatively and collaboratively, particularly if the content of the cohort's academic work is focused on conventional learning and problem solving as group rather than individual activity.

Second, and directly related to the parallel teacher education reform intention of improving elementary and secondary schooling, teacher education programs can identify and collaborate over time with selected school settings. These settings, sometimes called "professional development schools," become the sites where the teacher education students engage in all or a major part of their practical learning opportunities, where teacher education faculty have sustained intellectual influence upon curriculum and instruction in the schools, where school practitioners provide significant input into teacher education program review and improvement, and where there is a major investment by the university and the public school in creating norms of excellence and professionalism. Although it will be difficult to abandon the relatively unsystematic university-school relationships and alter what are currently individual-focused teacher education programs, the twin goals of school improvement and teacher education reform can contribute to teacher professionalism through reconceptualizations as noted here.

Learning from Teaching versus Only Learning About Teaching

If teacher education programs are to influence the professional status of teachers, it will be necessary for them to demonstrate a greater respect for and involvement with inquiry than is currently the case. It is fair to claim, with modest examples to the contrary, that teacher education has not been a major focus for disciplined research. Although there are current efforts to engage in inquiry about teacher education, they are generally located in only a handful of institutions of higher education.

Professional status for teachers will depend in large measure on the development and sustenance of two approaches to inquiry. First, because of the need for a profession to possess specialized knowledge that is unavailable to those not in the profession, it will be necessary to continue to develop the knowledge bases that, with some degree of certainty, ensure both safe and best teaching practice. It is interesting to note that the dominant forces for developing, discovering, and codifying this emerging knowledge come not from the teacher education community but from educational psychologists, who may or may not have some modest investment in the education of teachers (Doyle, 1988). It is important that teacher educators invest in the continued development of this specialized information, both for the general good in terms of teaching effects and for the development and refinement of the content of teacher education programs. Although it is unlikely that there will ever be one or even several ways to teach most effectively, linking teacher education to teacher professionalism and school improvement will require a much more intellectually sound decision-making basis than is currently the case.

Second, inquiry as a fundamental component of professional practice requires that teachers themselves be reflective, analytic students of their own practice. If teachers individually and collectively assume significant responsibility for discovering and inventing effective teaching practice, including an understanding of the relative effects upon student learning of alternate curriculum approaches, it is unlikely that they will be receptive to the growing centralized decision making about curriculum and instruction that is the theme of this book. It is more likely that teachers who are knowledgeable about and skillful in systematic problem-solving and inquiry strategies will be prepared to assume professionally relevant leadership roles in school change efforts. Further, if teacher education programs help prospective and practicing teachers develop an inquiry orientation, it is hoped that the various fads and nostrums, under the guise of panaceas for all problems, will be more rigorously studied and significantly revised or discarded before they prove to be relatively useless in educational settings.

Teacher education programs, then, can contribute to the realization of the professional teacher through systematic and rigorous research on teaching and on teacher education effects and through the development and implementation of opportunities for teacher candidates and experienced teachers to learn about the various inquiry strategies and their utility in teaching situations.

Preparing for Leadership versus Followership

As the discussion earlier in this chapter noted, teachers most often are viewed as at the bottom or near the bottom (students sometimes usurp the lowest rung) of the educational hierarchy. This is both a cause and an effect; it makes new teachers believe that they have little or no say about what schools should be about beyond their own classroom walls, and it is an effect in that the systems of preparing teachers give little, if any, attention to teachers as educational leaders. Educational leaders, it is assumed in most higher education institutions, are those persons, often experienced teachers, who engage in advanced study and prepare themselves for administrative or supervisory roles.

Yet in schools that are characterized by high levels of student achievement as well as positive teacher morale and a sense of efficacy, there is consistent evidence that teachers take leadership roles in a variety of arenas, including curriculum ones (Rosenholtz, 1989). For example, the finding that effective schools are characterized by high levels of teacher participation in goal setting combines the elements of teacher leadership and curriculum planning, for what are goals but a fundamental element of curriculum? (See Chapter 2.) The finding that these same schools also are characterized by consistent expectations across classroom groups and subject areas illustrates horizontal articulation, a central tenet of curriculum planning.

Usually, although far from a certainty, the teacher leadership that can be seen in elementary and secondary schools emerges over time as an effect of a school principal's vision combined with an expecially talented teacher faculty group. It would be difficult to claim and prove that teacher education programs had any major input into developing the disposition in their graduates to assume these leadership roles.

Unfortunately, the largest number of teacher education programs appear to be focused on some minimal level of teaching technique rather than upon a vision of excellence. And it is difficult to think of teachers as leaders when the dominant expectation for teacher candidates is the demonstration of individual teaching style, however highly valued. Teachers as leaders will emerge when teacher education programs, for novice as well as experienced teachers, provide participants with opportunities to lead and help them acquire the disposition toward leadership as a consequence of those opportunities.

It is also reasonable for teacher education programs to give specific attention to those arenas of educational practice that are natural vehicles for professional teacher leadership, perhaps in the form of minispecializations for novice teachers and concentrations of effort for experienced teachers. One of these, naturally, could be curriculum planning, implementation, and evaluation. In the same way that some teachers become reading specialists, others could become curriculum specialists. Even for new teachers, a specialization in the basic properties of curriculum planning, as noted throughout this book, would result in a much-needed and highly marketable combination of teacher knowledge and skill

What is called for in terms of preparing teachers for leadership and not just to fit into an existing flat educational organization are teacher education programs that engage their students in the problems and prospects of leadership. The purpose is for students to be inclined to exert leadership when appropriate. Teacher candidates and teachers need to have experience with the content of leadership. This change in teacher education would promote professional status for teachers, provide much-needed intellectual resources for schools, counter the trend toward centralization of decision making because requisite expertise would be distributed throughout the school system, and provide prospective teachers, in particular, with a view of teaching as a career with expanded opportunities rather than a job that is repeated again and again and again.

Ongoing Investments in Learning to Teach

As suggested in the preceding paragraphs, teacher education is not simply those preservice programs leading to a degree and certification. Teacher education is a continuum of experience and opportunity to improve over the length of a teaching career. The professionalism of teaching requires that this conception of teacher education over time be taken considerably more seriously that is currently the case. It must be remembered that one of the hallmarks of a profession is its continuous attention to the intellectual and technical needs of its members.

It is an unfortunate truism that teachers in today's schools neither invest significantly in their own professional development nor are supported by their professional organizations or workplaces in continuing to learn to teach. Also, there are few instances where teachers engage in professional development in order to become teacher leaders with specialized skills and functions while continuing to work with children and youth. These specializations are almost always part of programs designed to prepare teachers to move out of teaching, as noted earlier.

Further, the occasional and disconnected professional development options that are available to teachers are seldom characterized by attention to true professional growth, but are instances of either shoring up a perceived deficit in the teaching ranks or preparing teachers to implement decisions made by others, as in the example of packaged curricula and prescriptions for teaching practice. Teachers may be required to earn advanced degrees, most often master's degrees, in order to obtain permanent state certification, but these degrees are typically unconnected to the persistent dilemmas and possibilities of elementary and secondary schooling. They also may be required to attend a specified number of district-level workshops or "in-service" courses, but these, too, are usually planned to accommodate the wishes of persons removed from teaching situations or to ensure compliance with some centrally mandated requirement for teachers, such as the implementation of a mastery learning model of instruction or a hands-on science curriculum.

What is needed, both for the professionalization of teaching and the complementary increase in the capacity of the individual school to engage in rational curriculum work, is a major investment in and by teachers toward the end of ongoing professional growth. As a rule, teachers are unaware of recent research on teaching, models for curriculum improvement, or organizational variables that contribute to school effectiveness. Also, they are unaware of the potential influence they can have on school programs if they had at hand these and other bodies of knowledge and skill. In effect, most teachers are disenfranchised as professionals because of limited expectations for rigorous and ongoing career development opportunities. This condition directly feeds the centralization of curriculum decision making as well as other critical school features because few investments are made in recreating the intellectual leadership cadre to include professional teachers as well as designated school and district officers.

Teacher education takes place in a variety of settings and takes a number of forms. Most obvious are those programs situated in colleges and universities. These programs must take more seriously the professional requirement of continuing teacher education beyond an initial entry-level degree, and must include in their offerings opportunities for teachers to gain the requisite knowledge of and develop the disposition toward leadership, collegiality, and specialized information.

Teacher education also is a function of individual school systems and, in some instances, of state departments of education, particularly in terms of teacher induction programs. These opportunities for teacher growth must face the reality of the coming shortage of educational practitioners and must invest in preparing members of the teacher cadre to take responsibility with their colleagues for important matters of curriculum, working with novice teachers, developing appropriate measurement procedures and coordinating home and school activities, for example. For school systems to continue to offer unrelated and often trivial in-service workshops and institutes in order to satisfy a district or state rule is to deny the possibilities for ongoing teacher education to enrich schooling for children and youth and to blunt sharply the probability that teaching can be considered a true profession.

Conclusion

This chapter has presented a set of related issues that are believed to influence the degree to which the current move toward centralized curriculum decision making will be increased or diminished in the future. Because centralization of authority for important decisions is rooted in an assumption about who should control education opportunity, it was argued that the typical pattern of the school hierarchy should be challenged. Because such a challenge depends upon a new conception of teachers as leaders in schools rather than as followers of others' dicta, features of teaching as a profession were presented with particular reference to how those features might influence curriculum work. And, because a primary influence upon the nature and status of teaching can be the various teacher education opportunities available to prospective and experienced teachers, the potential of teacher education to influence both the professional status of teachers and school improvement was suggested.

Clearly, this chapter has taken the position that professional status for teachers is desirable and necessary, particularly in view of the need to rethink the growing centralization of decision making, in this case decisions about school curriculum. It is important, however, to realize that professionalization of the teaching force must not be simply empty rhetoric, calls for change of status but not for changes in the intellectual and practical underpinnings of the real work of teaching. Professionalization must be earned and will serve schools well when it is rigorously conceptualized, rooted in theoretical and research-derived knowledge, and linked to important societal imperatives. It is this approach that has potential for altering the role, function, and effectiveness of teachers in this nation.

References

California Commission on the Teaching Profession. (1985).*Who will teach our children?* Sacramento: California Commission on the Teaching Profession.

Carnegie Forum on Education and the Economy. (1986). *A nation prepared: Teachers for the 21st century.* New York: Carnegie Corporation.

Corey, S. M. (1953). *Action research to improve school practices.* New York: Teachers College Press.

Darling-Hammond, L. (1988). Policy and professionalism. In. A. Lieberman (Ed.), *Building a professional culture in schools.* New York: Teachers College Press.

Devaney, K., & Sykes, G. (1988). Making the case for professionalism. In A. Lieberman (Ed.), *Building a professional culture in schools.* New York: Teachers College Press.

Doyle, W. (1988). *Curriculum in teacher education.* Invited address at the annual meeting of the American Educational Research Association, New Orleans.

Etzioni, A. (Ed.). (1969). *The semi-professions and their organizations: Teachers, nurses, social workers.* New York: Free Press.

Good, T. L. (1981). *Research on teaching: What we know and what we need to know.* Austin, TX: University of Texas at Austin, Research and Development Center for Teacher Education.

Goodlad, J. I. (1984). *A place called school.* New York: McGraw-Hill.

Griffin, G. A. (1985a). *The paraprofessionalization of teaching.* Paper delivered at the annual meeting of the American Educational Research Association, Chicago.

_____. (1985b). The school as a workplace and the master teacher concept. *Elementary School Journal, 86*(1), 1–16.

_____. (1986). Thinking about teaching. In K. K. Zumwalt (Ed.), *Improving teaching. 1986 yearbook of the Association for Supervision and Curriculum Development. Alexandria, VA: The Association.*

_____. (1988a). Leadership for school improvement: The school administrator's role. In L. Tanner (Ed.), *Critical issues in curriculum.* Eighty-seventh yearbook of the National Society for the Study of Education. Chicago: University of Chicago Press.

_____. (1988b). *Learning to teach in schools: Lessons from The Gatlin Brothers, Stephen Sondheim, Les Miserables, and Winston Churchill.* Invited address at the annual meeting of the American Association of Colleges for Teacher Education, New Orleans.

Griffin, G. A., & Barnes, S. (1986). Using research findings to change school and classroom practices: Results of an experimental study. *American Educational Research Journal, 23* (4), 572–586.

Hoffman, J., Barnes, S., Griffin, G., O'Neal, S., Edwards, S., Paulissen, M., & Leighty, C. (1986). *Teacher induction: Final report of a descriptive study.* Austin, TX: University of Texas at Austin, Research and Development Center for Teacher Education.

Holmes Group, The. (1986). *Tomorrow's teachers.* East Lansing, MI: The Holmes Group.

Lanier, J. E. (1986). Research on teacher education. In M. C. Wittrock (Ed.), *Handbook of research on teaching* (3rd ed.). New York: Macmillan.

Lieberman, A., Ed. (1988). *Building a professional culture in schools.* New York: Teachers College Press.

Rosenholtz, S. (1989). *Teachers' workplace: The social organization of schools.* White Plains, NY: Longman.

Sarason, S. (1971). *The culture of the school and the problem of change.* Boston: Allyn & Bacon.

Schon, D. A. (1983). *The reflective practitioner: How professionals think in action.* New York: Basic Books.

Schulman, L. (1988). *Classroom processes.* Invited address at the annual meeting of the American Association of Colleges for Teacher Education.

Sprinthall, N. A., & Thiess-Sprinthall, L. (1983). The teacher as an adult learner; A cognitive-developmental view. In G. Griffin (Ed.), *Staff Development.* Eighty-second yearbook of the National Society for the Study of Education. Chicago: University of Chicago Press.

Tikunoff, W. J., Ward, B. A., & Griffin, G. A. (1979). *Interactive research and development: Final report.* San Francisco: Far West Laboratory for Educational Research and Development.

Tyler, R. W. (1949). *Basic principles of curriculum and instruction.* Chicago: University of Chicago Press.

Ward, B. A. (1987). State and district structures to support initial year of teaching programs. In G. Griffin & S. Millies (Eds.), *The first years of teaching: Background papers and a proposal.* Chicago: University of Illinois at Chicago.

Zumwalt, K. K. (1988). Are we improving or determining teaching? In L. L. Tanner, (Ed.), *Critical issues in curriculum.* Chicago: University of Chicago Press.

7 Centralized Curriculum: Effects on the Local School Level

Martin G. Brooks

The argument in favor of state mandated curriculum goes something like this: because students in some school districts perform below state expectations, the state needs to set clear and high standards for student performance and then require all school districts to meet these standards. From the state perspective, the most direct method of setting clear and high standards is to develop mandated syllabi for each curriculum area, and the most powerful way of ensuring adherence to the objectives of these syllabi is through an extensive testing program. Although this argument seems logical, it is generating vigorous resistance, particularly at the local school district level. In the seven years since *A Nation at Risk* (National commission on Excellence in Education, 1983), there is little evidence to indicate that the approach to school reform supported by this argument has improved the quality of education in this nation (Airasian, 1988).

This chapter will discuss the growing disaffection with centralized curriculum, identify the subtle and direct messages received at the local level through implementation of state-centralized curriculum, list some changes occuring at the local level in response to state-mandated curriculum, and state some recommendations for the future. Throughout the paper, examples will be cited from New York State, since that is the state with which I am most familiar.

Responding to the Call for Reform

New York State was quick to embrace state-mandated curriculum as policy and practice, fueled in part by its desire to be at the forefront of

151

the educational reform movement. In 1983 the New York State Board of Regents issued the first draft of its *Proposed Action Plan to Improve Elementary and Secondary Education Results in New York State* (The University of the State of New York, 1983). This plan was developed on the heels of several educational reform reports, most notably *A Nation at Risk* (National Commission on Excellence in Education, 1983), which focused national attention on perceived deficiencies and was similar in content, scope, and methodology to plans under development in other states.

Note that the plan, as emphasized in its title, seeks to improve educational *results*, an emphasis not lost on educators at the local school district level. As anticipated, the plan required the use of state-mandated syllabi and enforced usage of the syllabi by broadening an already formidable statewide testing program. The results of statewide tests, not improvements in instructional practices, would be used to gauge local school district efficacy. The authors unashamedly wrote that the plan "places a heavier emphasis on results or evidence of pupil performance than on technique or instructional practice" (The University of the State of New York, 1984, attachment #2).

A series of hearings on the plan was held throughout the state during the fall and early winter of the 1983–84 school year, and a revised plan was published by the regents in 1984. The revised plan purported to drop the required use of state-developed syllabi as well as procedures and time minimums, stating that these requirements would still apply "only to certain low performing schools" (The University of the State of New York, 1984, attachment #2, p. 8). The revised plan, however, also stated, "We must insist that the goals, objectives, standards and requirements of our Plan apply to *all* students" (The University of the State of New York, 1984, p. 2), a contradiction that continues to perplex local district educators.

Although required use of state-mandated syllabi is, in fact, dropped in the revised plan, local school district adherence to the objectives of the syllabi remains stringently enforced through the comprehensive program of state testing. Furthermore, the state's plan requires each school district to prepare annually for its board of education a comprehensive assessment report which lists district scores on all state-mandated tests. Each district's scores are also released to the media, which annually publish lists of state-mandated test scores for all school districts in the area.

Messages Received at the Local Level

In discussing the messages received at the local level, it is important to note that state-mandated curricula and their concomitant state-mandated tests can be, and have been, useful for the small number of school districts that historically have offered an inadequate, deficient curriculum to their students. These school districts have been forced to upgrade the standards of their programs by meeting the objectives set forth in state syllabi. In attempting to improve the quality of education results in those districts, however, the state has painted with an unnecessarily broad brush, thereby communicating to local educators throughout the state some unfortunate messages.

Message #1: "Curriculum development is not your responsibility."

Curriculum development historically has been the responsibility of local school district educators (see discussion in Chapter 8). State education departments identified for local school districts those curriculum areas which must be taught, such as language arts, science, social studies, and the arts, and set suggested skills and objectives in each curriculum area, commonly known as a syllabus. Local school personnel would then develop or select appropriate materials, activities, and modes of instruction, commonly known as a curriculum.

The growing phalanx of state-mandated tests has interfered dramatically with this process. By focusing so much attention on the skills listed in state-developed syllabi, the tests have, in effect, eliminated differences between syllabi and curricula, making them interchangeable terms for local district educators. Teachers who wish to deviate from the syllabi must do so in the hope that the materials and activities they develop or select will equally prepare their students to demonstrate acceptable results on the required tests. Naturally, this set of circumstances has affected teacher initiative: why spend time and effort developing innovative curricula if such curricula are not valued, and, in fact, place the teacher and students at some risk?

This change is not without irony. Recent reports on the status of teaching as a profession, most notably the Carnegie report (1986) and the Holmes Group report (1986), advocate an expanding role for the teacher. Those who argue in favor of state-mandated curriculum, although professing to respond to the same call for reform, are in fact narrowing the teacher's role considerably. They have, in effect, drawn a clear distinction between curriculum development and curriculum delivery: the state's responsibility is the development of curriculum, and the local school district educator's task is delivering it. Teachers feel far less professional under this system.

Message #2: "Testing drives instruction."

The role of testing has shifted strikingly. In years past, before the proliferation of state-mandated, criterion-referenced tests, most school districts administered only nationally normed achievement tests, designed to measure how the student population in a district compared with the overall national group of age and grade peers. This practice by itself was questionable, given what we now know about the validity of these tests (Gifford, 1989). With the reform reports arrived a slew of state-mandated tests, which have a very different purpose: they measure the adherence by a school district to the specific criteria (objectives) included in state-developed syllabi.

It did not take long for educators at the local district level to figure out that their efficacy and that of their districts would be judged by the results their students produced on state-mandated tests. Popham (1987) writes the following:

> Measurement-driven instruction occurs when a high stakes test of educational achievement, because of the important contingencies associated with the students' performance, influences the instructional program that prepares students for the test...Teachers tend to focus a significant portion of their instructional activities on the knowledge and skills assessed by such tests. A high stakes test of educational achievement, then, serves as a powerful *curricular magnet.* (p. 680)

This realization has rekindled for many teachers the classic paradox of means versus ends. It has convinced many teachers that, for reasons of self-protection (and for some, self-aggrandizement), they ought to *teach to the test,* breathing new life into the old saying, "What gets tested gets taught." Weiss and Fege (1988) discuss the possibility that the National Assessment of Educational Progress (NAEP) may someday oversee state-by-state comparisons of test scores, and write the following:

> Beware the consequences of state-by-state comparisons... Newspapers across the U. S. will publish the results; in low scoring states elected officials will cry out for school reform; pressured to improve scores, school people will begin encouraging teachers (subtly, at first) to teach to the tests. Ultimately, instead of measuring the success of the public education system, standardized tests will dictate what is taught. (pp. 13–14)

Teaching to tests, as a practice, has a number of disturbing ramifications. First, it permits tests to define what is important to know: if it is not tested, it is not important. Second, since tests typically seek one correct answer to each question asked, teaching to tests results in the creation of educational environments that favor one correct answer, one truth, rather than the complexity of multiple options. Third, higher-order thinking is devalued by teaching to tests because most tests focus on basic skills, not inferential, analytic thinking (Fiske, 1988). (See also Chapters 8 and 10.)

Many state education department officials claim that their tests are flexible and accommodating, that they may be used much in the same manner as a reading management system—freeing the teacher to use a wider variety of reading materials by ensuring that the basic skills are being taught. At the local level, however, the tests have caused a constriction of materials, objectives, and approaches, pruning away most of those that do not directly address what is tested. Again, an irony exists. In an attempt to respond to the clarion call of the reform reports to "produce" more creative, complex thinkers, state education departments have created a testing and accountability monster that is blocking attainment of this very goal. Means such as inquiry and discovery have been overwhelmed by a growing obsession with ends, redirecting the focus of classroom instruction across the nation.

For example, several teachers in our district's high school (Schutzman et al., 1988) recently completed an analysis of the revised curriculum and test from the state for Global Studies II, a tenth-grade course. They found both to be largely fact oriented, and concluded that in order to prepare their students to score well on the test, they needed to (1) eliminate team teaching between social studies teachers and English teachers because it is too time consuming, (2) significantly reduce in-depth study and related activities such as a comprehensive three-week unit on the Holocaust because of time constraints, (3) banish certain units and themes from the curriculum, such as nuclear issues and parts of the world today, because the test ignores them, and (4) excise completely or reduce the time given to certain teaching methodologies and approaches such as cooperative learning, class debates, and theme papers. In place of these activities, students would be required to memorize facts such as the purpose of the Council of Trent or the significance of the Archduke Ferdinand of Austria. Although Hirsch (1987) may applaud this transmutation, the results have been depressing to these teachers, who ended their report by writing, "We are discouraged about the exam and its effect on our courses. We all have a great deal of work to do in order to meet the [new] demands" (Schutzman et al., 1988, p. 1). In response to the suggestion that they retain the current curriculum and make none or only a few of the changes discussed above, they indicated that doing so would place their students at a disadvantage when compared with students from other districts. The test results are used to compare students across the state and are considered by universities when students apply for admission.

Message #3: "It is more important to cover material than to learn it."

Recently, I spoke to a group high school teachers from several districts about the importance of considering cognitive developmental principles when creating lessons and choosing instructional strategies. While agreeing that hands-on experiences, discovery activities, simulations, and student-generated goals all enhance learning and make for an exciting classroom environment, the group unanimously indicated that structuring lessons to account for the developmental abilities of students was valued less by the educational system than *covering the material* on which their students would be tested. In order to "cover the material," most teachers opt to behave didactically, presenting themselves as the sole possessors and disseminators of knowledge in the classroom. These teachers extend to their students a very different set of educational experiences than do "constructivist" teachers, who function as mediators of the school-based experiences through which students construct their own knowledge (Dewey, 1916; Piaget, 1954).

Related to this, Goodlad (1984) pointed out that "teacher talk" dominated the classrooms in his sample, leaving little time for student exploration, discovery, hypothesis testing, and problem solving. Yet another irony: state-developed curricula and tests place more pressure on teachers to dominate classroom interactions, a practice that runs counter to good teaching practices (Dunkin & Biddle, 1974; Rosenshine & Furst, 1971; Jackson, 1968) and that has been roundly criticized in some of the very same reform reports to which their supporters claim to be responding.

Message #4: "Minimum competence is the desired outcome."

Most state-mandated syllabi establish lengthy lists of behavioral objectives to be achieved by students and set minimum standards of achievement to be measured through batteries of tests. Performance on most state-mandated tests is measured against a state reference point—the minimum number of correct answers the state expects all students to obtain. Students who fall below the state reference point on a given test are earmarked for remedial services.

In many states, district results are not reported by mean raw scores. Instead, they are reported by the percentage of students falling below the state reference point. For example, assume that one hundred students in district X take a 50-item test, and the mean raw score is 41 with thirteen students falling below the state reference point. In district Y, the mean raw score for one hundred students is 38 with only nine students falling below the state reference point. Although more students achieved higher scores in district X, the scores of district Y are perceived as better by the state because a smaller percentage of students fell below the state reference point.

This sort of emphasis creates a minimum competency baseline toward which lower-achieving students are aimed. The problem with aiming at minimum competence for *all* students is that "you get what you ask for." Many teachers have determined that spending time with those students who are well above minimum competence levels is not as highly valued by the state as spending time with those who are below minimum competence levels. Extension and enrichment activities are being crowded out of the curriculum by classroom remediation of skill deficiencies, creating for many districts a regression to the mean. Minimum competence is becoming the expectation for all students. Airasian (1988) states that minimum competence has become an important public symbol of educational reform, engendering misguided faith in test scores as indices of improvement:

> It is hard to be against competence, standards, or functional literacy, and few politicians or school board members would be likely to state in public that they are not in favor of such constructs. What, after all, is someone who is against competence for—incompetence? The language of state-mandated high stakes testing programs helps crystallize public acceptance because words like *competence* and *standards* conjure up symbolically potent images. (p. 308)

A disturbing by-product of the increased emphasis on minimum competence and remediation has been that special education students are further squeezed out of the mainstream. Districts concerned with improving test scores and reducing the percentages of students who fall below state reference points have pulled special education students out of their mainstream classes for larger doses of skill-based remediation. Another incentive for separating special education students from their mainstream classes is found in the fact that many states do not include the scores of special education students when reporting district data, increasing the likelihood that these districts will have better results.

Message #5: "We don't trust you!"

The imposition of state-mandated syllabi has occurred through a militarylike, hierarchical system of accountability in which a state board directs the state education department to improve educational *results,* the state education department directs local boards of education, local boards direct superintendents, superintendents direct building administrators, and building administrators direct teachers. All participants in this system are held accountable by the tests. Sedlak et al. (1986) write the following:

> Reformers have attempted to change public education from the top down with mandates to address a particular problem; with rules, procedures and standards generated to facilitate goal attainment, and with monitoring and evaluation to assess progress. What has been missing has been an appreciation of how such programs would actually affect the daily lives of students and teachers. (p. 185)

Teachers in such systems are beginning to feel that they are trusted neither to develop or select curriculum nor to teach it appropriately. This message is rather disheartening for many teachers since academic freedom and autonomy are two of the precious few job satisfiers which offset for them a multitude of dissatisfiers, such as the perceptions of relatively low pay, inadequate working conditions, misbehaving students, critical parents, and a general lack of public support. Local school district educators correctly perceive that state education departments have little interest in understanding the idiosyncratic cultures in which local education programs have developed, seeking instead to treat them all as similar for the purpose of control.

Moreover, in New York one must wonder about the state's professed desire to professionalize teaching in light of the continuing constriction of responsibilities attached to teachers' roles in the state. The Commissioner's Task Force report (1988), in discussing obstacles to reform, states the following:

> Other barriers have arisen from a lack of trust among adults. Because some students fail to learn and/or some teachers do not know how or are unable to reach them, the behavior of all is regulated. What we have learned, however, is that the system which has been designed and redesigned to perfect top-down control has only a limited capacity to respond to individual student needs. Before the structure can be changed to allow

those school personnel closest to students—the teachers—to respond directly to their needs, there must be a commitment to establishing trust in teacher competency. (p. 8)

Until these two contravening voices can be reconciled, teachers will continue to receive confusing, mixed messages.

Message #6: "Past effectiveness does not matter."

Many and quite likely most school districts throughout the nation offer sound, comprehensive educational programs to their students. The effectiveness of these programs is manifested through parental support, student self-esteem, curriculum and extracurriculum accomplishments, and "the hard data set," such as student test scores, attendance and dropout rates, and percentages of students in remedial or special education programs. In fact, past statements by the commissioner of education in New York, members of the New York Board of Regents, and state-level politicians have consistently attested to the high quality of public education offered in the state.

Despite indices of past efficacy, all school districts are treated by state education departments in the same manner as are those few districts that historically have been deficient. All districts are held equally accountable for adherence to the objectives of state-mandated syllabi. Innovative programs, unique cultural variations, and long-standing commitments to local curriculum and material development are devalued by state-mandated syllabi and tests that increasingly encourage interdistrict homogeneity. Sizer (1985) warns that reformers often "confuse standardization with standards...We trivialize the process of learning by oversimplifing it; and by the over simplification represented by mandated standard practice, we lessen the potential of teachers" (p. 23).

Message #7: "More and sooner and quicker and tougher is better."

Throughout the nation, state education departments have been focusing attention on improving early childhood education and on reducing high school student dropout rates, two noble goals. Some states, however, have chosen some rather curious ways to proceed. The former commissioner of education in New York, for example, pushed for years to have students enter school at four years of age and graduate at sixteen. This proposal contradicts much of what we know about child development and learning (Elkind, 1981). "More and sooner and quicker" may sound responsible, particularly in light of the reformers' calls for higher standards and increased emphasis on academic achievement, but it may result in greater numbers of students feeling the frustrations associated with being asked to learn concepts for which they cognitively are not yet ready. Development accounts for learning, not vice versa. Students who are asked to learn material for which they are not developmentally ready will fail or will compensate by memorizing that which is necessary to pass the tests—and then quickly forgetting it.

Several years ago, a number of teachers in our district analyzed the newly developed state elementary mathematics syllabus. The teachers indicated that some of the skills, concepts, and objectives were developmentally inappropriate for the grade levels in which they were placed. The teachers expressed concern that the students would not be able to understand the inappropriate material, and asked if these skills, concepts, and objectives could be taught in later years, by which time most students would have developed the cognitive schemes necessary to grasp them. Although we granted permission, we did so apprehensively, believing the changes to be in the best educational interests of the students but fearful that the public profile of the district might suffer.

It is also important to mention that a major, perhaps *the* major, thrust of most state reform efforts is to toughen standards for high school graduation by increasing the number of credits needed for the diploma, requiring sequences in a specified number of academic areas, and offering accelerated tracks for able students. States are transmitting a confusing message to their local educators and students. On the one hand, they appear to be devoting a good deal of time, energy, and resources to reducing student dropout rates and keeping students in school. On the other hand, by toughening course standards and establishing minimum competence requirements for high school graduation, they may be forcing more and more students to drop out before graduation, particularly poor and minority inner-city students, who often wind up in the lowest high school tracks (Goodlad, 1984). A strong case could be made, I think, that the national thirst for tougher high school standards is, at least in its operational form, inherently discriminatory.

Effects at the Local Level

It is important to reiterate that, for some "miscreant" school districts, state-mandated curricula have helped improve education for students. That said, I will briefly discuss the unfortunate effects felt by the majority of school districts.

First, state imposition of curricula and tests has signaled to local school district educators a perpetuation of the very same system that created the need for reform, a system that overtly values standardization of knowledge more than learning. Teacher thinking and student thinking appear to be less valued than good test scores.

This is closely tied to the second effect: qualitative measures of local school district efficacy have become subordinate to quantitative measures. Teachers, administrators, boards of education, and parents all are asked to judge the quality of educational programs by how well their student populations score on state-mandated tests. This creates for state boards a paradoxical, self-fulfilling prophecy: as teachers are forced to pay more attention to test results, test results improve; as test results improve, so, too, does the belief of boards that their state-mandated curricula are, indeed, improving the quality of education.

Third, many districts have experienced an epistemological constriction, an abridgement of the curriculum and experiences to which students are exposed. In "teaching to the test," teachers have narrowed the range and depth of learning. As the range of learning has narrowed, so, too, has the range of teaching methodologies and strategies to which students are exposed. A significant body of research exists that suggests that humans learn best orthogenetically, that is, whole to part (see, for example, Bruner, 1985). State curriculum guides and syllabi organize the curriculum and test the curriculum by parts, not wholes. Many teachers perceive that state education departments are pressuring them to teach in ways that run counter to what they know to be in the best interests of their students.

Local curriculum development and curriculum review as standard practices have become essentially moribund. The incentive to write curriculum, develop one's own materials, and try innovative approaches has been significantly lessened because locally developed curricula are not tested by the state.

All these factors have coalesced to erode teacher innovation. The hierarchical, top-down system of accountability described earlier places considerable pressure on teachers to conform to the guidelines of the state. Refusal to do so places teachers and students at some risk because low test scores redound poorly to teachers and require students to participate in remedial programs. It is difficult for many teachers to withstand the weight of this pressure.

A Look to the Future

As minimum competence is raised to an exalted status, those who receive the most attention are students who score below state reference points, largely because school districts target a disproportionate quantity of resources toward these students to improve their test scores. In most districts and exclusive of the large cities, we are talking about a minority of students. Since time, material, and personnel are limited resources, what is given to one group is, by necessity, taken from another group. Those students who fall above the state reference point, in most cases the majority of students, will continue receiving less as a result of this change.

I fear that state-mandated curricula and tests may represent the beginning of a larger erosion of the authority historically delegated to local school districts. It does not take an oracle to speculate that if the state is telling local school districts *what* to teach, it will not be too long before the state begins telling local school districts *how* to teach. In fact, this is already happening to some degree. For example, in California, prospective teachers cannot receive their teaching credentials unless they have been trained to use the techniques associated with the so-called "Madeline Hunter" model (Hunter, 1982), and this model is used for the yearly evaluation of teachers throughout the state (see also Chapter 10). I worry that mandating methodology as well as content likely will sap what little autonomy remains for teachers and will further the standardization process. It is teacher creativity, not uniformity of content and practice, that generates student excitement about learning.

A related fear about the future has to do with statewide adoption of textbooks and materials. Local school districts historically have had a free hand in selecting appropriate texts and materials. Publishers and developers of materials, however, recognize the emerging trend and are rushing to bring their texts and materials in line with state objectives. Similarly, some state education departments have sought to bring their curricula and tests in line with adopted textbooks (English, 1986–87), a trend euphemistically called "curriculum alignment."

The Council for Basic Education (CBE) has reported that twenty-two states already have mandated statewide adoption of textbooks and have sought to align the textbooks with their statewide curricula and tests (1988). The CBE report noted that increased attempts to regulate the content of textbooks render them less useful for students locally and nationally. Competition among publishers to bring their materials in line with state criteria is narrowing the range of choices available to local school district educators.

Recommendations

The desire to improve the quality of education is laudable, but the belief that improvement can be mandated through a top-down system of accountability for all is misguided. Changes must be targeted specifically toward those districts that require them. State education department officials can easily identify those districts that require intervention. Most of those districts have long records of deficient performance, including parent complaints, unstable boards of education, high dropout rates, and consistently low student achievement. The energies of state education departments ought to be directed at such districts, leaving alone those districts with long records of successful performance. The broad brush needs to be tapered.

State education department assessments of local school district efficacy need to be more qualitative in nature, not solely quantitative. Research indicates that managing large organizations through top-heavy systems of quantitative accountability has not been effective (Schein, 1985; Argyris & Schon, 1976; Levinson, 1973; Ouchi, 1981). In their zeal to replicate management practices from the business world, school executives at the state level are adopting the very same practices that business executives are jettisoning after years of frustration. Instead of falling into this trap, state education departments can play a helpful role by assisting local school districts in qualitatively examining their programs; it is helpful to have a fresh set of eyes with a broad, statewide perspective examine a long-standing math or language arts program. With the resources saved by attenuating or modifying the statewide curriculum development and testing efforts, state education departments could send, perhaps once every five years, a team of two or three of their associates and teachers from other districts into each district for one week to help local school district educators analyze current practices. Doing this would not only place the state education department in the position of playing a helpful role in local school improvement, but would enable teachers throughout the state to visit other districts, offer suggestions and insights to those districts, and bring suggestions and insights from those districts back to their own schools. Finally, the establishment of teams would enable the state to examine environments in a local context rather than through the unproductive paper audits currently used.

The school improvement process also could be helped by decentralizing the bureaucracy that exists in virtually all state education departments. Establishing regional school improvement offices staffed by state education department associates would give the states easier access to such qualitative data as indices of student thinking, peer reports, student projects, student work portfolios, teacher instructional methodologies, information on parent support, and student and teacher observations.

All schools in each state should be required to be registered by their state education departments. Schools passing muster every five years should be automatically re-registered and permitted to continue along their own paths, free to use the expertise of regional offices as needed. Schools found wanting should be issued a provisional two-year registration. During these two years, state aid should be increased to support the change process. I am aware that this suggestion flies in the face of conventional wisdom, which dictates that delinquent schools should be punished, not rewarded. If change is to occur, however, it needs to be supported financially. Furthermore, teams from the state education department and the regional offices should spend seven or eight weeks per year intervening in deficient schools. The intervention should include ongoing team meetings with local boards of education and top-level administrators about possible changes in policies, practices, and procedures; meetings with teachers and school-level administrators regarding instructional practices and in-service education needs; meetings with parents and community members about support (both psychological and fiscal) for the school(s); and meetings with students about commitment to learning. Using these meetings as catalysts, districts should be allowed to renew themselves without imposition of specific remedies by the state education department. After two years, however, if education has not improved appreciably, schools should be subject to more directive—and possibly punitive— measures, such as the imposition of specific guidelines, regulations, and procedures; mandated in-service education courses for staff and administrators; mandated use of state-developed curriculum; and, if necessary, revocation of registration, which would then free parents to send their children to other schools.

I want to emphasize the need to funnel more funds into teacher in-service education and follow-up activities. Teachers make more of a difference than mandated curricula. If aspects of the educational program of a district need improvement, regional in-service courses— and appropriate follow-up activities in the classroom—targeted at those aspects and taught by state education department associates, state university professors, or educators from other school districts are likely to have a greater direct impact on them than a series of state-developed syllabi and tests designed to regulate and homogenize the behaviors of all teachers. Mandated syllabi should be used only with districts that are consistently judged to be substandard and that have been unable to demonstrate the ability to improve themselves.

The centralization of curriculum is not the remedy for what ails education. The imposition of centralized curricula by state education departments creates many needless problems for local school district educators and students. State education departments have a right and a responsibility to intervene in local districts that require improvement. I am reminded of the teacher who, about to send the class to recess, notices two students misbehaving. The choice: send the remainder of the class to recess and deal with the two students by holding them in the room, or hold the whole class in the room for the misbehavior of the two. Throughout the nation, state education departments are making their positions on this choice clear.

References

Airasian, P. W. (1988, Winter). Symbolic validation: The case of state-mandated, high-stakes testing. *Educational Evaluation and Policy Analysis, 10,* 301–313.

Argyris, C., & Schon, D. (1976). *Theory in practice: Increasing professional effectiveness.* San Francisco: Jossey-Bass.

Bruner, J. (1985). *Models of a learner.* Invited address, American Educational Research Association annual conference, Chicago, Illinois.

Carnegie Forum on Education and the Economy. (1986). *A nation prepared: Teachers for the 21st century.* Hyattsville, MD: Carnegie Forum on Education and the Economy.

Commissioner's Task Force on the Teaching Profession. (1988). *A blueprint for learning and teaching.* Albany: New York State Education Department.

Council for Basic Education. (1988). *A conspiracy of good intentions: America's textbook fiasco.* Washington, DC: Council for Basic Education.

Dewey, J. (1916). *Democracy and education.* New York: Macmillan.

Dunkin, M., & Biddle, B. (1974). *The study of teaching.* New York: Holt, Rinehart & Winston.

Elkind, D. (1981). *The hurried child.* Reading, MA: Addison-Wesley.

English, F. W. (1986, December/1987, January). It's time to abolish conventional curriculum guides. *Educational Leadership, 44* (4), 50–52.

Fiske, E. (1988). America's test mania. *The New York Times,* April 10, 1988, p. 16.

Gifford, B. (1989, January). Testing: Perils and promises. *The Educator,* University of California at Berkeley, 3, (1), 4–7.

Goodlad, J. (1984). *A place called school.* New York: McGraw-Hill.

Hirsch, E. D. (1987). *Cultural literacy: What every American needs to know.* New York: Vintage Books.

The Holmes Group. (1986). *Tomorrow's teachers: A report of the Holmes Group.* East Lansing, MI: The Holmes Group.

Hunter, Madeline. (1982). *Mastery teaching.* El Segundo, CA: TIP Publications.

Jackson, P. (1968). *Life in classrooms.* New York: Holt, Rinehart & Winston.

Levinson, H. (1973). *The great jackass fallacy.* Cambridge, MA: Harvard University Press.

National Commission on Excellence in Education. (1983). *A nation at risk: The imperative for educational reform.* Washington, DC: U.S. Government Printing Office.

Ouchi, W. (1981). *Theory Z.* Reading, MA: Addison-Wesley.

Piaget, J. (1954). *The construction of reality in the child.* New York: Basic Books.

Popham, W. J. (1987, May). The merits of measurement-driven instruction. *Phi Delta Kappan, 68* (9), 679–682.

Rosenshine, B., & Furst, N. (1971). Research on Teacher Performance Criteria. In B. O. Smith (Ed.), *Research in teacher education.* Englewood Cliffs, NJ: Prentice-Hall.

Schein, E. (1985). *Organizational culture and leadership.* San Francisco: Jossey-Bass.

Schutzman, L., Mann, K., Miner, M., & Casey, J. (1988). An unpublished analysis of the Global Studies II exam. Shoreham, New York.

Sedlak, M. W., Wheeler, C. W., Pullin, D. C., & Cusick, P. A. (1986). *Selling students short: Classroom bargains and academic reform in the American high school. New York: Teachers College Press.*

Sizer, T. (1985, March). *Common Sense. Educational Leadership, 42* (6), 21–22.

The University of the State of New York. (1983). *New York state board of regents proposed action plan to improve elementary and secondary education results in New York.* Albany: The University of the State of New York, The State Education Department.

———. (1984). *New York state board of regents proposed action plan to improve elementary and secondary education results in New York* (revised). Albany: The University of the State of New York, The State Education Department.

Weiss J., & Fege, A. F. (1988, October). Warning: Standardized tests will dictate your curriculum. *The Executive Educator, 10,* 13–14.

8

Organizational Metaphors, Curriculum Reform, and Local School and District Change

Audrey James Schwartz

The consequences of recent externally developed curriculum reforms for local board members, educators, and students are discussed in this chapter. It will be seen that policies emanating from state and federal levels affect organizational roles in local districts far more than they produce intended educational outcomes. Most of the acknowledged failures in implementing top-down curriculum mandates (Elmore & McLaughlin, 1988; Rosenholtz, 1989) come from underlying notions about education that are inconsistent with the realities of schooling. The way in which state and federal policy makers understand education has major implications for the quality and feasibility of the educational reforms they propose. When assumptions about how schools work are in error, mandates to change them are seldom effective.

Metaphors for Curriculum Reform

Proposals for educational change usually are supported by one of two metaphors associated with schools of thought in organizational theory (Burrell & Morgan, 1982; Foster, 1986). The *machine* metaphor, evident in descriptions of American industrial beginnings, was integral to the thinking of early twentieth century school reformers, as Cubberly (1916) made clear in his well-known analogy of schools to factories. This industrial perspective has survived in education for more than half a century and is prominent in most top-down educational reforms.

The second metaphor emphasizes interacting social factors. In its original form, social systems were conceptualized as giant *organisms* composed of interrelated parts struggling for survival through evolutionary processes. The organic analogy was used to argue for the independence of business organizations from external governmental controls. This was seen in Sumner's (1906) dictum that stateways cannot folkways make, which implied that each system moves along a unique path with overarching concern for its own autonomous development. Although many of the evolutionary trappings of the organic metaphor have been dropped, it continues to emphasize survival of the system in a larger environment as well as structural looseness among its parts. This is the guiding metaphor in social system theories that have a socio-psychological perspective, as in progressive education, and in those that have a sociotechnical perspective (Foster, 1986, pp. 124–127). It also is present in proposals urging that educational policies be developed by the people who implement them, such as in backward mapping (Elmore, 1980) and bottom-up reforms (Committee for Economic Development, 1985).

Educational systems derived from the machine metaphor are evaluated by criteria of effectiveness and efficiency, that is, by the number and quality of their outputs and by the economy realized in transforming inputs into outputs (Scott, 1987, p. 321). Bureaucracy is their most distinguishing characteristic. Two bureaucratic features in particular are salient to the implementation of top-down curriculum change. One is the hierarchical structure of authority, in which educators are supervised by and report to people immediately above them. The other is explicit rules delineating the responsibilities of each educator. The machine metaphor implies a logical connection between the goals of education and the means prescribed to attain them; once solutions to educational problems are identified, they can be mandated in centralized policies. With this metaphor, then, legislation of goal attainment is sufficient for goal attainment to occur (Wise, 1979, p. 357).

From the perspective of the organic metaphor, schools are social organisms struggling to adapt to demands from within and beyond their boundaries (Waller, 1932). Bureaucracy is important only in that it gives general form to the system, and hierarchical authority is not axiomatic, since administrators earn their right to lead through positive interpersonal relations and demonstrations of superior knowledge. Prescribed rules do not control the system totally in that separate units function with quasi-independence as they pursue self-serving objectives. The teaching act is understood to be more art than the application of scientific findings because students are seen as diverse, with different aptitudes, interests, and needs. The organic metaphor fosters curriculum development at the level of implementation. To the extent that educational policy is formulated outside the local district, it calls for participation by local educators, both for their professional expertise and for their future cooperation in its implementation.

These two organizational metaphors are abstractions or ideal types accenting real differences in orientation toward public schools. The machine metaphor leads to a rational view of schools in which teachers are compliant, semiskilled practitioners of routinized work and students are compliant receivers of prescribed, standardized curriculum. The organic metaphor leads to a view of schools as complex systems in which teachers are autonomous professionals, knowledgeable in their subjects and in the psychological and sociological principles of teaching and learning and with motivations linked to the successes of their students. It recognizes that students differ in degree of compliance and in response to educational strategies and do not always share the educational goals developed for them.

In summary, the machine metaphor implies universalism in the approach to students and the appropriateness of a common curriculum; the organic metaphor implies particularism toward students and a differentiated curriculum. Further, the machine metaphor suggests that classrooms are controllable through application of the science of education; the organic metaphor suggests that the teacher's discretion is essential because classroom events derive from complex in-school and out-of-school factors not fully understood.

Organizational Metaphors and American Educational Policy

Both metaphors have supported policies articulated for American public schools, and both have had periods of dominance. The organic view, with its emphasis on community control, was present in colonial times and persisted through the Common School era of the nineteenth century. The machine perspective was brought into play in the early twentieth century to coordinate and control expanding school districts as they responded to changing work patterns. The organic metaphor reappeared in the 1930s in a more sophisticated form when terminal secondary school students outnumbered those expecting to transfer to college and differentiated curricula were introduced emphasizing citizenship, life adjustment, and that which is useful.

The school organizational metaphor shifted back to the machine in the 1950s when the federal government unambiguously moved into the arena of educational policy as a result of the Soviet space satellite launching in 1957. This gave impetus to federally supported curriculum activity and the U.S. Supreme Court's *Brown v. Board of Education* decision in 1954 declaring unconstitutional the deliberate separation of students by race. The *Brown* ruling ushered in the drive for educational equity that has characterized federal policy ever since. Although curriculum changes were not specified by Congress in the Civil Rights Act of 1964 or the Elementary and Secondary Education Act of 1965 (ESEA), the consequences of the regulatory and judicial actions that followed affected curricula through alterations in school structures and procedures. Learning environments across the nation were modified by school desegregation, bilingual education, and mainstreaming of special-education pupils.

As the social turmoil of the 1970s reached schools, organic assumptions were manifested once again. The federal judiciary significantly affected the latent or unintentional curriculum of secondary schools through decisions acknowledging the heterogeneity of students and the importance of school procedures to what they learn. General recognition of the problems of youth had an undeniable influence on secondary curriculum, and organic assumptions continued with federal legislative emphasis on vocational studies, including apprenticeships, career education, and school credit for work experience.

Organic assumptions also were seen at local levels as courses were added in response to perceived needs and interests of youth. Many school staffs embarked on endless searches to find something to interest each student, under the assumption that if they could, educational needs would be met (Cusick, 1983, p. 44). But little positive can be said about the depth of the curriculum or the standards to which students were held during the 1970s. Grade inflation was common, and the slump in national achievement scores could no longer be explained by the demographic characteristics of the new secondary school students. Ironically, the largest decline was in the area of civics, which apparently was unaffected by the lessons schools provided in democratic rule and peaceful coexistence (Hampel, 1986, p. 140).

The machine metaphor dominated educational policy through the 1980s, accompanied by unprecedented involvement of states in local district activities. This was prompted by three factors. First was the national policy of new federalism manifested in the Education Consolidation and Improvement Act (ECIA) of 1981, which reduced the federal role in local program development and gave state educational agencies greater authority in how federal money was spent. Second was the assumption by many states of more of the costs of local education. Third was wide dissatisfaction with schools, expressed variously as loss of school authority over students, poor scholastic outcomes, and purposelessness of the curriculum. The crisis rhetoric of commission reports released in the early 1980s elaborated on and exacerbated these concerns. Diminished confidence in education stimulated reform movements with assumptions derived from the machine metaphor, such as back to basics, minimum competencies, core curriculum, and stricter promotion standards and graduation requirements.

Scientific management principles embedded in the machine metaphor were evident in the reform activities. At first, most school problems were diagnosed as managerial, and plans to address them urged practices used in industry, such as management by objectives and program budgeting. Accompanying curriculum proposals characteristically dealt with quantitative changes, including more hours of instruction each day and more days each year. By the mid-1980s, state reforms also emphasized instructional quality, with many prescribing classroom curricula accompanied by outcome assessment measures.

With the entry of state legislatures into classroom practices, differences in basic assumptions among educational policy actors began to surface. Proposals affiliated with the machine metaphor were inconsistent both with the traditional culture of professional educators, which had greater identity with the organic metaphor, and with recommendations drawn from empirically based studies of school social systems (e.g., Boyer, 1983; Cusick, 1983; Grant, 1988; Lazerson, McLaughlin, McPherson, & Bailey, 1985; Sizer, 1984). While alarmed legislators increasingly urged uniformity in curriculum, instruction, and accountability, educators became more vocal in their opposition to the universalistic practices such legislation implied.

The Effects of Externally Imposed Reforms on Educational Roles in Local School Districts

By the late 1980s, the stage was set for clashes in curriculum policy between the underlying machine metaphor of central control and the strengthened organic metaphor. With mixed metaphors driving educational policies, local school districts were responsible for activities based on inconsistent assumptions. The effects of top-down curriculum policies on school board members, administrators, teachers, and students are discussed in the pages that follow.

Effects on Local School Board Members

From the inception of American public education, the local school board was assumed to be the official governing body. And so it was in the nineteenth century Common School that boards had total responsibility for local education and performed both policy development and administrative functions. This also was true in the early twentieth century, when boards, having yielded most administrative functions to professional school managers, retained responsibility for policy. In the second part of the twentieth century, however, the intrusion of federal and state mandates into local districts dramatically diluted the monopoly of school boards, and they changed from an independent body representing local constituents to directors of a local educational bureaucracy nested within a larger state bureaucracy which, in turn, was nested in the federal bureaucracy. Although boards now have nominal control over local schools, in reality they are responsible to external governmental agencies more than to the citizens who select them.

Until the 1954 *Brown* decision, school boards supplied curricula that reinforced local culture and maintained local social patterns. This began to change with the national civil rights movement, which showed that schools themselves were implicated in the preservation of inequities (Grant, 1988, p. 128), and it changed even more in the 1980s with state legislative policies designed to eradicate the mediocrity believed to be a product of local control.

Sanctions that have been effective in imposing state curriculum policies link resources to curriculum practices and student outcomes or tie high school graduation to students' demonstrations of competence. A new state tactic directly affecting school boards is to declare districts academically bankrupt if they are perceived as too weak to carry out educational functions. This permits state intervention in the management of schools, as occurred in Jersey City in 1988, or the elimination of a central school board, as occurred with the restructuring of Chicago schools in 1989.

Some states are involved routinely in the functioning of local boards and in their relationships with schools, parents, and communities. An example is the California requirement that annual school improvement reports be prepared by local school councils (composed of representatives from teachers, students, parents, and community) and that a written appraisal of each report by the local board be submitted to the state. If the state is not satisfied with a school, it can send a review team to recommend strategies for change (Timar & Kirp, 1988, p. 105). A modified version of this practice is mandated for districts receiving Title I funds by the Hawkins-Stafford Elementary and Secondary School Improvement Amendments of 1988.

Educational goals developed by state legislatures tend to be minimalist in that they emphasize traditional basics on which there is strong consensus and ignore or mute socialization and human-skills development functions, about which there usually is disagreement. Thus, controversial issues derived from history, social science, and differences among subpopulation groups typically are absent in state-mandated curricula, leaving them narrow and often bland (see also Chapter 10). When such issues are addressed above the level of platitudes, they usually come from local boards.

State educational agencies (SEAs) also are involved in developing educational goals. Approval of textbooks by a state department of education is a common example. The adoption of a text, which is often the same as the adoption of a curriculum, makes manifest the ideas to which students are to be exposed. Many SEAs publish guidelines for textbook adoption, and about half of the states have state-level committees to approve books, which further dilute local board control over curriculum policy.

In addition, publishers play a major part in circumscribing curricula, since texts can be selected only from those available. A common practice contributing to superficial curricula is the exclusion of material that is objectionable to any articulate group in order to gain widest possible adoption. Vocal critics have pointed to the low intellectual level and banality of textbook content, and some SEAs have rejected mathematics and English literature texts, charging "shallowness" and "trivialization" of the subjects.

When relatively noncontroversial areas of the curriculum are usurped by state policy, local school boards are left to grapple with difficult decisions involving the personal values of their constituents. Boards can minimize local conflict by limiting their districts' goals to those set at other levels. In that case, purposely selected narrow goals on which there is broad consensus displace traditional social and political objectives of education, producing uniform, superficial curricula in many districts. Nevertheless, even an apparently noncontroversial curriculum can precipitate conflict if it reflects a worldview different from that of community members. There are many examples of rejection of external policy based on value conflicts with local cultures. One is the carefully constructed social studies curriculum, "Man: A Course of Study" (MACOS). Local citizens, determined to control the values transmitted in schools, found threatening the comparisons in the MACOS curriculum between the development of humans and animals. MACOS virtually disappeared from public schools as a result of citizen pressure on school board members and congressional representatives (Ravitch, 1983). Sex and drug education are other examples of issues that produce local controversy, as is the newer policy of no-pass no-play, prohibiting students without acceptable achievement from participating in extracurricular activities. The

U.S. surgeon general's proposal to provide information about AIDS garnered opposition in many school districts.

Courts have become active in adjudicating some of the challenges to curriculum. The celebrated 1987 Tennessee decision in *Mozert v. Hawkins* ruled that children could be excused from reading materials that offended the religious values of their parents and that schools must provide greater diversity in their means to reach prescribed ends. Compliance with this and similar judicial directives can be compelled by police action. If boards do not balance the competing perspectives of external and local constituents, they may have to contend with judicial decisions.

Reconciliation of competing curriculum demands is a major function of contemporary school boards. Since curriculum controversies are controversies over what is believed desirable for society, tensions arise within districts over what should be taught. Development of consensus about curriculum is especially difficult in heterogeneous communities with fighting coalitions. The problem is exacerbated where board members represent geographic areas with different social characteristics and unique policy agendas. Furthermore, where board elections have no local tax implications, as in states that assume most of the school funding, voter turnout in school elections is low. Without the meliorating influence of all citizens, educational policy is left to those with special interests. In the absence of local consensus, boards deal with controversial issues by using broad, ambiguous terms accompanied by behind-the-scene negotiations.

Schools perform many educational functions, including those not made explicit. Nonetheless, most local boards accept formal responsibility for more goals than time and resources allow and for goals and practices that may be inconsistent, such as commitments to the transmission of national and local cultures and to behavioristic and child development pedagogies. New goals are adopted in response to new community demands, often without surrendering existing ones. Commitment to far too many goals helps to explain why local curricula often appear as broad objectives which are difficult to operationalize and measure.

In addition to transmitting and articulating curriculum policy, boards protect individual schools from unwarranted intrusion by local constituents. Schools traditionally have been closed to lay inspection except at designated times, with board meetings the legitimate setting for protests against established practices and arguments for change. With community and parental involvement in schools, the gatekeeping function has become less important. For example, Chapter I of ECIA (1981) as well as other entitlements require that parents be consulted in program design and implementation, which guarantees that at least some people have direct access to local school facilities.

Other challenges to local board authority over curriculum policy appear in recent proposals in which states would continue to provide educational standards but the method to attain them would be determined at the local school. If the next wave of school reform bypasses district boards, their formal role will become largely symbolic. In fact, according to the reigning machine metaphor, school boards are relatively unimportant at present because most of their policy and resource functions have been acquired by state and federal governments, and, as has been seen, boards can be disbanded by state legislatures. Viewed from the organic perspective, however, the role boards play in maintaining local schools in often turbulent social and political environments is crucial. They accomplish this through traditional board meetings in which the views of diverse constituents and the district are presented, challenged, and compromised. If there were no school boards, a substitute mechanism would have to be developed to reduce local tensions and reconcile the concerns of local citizens so that educational activity could be carried on without undue interference.

Effects on School Superintendents

To the extent the school superintendency existed in the nineteenth century, it was no more than a simple school caretaker role concerned with daily physical maintenance. Its transformation into a professional, educational executive officer began at the turn of the century with reforms creating bureaucratic school districts independent of local government. Controversies with boards of education over their relative power were settled by the end of the first world war, when superintendents became the established educational experts of local districts. Consistent with the organizational metaphor of the time, scientific management principles were incorporated into the superintendency, and for the following half-century superintendents had formal authority in most areas formerly controlled by boards, except for curriculum policy. Even so, curriculum matters typically were initiated by superintendents for board approval and delegated to building principals for development and implementation. Superintendents were the acknowledged educational leaders of their communities; they defined the purpose of schools, protected educational values, and supplied vision to the districts.

The superintendents' leadership role in educational matters was less important after the 1950s as judges and legislators forced schools to be accountable beyond traditional governance structures and as ideological splits permeated school governance. Successful superintendents began to emphasize political over educational leadership; they became political strategists, makers of compromise, and coordinators of policies made elsewhere. Like managers of most contemporary organizations, superintendents devoted as much energy to managing their environments as to managing their production systems (Blumberg, 1985; Scott, 1987). In summary, superintendents were forced to adopt the organic perspective in managing their districts.

The relationship between local superintendents and state educational agencies (SEAs) took on new meaning. Superintendents could no longer ignore the SEAs, which had been strengthened by Title V of the ESEA and had acquired additional functions. In varying degrees SEAs were involved in school accreditation, program monitoring, allocation of state and federal money, development and enforcement of standards, and dissemination of state curriculum frameworks and guides. With these new functions came increases in their size, expertise, and power, so that prudent superintendents went out of their way to communicate with the state personnel who made major decisions affecting their districts.

The formal educational leadership aspects of the superintendency were diminished further by those SEAs requiring tangible evidence of compliance with mandated changes. Where outcome assessments were required, outward conformity to rules designed to bring about implementation no longer sufficed. Acceptable scores on standardized tests became the most critical concern of many superintendents, often taking precedent over professional judgment.

The initial reaction of most superintendents to externally mandated change is to give an innovative appearance through lip service to each proposal. In reality, their attitudes are more that of wait and see, knowing from experience that many proposals go away. Consideration of external reforms tends to be delayed as long as possible so that superintendents can attend to other problems competing for their time.

The reactions of superintendents to external mandates that cannot be ignored largely depend on their own perspectives of the superintendency. Professionally secure superintendents with cosmopolitan orientations are the most accepting. They have many professional contacts who can supply information about proposed changes, and they are less likely to be locked into local ways of doing things. Moreover, they may see innovations as positive and accept them on their merits. Or, more cynically, superintendents may adopt externally initiated reforms to project a forward-looking image for themselves or their districts or because the changes are accompanied by additional funds.

In contrast, superintendents who are less secure in their professional role with a local orientation are not as likely to accept externally induced change. They may be unfamiliar with its origin and the experiences of other districts, or they may have invested emotionally in their own program for the district. A mandate for change often appears threatening to the locally oriented superintendent—to be held responsible for results that depend on the work of others usually provokes a cautious, low-risk, play-it-safe attitude (Kanter, 1977, p. 192). The more concern superintendents have about adopting a mandated change, the more likely they will issue rules and regulations which tend to be followed by additional rules at the school and classroom levels. Thus, increased bureaucratization is a common consequence of externally generated change, particularly under conditions of professional insecurity.

In implementing external initiatives, superintendents use either a soft or hard sell (Wolcott, 1977). With the soft sell they may stress the similarity of the reform with what currently takes place in the school, merely provide guidelines for its implementation, bargain with teachers and administrators over implementation, or encourage teachers to participate in decisions that already are decided. With the hard sell they may exercise formal authority, develop informal influence through teachers' spouses and friends, withhold critical information, or intimidate teachers and principals. When neither the soft nor hard technique is effective, superintendents usually retreat from the proposed innovation and turn their attention to other problems (Wolcott, 1977).

Recent proposals for school district organization recommend that much of the formal authority of superintendents, like that of school boards, be delegated to local schools. This recommendation comes from the realization that external policies have not brought about anticipated results. Support for curriculum development in local schools is found in two peripherally related factors. One is the recognition that many decisions about externally generated reforms have been made de facto at the school site (Cohen, 1982, p. 489). And second is the shift in the metaphor underlying contemporary American industrial policy from the machine to the organic perspective. Recognition that top-down reforms have not been implemented as intended in classrooms has opened the assumptions of the machine metaphor to scrutiny and brought the issue of highly centralized control of schools into question.

Accordingly, many proposals now argue for problems to be solved at the level of operation, which usually is the classroom. The Committee for Economic Development contends in its 1985 report, *Investing in Our Children,* that the states should set standards and provide guidance and support, but must allow for school-level flexibility. The California Commission on Educational Quality (1988) goes even further in its recommendation that curriculum frameworks and model curriculum standards be advisory and permissive so that decisions about teaching methods can be made locally. Assumptions of the organic metaphor, which take into account variations in internal and external environments, are finding their way into practice. Districts that have implemented school-based management, such as Rochester, New York and Miami-Dade, Florida, provide two examples.

The growing division of educational decisions between state and school levels reduces the formal leadership roles of superintendents and central office personnel. If the trend toward school-level control continues, the office of the superintendent may be limited to providing educational support services and advice and to transmitting information between local schools and the SEA. On the other hand, the federal Hawkins-Stafford School Improvement Amendments of 1988 suggest that the state role in administering federal categorical programs will be reduced. Local districts, then, would be expected to be more active in developing and implementing policy for low-income and minority students. If this is so, superintendents would play a larger part in educational leadership than they have in the recent past.

Effects on Building-Level Principals

From the perspective of the machine metaphor, the building principal is the chief administrator of a local bureaucratic unit within the larger school district bureaucracy. Principals function as linking pins between the two by transmitting rules and expectations, some of which pertain to externally mandated curriculum, from the central office to classroom teachers. That so little change has occurred in classrooms following the reforms of the 1980s has puzzled those who accept the machine metaphor. Yet resistance to change at the school level can be understood within this metaphor, although the organic metaphor has greater explanatory power, as will be seen below.

When viewed through a bureaucratic lens, the main shortcoming of top-down reforms is their tendency toward hyperrationalization (Wise, 1983), or proliferation of rules, which transforms the principal's role from educational leader to a bureaucratic functionary who administers regulations made elsewhere. Most principals accept responsibility for implementing top-down mandates, even those with which they disagree, not only because it is one of their role responsibilities but because change or the appearance of change gives them career-enhancing visibility.

Nonetheless, principals alone cannot accomplish curriciulum reforms. In the final analysis, teachers bring educational change, and the assumption they are as motivated as principals by the rewards school districts offer is unwarranted. Teachers as a group are less career oriented; most are secure in their tenure and many are from two-career households, which gives them some financial independence while inhibiting their geographic mobility. Since an innovative reputation is not as important to teachers as it is to principals, they are less likely to embrace educational policies that conflict with their own views. If principals are to bring teachers' perspectives in line with mandated changes, they must emphasize leadership more than administrative techniques.

In addition, the principals' effectiveness in carrying out reforms is severely affected by the culture of teachers in their schools. For example, teachers often expect the principal's linking-pin function to be the transmission of their communications to the district office. But although bureaucracies call for feedback from messages sent downward, it usually comes back as a "whisper" (Hanson, 1985) to the irritation of most teachers. Moreover, professionally oriented teachers oppose external mandates pertaining to classroom functions, for their culture holds that they are the educational experts. Thus, the acceptance by teachers of externally generated rules is never ensured, even when supported by talented principals. More likely, informal teacher groups refer to their own values and objectives to determine when to comply. State-mandated outcome assessments provide a major exception, but accountability is not the feedback teachers seek to give. Obligatory testing presents an additional conflict with teachers' cultures, thereby increasing the need for principals with interpersonal and leadership skills.

Principals who are personally threatened by the opposition of teachers to external mandates tend to overemphasize their own bureaucratic authority. Like other administrators who believe themselves relatively weak, they become rule-minded with the hope that rules will be power tools to bring their objectives about (Kanter, 1977, p. 192). Nevertheless, an authoritarian stance usually undermines compliance since formal rules unabashedly move principals into the teachers' traditional sphere of influence over classroom matters (Hanson, 1985). For principals to rely solely on rules to control teachers does little more than generate hostility and possible conflict.

How closely units of a school district are coupled is an important variable in analyzing the implementation of external mandates.

Schools with tight couplings have highly interdependent units and, as implied by the machine metaphor, open communication, much coordination, and mutual accountability. The probability that principals implement top-down reforms is greater in tightly coupled than in loosely coupled schools since they will know how and if curriculum mandates are carried out. Even so, most schools are loosely coupled (Weick, 1983), although the strength of the coupling may vary.

Coupling between the central office and local schools also differs. If it is weak, district messages may be garbled and feedback minimal, giving principals flexibility in choosing which mandates to implement. Where coupling is tight, principals have few options but to seek compliance from teachers. Outcome assessments that rely on students' scores on authorized tests strengthen vertical couplings between educational units. Even when state communications about curriculum content are imprecise, return messages in the form of standardized examination results leave little ambiguity. The irony of this is that although students' scores are influenced by many factors outside the control of principals, the principal's professional reputation often rests on them. When test scores are uppermost in administrators' thoughts, they tend to emphasize bureaucratic means to raise them and, like superintendents, promulgate additional rules, which only accentuate their difficulties with professionally oriented faculty.

With the opening up of public education to environmental and political pressures, the participation of school principals in curriculum development has decreased. Not only are most formal curriculum policies developed outside the local school, but other responsibilities compete for principals' time. In addition to those related to requirements of federal and state programs, local schools have become lightning rods for community civil rights and special interest activities. The need to put out fires and to negotiate with disaffected students, teachers, and parents has modified the principal's role considerably, leaving less time for the instructional process. Recent proposals for principals to become school-level instructional leaders may be a backlash from their reduced attention to the curriculum.

The concept of principal as instructional leader evolved from school effectiveness research, much of which contends that schools most successful with at-risk students are those in which principals are active in matters of curriculum and instruction. This is not the place to review the shortcomings of this literature (see Purkey & Smith, 1983) except to note the major finding from a reanalysis of the most successful schools studied. Stedman (1987) found from his comprehensive review of those data that shared governance with teachers and sometimes with parents occurred in many of the effective schools, contrary to the prescription from effective schools research for a single, strong instructional leader. An executive or steering team of teachers helped run the instructional program in some schools, and in others parent-teacher councils helped to bridge the gap between school and community, which made schools more responsive to parental concerns. The implication of his findings is that instructional leaders need not be principals, although the function of instructional leadership must be performed.

The imposition of external mandates not only changes the role of principal but may effect a reconfiguration of district- and school-level roles or lead to the creation of new positions. In many districts subject matter supervisors, curriculum coordinators, and consultants have been added to the central office, and outreach consultants have been hired to coordinate work in local schools. Within schools, curriculum functions now are allocated in a variety of ways. In larger schools, they often are given to vice principals for instruction, whose initial responsibilities are divided among other vice principals or who may retain their other duties, which then compete for their time (Cusick, 1983). Department chairs sometimes are expected to assume curriculum responsibilities, although evidence suggests they do not have the inclination or informal authority to affect what happens in colleagues' classrooms. At the elementary level, principals are nominally in charge of curriculum but may have specialist assistants, variously called "curriculum coordinators," "master teachers," or "teachers on special assignment," to deal with the technical core of the school. Since new positions often parallel curriculum consultants in the central office charged with similar functions, problems of turf and difficulties in coordination often arise.

The machine metaphor upon which much of the preceding discussion of school-level leadership rests does not account adequately for the functioning of schools. Although it is true that the local school is a technical unit of a larger bureaucratic organization, the unit itself is best explained from the organic perspective. Each school is a dynamic social system with a unique climate created from the interaction of its culture, ecology, and social milieu. Educational professionals do act rationally, as the machine analogy implies, but their motivations may derive from their individual units or their own personal agendas, not from the school as a whole.

The notion of the local school as a classical bureaucracy is rejected in much of the newest educational research in favor of the view that schools are social and political systems (Hanson, 1985). Some scholars now conceptualize schools as open systems encompassing a series of loosely coupled, interlocking subsystems, often with their own

boundaries, identities, values, and interests (Weick, 1983). Although
the increased bureaucratization of school districts has constrained the
formal role of the principal toward bureaucratic manager, the role
remains multidimensional. From the organic perspective, effective
principals focus on the social and emotional aspects of the school social
system as well as on organizational tasks. In a recent study of
administrative styles of secondary school principals (Schwartz, 1988), it
was found that all principals were perceived by their faculties as
placing greater emphasis on personal aspects (human relations,
consideration, and integration, for example) of the role than on
administrative aspects (task, production and initiating, for example).
Every principal studied recognized the importance of realizing educational objectives, but each chose to motivate teachers through the
exercise of personal leadership, which directly influences the ethos of
the school more than its instructional activities.

Mitchell, Ortiz, and Mitchell (1987) point out that principals fall into
one of two camps: those who believe that classroom effectiveness
depends on teachers' dedication and the qualities of the school
organization and those who believe effectiveness depends on the
techniques teachers employ. Principals in the first camp cast their own
role in terms of leadership and try to inspire, rather than direct, teacher
performance. Those in the second camp see themselves as managers
with responsibility for coordinating school resources and supplying
training to help teachers capitalize on their strengths and overcome
their weaknesses.

The concept of school-based management derived from the organic
metaphor is consistent with the first view presented above in that
schools are seen as much more than bureaucratic organizations and
cannot be governed solely by management practices. School-based
management flattens the school district organization and allows for
educational decisions such as faculty selection, curriculum and instruction at the school level, and the allocation of resources to be made
where most is known about their implications. With managerial and
policy decentralization, principals can adjust curriculum mandates to
local conditions and package them so that they are more credible to the
faculty and school community. In this sense, principals become
community representatives to the district, rather than the reverse.

Although decentralization gives principals additional formal
authority, it also provides them with greater opportunities to exercise
leadership and make schools more satisfying places in which to work.
Decentralization permits principals to take social context into consideration as they develop plans for their schools. Principals who are not
burdened with accountability have more potential for shaping the

culture of the school toward one that values and expects student achievement and is hospitable to constructive change. With the absence of rigid external directives, principals can allow those who are affected by decisions to participate in their development. Teams of teachers can be created to deal with specific educational issues; these teams not only produce solutions to problems but also foster professional interaction, thereby strengthening the school culture and increasing teachers' commitment. Involvement of teachers in planning the educational program will go a long way toward implementing sound educational practice.

Effects on Classroom Teachers

Thus far the policy and administration of formal education have been discussed. The focus now shifts to the task level, where educational goals are realized. Assumptions of both the machine and organic metaphors are germane to this discussion, since the implications of each about how classrooms function are vastly different. What is more, the incongruities between the machine metaphor, underlying the thinking of most policy makers and administrators, and the organic metaphor, underlying the behavior of most teachers, inhibit the implementation of external curriculum policy.

The role of classroom teacher from the machine perspective is that of a lower-level employee in a pyramid-shaped bureaucracy. Teachers' motivations are extrinsic, and their activities are controlled through rules and close supervision. The instructional model implied in related reform proposals is means-end-oriented in that teachers apply specified procedures derived from the technology of teaching to produce student products that meet curriculum objectives. Consistent with this, teacher-proof materials often are advocated to minimize teachers' discretion in implementing curriculum mandates. In this view, the primary function of the classroom is the incorporation of critical basic skills into children who are seen as vessels to be filled (Metz, 1978).

Because outcomes of top-down curriculum mandates have not received high marks overall, teachers have been identified as the weakest link in the educational organization chain. Accordingly, reform proposals emanating from the machine perspective often include strategies to change teachers' behaviors, such as closer supervision and coaching, in-service and staff development programs, modeling of appropriate behaviors, and positive or negative financial incentives (see Fullan, 1982). It is unlikely that these activities will bring teachers to accept curriculum modifications with which they disagree, since they are based on inadequate understandings of the teacher role.

Most teachers do not see themselves as lower-level employees in that their interests center around individual classrooms and, to a lesser extent, their own schools. In addition, teachers contend that they are more expert than others in what constitutes good teaching and what ought to be taught. Many are skeptical of changes imposed from above. In fact, teachers often protect their students from the school organization by offering their own alternatives to mandated curricula (Powell, Farrar, & Cohen, 1985; Rosenholtz, 1989).

Even if teachers were convinced of the wisdom of externally imposed curriculum, there are personal reasons that militate against its acceptance. Professional insecurity is a major factor in resistance. Teachers who have invested physically and emotionally in existing curriculum may be anxious about any change. They may not understand what it requires of them or may not have the requisite knowledge to meet new expectations. In the extreme, the prospect of a curriculum so radically different that teachers can no longer work in the areas of their own preparation is devastating.

The measures for gaining teachers' compliance implied by the machine metaphor are not practical. Since most teachers come to education because of their own service orientation, they are relatively unmotivated by prestige, power, or moderate increases in salary. In spite of occasional bitter contract disputes, extrinsic rewards are less important to teachers than those derived from the direct part they play in the social and academic development of their students. Their work is most satisfying when they can claim responsibility for raising student achievement and when students respond with warmth, enthusiasm, and appreciation (Mitchell et al., 1987, p. 13). The reluctance of faculty to conform with external mandates, then, may be an attempt to protect the domain from which they receive their most joy.

The probability that teachers will implement an external curriculum policy increases if they understand the policy and share in its objectives or, as often happens, if it is consistent with ongoing classroom practice. Teachers also are motivated by outcome assessments that call for students' scores on standardized tests of achievement. Even so, implementation does not ensure desired learning. Attainment of specified objectives depends on a host of factors, including the wisdom of the curriculum, its appropriateness for targeted students, the methods prescribed, and teachers' skills.

That the imposition of curriculum will affect faculty adversely and, consequently, reduce overall educational quality also must be considered. Teachers usually resent intrusion into their special domain. Most likely the initial reaction is to ignore external mandates or, if pushed, to resist through passive measures such as foot dragging, martyrdom, or adopting the posture of the "old hand" who has seen these reforms tried before and fail (Kanter, 1977, p. 156). Indeed, cycles of reform are endemic to American education, so much so that a recent history of school reform was given the title *Steady Work* to emphasize the fact that one reform is never completed before a new one appears (Elmore & McLaughlin, 1988). It was noted in that same monograph that policies restricting teachers' discretion impede their effectiveness because flexibility is an important ingredient of a teacher's performance (p. vii). Many of the educational initiatives of the 1980s saddled good teachers with standardized prescriptions that reduced their ability to teach (Darling-Hammond, 1984).

Not only did these educational initiatives not produce greater overall student achievement, but they lowered the morale of the teaching force. Half of those who responded to a survey by the Carnegie Foundation for the Advancement of Teaching (1988) reported a decline in teacher morale since 1983, and 70 percent gave the reforms a grade of "C" or below. Intrusions into the classroom are resented most by the best-qualified teachers and pose a threat to their retention. Additionally, they make the recruitment of highly qualified persons more difficult (Darling-Hammond, 1984; Rosenholtz, 1989; cf. Heyns, 1988). A serious teacher shortage in both number and quality is expected in the 1990s because of retirements, lack of retention, and failure to attract able people. The supply of new teachers is projected to satisfy only about 60 percent of the demand (Darling-Hammond & Berry, 1988). While work circumstances created by mechanistic educational reforms repel the very individuals education should attract, this anticipated shortage is exacerbated by increases in other opportunities for women. It is ironic that the movement toward equality for all citizens has the effect of diminishing educational opportunities for low-income and minority children, who rely disproportionately on their teachers for skills and knowledge (Coleman, Campbell, Hobson, McPartland, & Mood, 1966; Carnegie Forum on Education and the Economy, 1986).

The organic metaphor produces a more personally satisfying description of the teacher role in which teachers' responsibilities come closer to what they actually do, to what they want to do, and to the realities of local schools. Although most districts take a bureaucratic form, linkages within schools are loosely coupled, giving teachers wide discretion. They, like other social service workers, are street-level bureaucrats who, because they are expected to perform tasks that exceed available resources, are left alone to improvise (Lipsky, 1980). The knowledge, beliefs, and values teachers share stress variability among students and classrooms and the need for personal judgment in maintaining classroom order and carrying out educational functions.

Teacher culture stresses autonomy and tolerance of classroom methods, probably because no consensus exists on what constitute good teaching. No one set of practices has been shown to be more effective than another (Lortie, 1975; Metz, 1978; Schwartz, 1987). Teachers who emphasize achievement outcomes tend toward tightly structured lessons and a businesslike atmosphere, whereas those who emphasize development adopt a more open, exploratory lesson structure (Mitchell et al., 1987, p. 198). Almost all teachers believe they do what is best for their students, and because public schools historically have been domesticated organizations in which survival but not effectiveness is guaranteed, they view external interference and evaluations as odious.

The organic metaphor leads to the recognition of one or more cultural systems within an educational organization. These systems function to interpret environmental factors and to craft behavioral responses to them. Wolcott (1977) observed a conflict between the culture of teachers, which emphasizes personal judgment in the application of their unique knowledge and skills, and the mechanistic culture of technocrats (administrators), which emphasizes modernity through the implementation of rational decisions by bureaucratic authority. Whereas teacher culture stresses classroom autonomy, the culture of technocrats stresses control. The affinity of differentiated staffing to technological culture may explain why some of the newer educational roles such as master teacher, peer coach, and mentor are slow to be accepted by faculty. Unless there is mutual trust at the school building level between administrators of external policies and those expected to implement them, most policies are doomed to failure regardless of their merits.

The organic metaphor also allows for consideration of the social and political subsystems influenced by the different cultures of the school. Teachers and administrators have their traditional spheres of influence within which independent decisions are made. Externally imposed curricula that hold principals responsible for classroom activities upset this established dichotomy and produce a contested area in which the two spheres overlap. The organic metaphor suggests that decisions within disputed areas can be reached if administrators attend to human relations and the personal and group needs of teachers, often employing political processes such as negotiation, persuasion, and manipulation (Hanson, 1985).

The organic model further suggests that schools vary in their openness to external social environments. In some communities, school boundaries are so penetrated that teachers' traditional spheres also are contested by the parents of their students. Conceptualizations of parents as consultants, consumers, or partners in the education of their children encourage this overlap. Parental pressures that differ from top-down curriculum demands reinforce teachers' traditional intransigence, whereas those that are congruent constrain teachers to comply in spite of private reservations. The opening of schools to local communities reduces teachers' prerogatives. When vocal parents agree with external mandates, teachers tend to go along and stress the universalistic aspects of the curriculum; when parents pressure for parochial interests, teachers, especially those with less experience or academic preparation, tend to emphasize local particularism. Thus, centralized curriculum policies are reinforced or undermined through the impact of parents on classroom teachers.

The newest proposals, consistent in part with the organic metaphor, view schools and classrooms as separate social, political, and cultural systems, and maintain that educational problems should be solved at those levels. Some proposals do not reject the need for tighter controls over teachers but depart from earlier ones in that teachers are targeted for resocialization more than for manipulation by mandated rules and rigid accountability. Programs that attempt to change teachers' values will have dubious success in light of teachers' commitment to classroom autonomy. In-service education, however, may provide teachers with the rationale for proposed changes, which might then convince them of their merit.

Teacher involvement in school-level decision is included in many of the newest proposals for school reform. This orientation, known variously as "teacher empowerment," "job enlargement," and "quality of job life," is supported by the majority of teachers (Moss, 1986) and is consistent with the decentralization of other decisions. Teacher empowerment assumes that teachers are experts in classroom matters and, because of their shared culture, can mold consensus among faculty on what should be taught and how. Further, curriculum changes will be implemented because teachers have ownership in the policies they develop.

The teacher empowerment model also assumes that participation in decisions enhances teachers' morale and productivity. The same assumptions are present in management literature in general. For example, Ouchi (1981) contends that the productive Japanese workers described in Theory Z corporations are committed to the organization and satisfied with their jobs because they are required to participate in decisions through quality circles. These workers are similar to teachers in that they are part of a large cohort whose jobs are front loaded with little opportunity for advancement. However, the two nations are so different culturally that the Japanese management model may not be applicable to American public schools. Whereas Japanese society traditionally stresses cooperative efforts, American society stresses individualism, which may impede cooperation among teachers. Further, American teachers work in isolation, and although they may be excellent leaders of students, their social and leadership skiills with peers may not be as well honed as those of Ouchi's Japanese workers. For teacher empowerment to be effective, teachers must acquire an orientation in which they are not only obligated to do what is best for their clients but must be willing to be controlled by the collective opinion of colleagues.

Even if cooperative participation among teachers comes to pass, effectiveness is not ensured. Group decision processes are costly in time, and when mandated may be interpreted less as an increase in power over work than as an infringement on other obligations or as more work without compensation (Kanter, 1977). Nor are group decisions necessarily wise, especially if made without adequate discussion or access to relevant information. Further, the process will lower teachers' morale and commitment if it is seen as manipulation designed to give the appearance of democratic management without incorporating teachers' views. Moreover, teacher empowerment can lead to controversy between teachers and principals if areas of responsibility are not delineated clearly. In the ideal empowerment model teachers are concerned with curriculum and instructional decisions, whereas principals coordinate school activities and attend to school maintenance functions.

It should be clear from the foregoing discussion that neither all top-down nor all bottom-up development of curriculum policies is appropriate at this time. Whereas centralized decision making does not expect enough of classroom teachers, total teacher control over decisions expects too much. This is not to say that teachers ought not assume most of the responsibility for curriculum in the future, but that it is counter to past practices, to teachers' professional preparation, and to their culture. Modifications in teacher education and the conditions of teaching are beginning which will prepare them for a more collegial, professional role. But until this orientation is institutionalized within the teaching force, the development of curriculum must take a middle ground with teachers, principals, and other curriculum experts working in partnership.

Effects on Students

Arguments for curriculum reform emphasize the benefits of schooling either for children or for society and sometimes for both. Reforms stressing excellence often are justified by the nation's need for a quality work force, whereas child-centered reforms accent appropriate education to meet the needs of individuals. Reforms based on equity argue for both, contending that the development of productive, effective adults comes through fuller educational opportunities for specified categories of students, namely, low-income minority children who have been underserved educationally.

Most reforms of the 1980s called for excellence and were aligned with the machine metaphor, whereas reforms stressing individual needs, as was characteristic of the 1970s, were closer to the organic metaphor. The movement for equity, beginning with the *Brown* decision (1954) that separate education can never be equal and expanded in federal education legislation of the 1960s, was based initially on the organic view. The machine metaphor, however, took over as regulations mounted to ensure local compliance with Congress' "supplement, not supplant" intention. A recent review of the effects of ESEA concluded that these regulations "introduced changes that generated modest aggregate benefits in the achievement of Title I students in return for fairly serious cost to school organization and practice" (Elmore & McLaughlin, 1988, p. 27). Local districts separated targeted students from their classmates to demonstrate that only those who were eligible received benefits from the funding. In a critique of pullout strategies, Kaestle and Smith (1982) note that the removal of disadvantaged children from the classroom relieves the regular staff of responsibility for these students' success and also fragments their educational experiences. Moreover, pullout programs affect the self-perceptions of targeted children and shape what their peers think about them. But in spite of these shortcomings, they became the model for compliance with other entitlements and judicial mandates. Only recently has the value of attending to the special needs of all children within mainstreamed classroom been recognized.

Different assumptions about classroom order and learning are implied by the machine and organic metaphors. The machine metaphor leads to the view of students as passive receptors of knowledge, and their activities are limited to drills that reinforce this knowledge and develop associated skills. From this perspective classrooms are orderly collections of students controlled by their teachers' bureaucratic authority and power through grades. In contrast, the organic metaphor presents classrooms as untidy social systems composed of small sub-systems or primary groups of students, each with a somewhat different subculture. The interaction of these subsystems creates a classroom ethos that can support or undermine its educational environment. From the organic perspective, effective teachers use intuitive judgment, creativity, and skills to mold a favorable classroom ethos, and their expectations about behavior and academic responsibility become the students' norms. The relationship between classroom ethos and students' academic achievement has been well documented (e.g., Brookover, Beady, Flood, Schweitzer, & Wisenbaker, 1979; Coleman & Hoffer, 1987; Purkey & Smith, 1983; Rutter, Maughan, Mortimore, & Ouston, 1979).

Why teachers are reluctant to implement externally mandated curriculum in their classrooms is discussed above. Nonetheless, teachers are likely to comply when student outcomes are monitored through standardized tests and accompanied by sanctions. Sanctions in current use directly affecting students include grade retention, denial of high school diplomas or admissions to postsecondary education, and exclusion from extracurricular activities. From the perspective of the machine metaphor, standardized tests are rational instruments to assess educational quantity; from the perspective of the organic metaphor, they have significance far beyond this original intention.

To begin, standardized tests tend to drive the entire curriculum, providing a minimal level for all students and at the same time placing a ceiling on what is presented. Teachers typically emphasize the content of tests and test-taking skills at the expense of other educationally important activities, and formal curricula center on or are limited to those tested by the state. (See also Chapters 7 and 10.) Statewide outcome assessment minimizes local input and experimentation and inhibits adaptation of the curriculum to local clientele. It also reduces students' input into their own education so that, on the one hand, they cannot select easy courses in order to build high grade point averages or reduce school workloads, and on the other, they have fewer relevant and rewarding offerings from which to choose.

The effects of a set of curriculum on the larger society also are considered in the organic perspective. With decreased diversity in the academic program, there is a commensurate reduction in the variety of skills, knowledge, and abilities of graduates. In effect, state-mandated curricula lead to greater homogeneity among adults and, consequently, fewer perspectives from which to view social and physical phenomena. In the long run, the implementation of externally derived curriculum may limit the number of people schools can make available to society with the capacity for critical and independent thought.

Pressure for satisfactory assessments stimulates deviant behavior throughout local districts. School administrators have reported in confidence some of the strategies used to raise the test scores of their students. For example, only students predicted to produce sought-after performances are tested, or the population of test takers is redefined by listing weaker students in grades not tested, such as identifying twelfth-grade students as eleventh graders if they are not expected to graduate. Massive cheating in which teachers change test responses has occurred as well. Students, too, resort to deviant behavior when test results do not impact them directly. One outcome of the California market incentives program, in which financial allocations depended in part on test scores, was that seniors in several schools purposely performed below their abilities after failing to blackmail school officials to commit the money earned from high test scores to senior class activities (Timar & Kirp, 1988).

The effect of mandated standardized tests on the values and attitudes of individual students is of considerable importance. These norm-referenced assessments, in which 50 percent fall below average by definition, increase the psychological costs of schooling. Test results divide students into winners and losers, often creating self-fulfilling prophecies about each. When test scores are used for tracking or grade level promotion, students' failures become public, leading to even greater frustration, loss of self-respect, and alienation from school. Whereas positive labeling may motivate students and support aspirations for high educational and occupational attainment, negative labeling is indicative of blocked opportunity, which may stimulate a search for status through deviant activities such as individual and youth gang delinquency (Schwartz, 1989). Adverse labeling of students in school too often leads to real or psychological school leaving, which culminates in fewer job and other adult opportunities.

Retentions in primary grades, especially in kindergarten, have increased nationwide as academic curricula have replaced traditional developmental programs. Judgments about the academic abilities of young children are premature in light of what is known about the accuracy of standardized tests and variability in development (Good & Brophy, 1987) and findings that the "runt of the liter" usually catches up with cohorts by third grade. Children who are retained learn that they are in some way less able than their peers and that they have disappointed their parents. The negative effects of retention in kindergarten through second grade far outweigh the benefits it is expected to provide. A more effective policy would be to develop multigrade classrooms for this highly variable age group with developmentally appropriate assignments.

Minimum competency tests for high school graduation to ensure that the high school diploma stands for something is another increasingly common practice. These tests are presumed to measure the knowledge, skills, and behaviors required for successful functioning in adult society. The basic problem with school-leaving examinations is that there is no consensus about what is entailed in successful functioning and, therefore, no way to measure it. Moreover, factors such as critical thinking, problem-solving abilities, and social intelligence, which probably should be on the list, are not measured adequately. In effect, minimum competency tests may unfairly exclude those who cannot master the articulated state curriculum from the advantages of a diploma.

None of this is to say testing should be eliminated, but to point out that accountability norm-referenced tests are seldom used for the improvement of the education of students taking them. It is more likely that these educationally inappropriate measures, with their high financial, educational, and psychological costs, drive out more educationally appropriate ones. Tests of ability in combination with other identification procedures have been used successfully in the implementation of the federal Education for All Handicapped Children Act of 1975. This top-down policy strongly affected education for students with special needs. It stimulated the adoption of sounder identification procedures and, more importantly, gave impetus to the case conference, in which individual educational plans are developed for each special education student by guidance teams of teachers, counselors, administrators, specialists as needed, and parents. In addition, the All Handicapped Chidren Act provided procedures by which parents can challenge the treatment given their children, thereby reducing the need for rigid external scrutiny of the program. The least restrictive environment clause of this act, which mandates mainstreaming where feasible, has worked against the social isolation of this special group, and in some instances has led to reconfigurations of self-contained elementary classrooms to the advantage of all students.

From the perspective of the organic metaphor, the mandated curriculum changes of the 1980s have the most negative consequences for students who are at risk of dropping out. In addition to the rigid criteria for promotion and graduation and the narrow curriculum focus, these policies cut into personally rewarding extracurricular opportunities. The interpersonal and other skills acquired through optional activities and their contribution to the holding power of schools are not recognized in these reforms. For example, the no-pass no-play policies that were part of some 1980s reforms affect those who need the activities the most. The combination of higher standards for achievement withour appropriate remediation and the reduction of in-school sources of satisfaction are expected to increase the proportion of youth who never earn diplomas (McDill et al., 1986). Of the youth who remain, many will derive satisfaction only from deviant behaviors. The presence of large numbers of alienated students in school requires a disproportionate effort on the part of teachers and administrators, thereby diminishing the educational opportunities of all students.

Summary and Conclusions

Organizational metaphors underlying educational thought reveal values and assumptions that bear on curriculum policy. These metaphors are mental comparisons between educational organizations and other objects which illuminate some of their characteristics and ignore others. Metaphors provide a way of viewing public education which, in turn, influences what is expected from it, how it should be structured, and the role prescriptions of those who participate in it. Two organizational metaphors commonly applied to American education were presented in this chapter. The machine metaphor, derived from the early industrial model, portrays schools as rational, closed bureaucracies with tightly coupled parts controlled through techniques of scientific management; and the organic metaphor, increasingly present in thinking about contemporary organizations, assumes schools are open, loosely coupled sociopolitical systems struggling to survive in turbulent environments.

Which organizational metaphor dominates conceptualizations about schools is determined by the societal concerns of the time. If school production is emphasized, the machine metaphor stressing uniformity is uppermost, as seen when public education expanded in response to changing labor patterns, when the United States was engaged in technological competition with the Soviets, and most recently, when attention focused on the productivity of American industry in a tightening world market. Reforms based on the machine metaphor concentrate on school structure and measurable output.

If the socialization of citizens and the integration of society are deemed significant, the organic metaphor is uppermost and broad value consensus is stressed. This was apparent during periods of massive immigration, the depression years preceding World War II, and the social turbulence of the late 1960s and early 1970s. Growing anxiety about neofascist violence against minority-group members portends an increased emphasis on socialization in the 1990s. Diversity is intergral to the organic perspective, which emphasizes the pluralistic character of the American society. From this perspective, the ethos of schools and classrooms is varied, as are the abilities, interests, and culture of the students. By building on these differences, the school is expected to make critical contributions to the society.

Both metaphors compete for attention as the decade of the 1990s begins, with the machine metaphor giving direction to state and national policy and the organic metaphor to policies about classroom implementation. That public education is not one homogeneous enterprise is recognized in many of the newest proposals for school reform, which note basic differences between the social systems of schools and classrooms and the bureaucratic organizations of central districts and state educational agencies. Proposals for change increasingly call for shared authority in policy formulation with the specificity of the policy directly related to the policy makers' proximity to the classroom.

The next wave of educational reforms is expected to alter the structure of local school districts. Their bureaucratic form will be flattened by administrative decentralization as school-based management takes effect, and the central office will be shorn of important curriculum functions as newly empowered, professionally oriented teachers help to fashion curriculum in local schools. The bifurcation of policy development with the state and federal government representing a broad universalistic perspective and the school representing local interests could be a sound compromise between the machine and organic perspectives. Larger issues of equity, excellence, and human resource priorities would then be addressed at the general level, and contingencies arising from local diversity and the needs of individual students would be met in local classrooms.

References

Blumberg, A. (1985). *The school superintendent: Living with conflict.* New York: Teachers College Press.

Boyer, E. L. (1983). *High school: A report on secondary education in America.* New York: Harper & Row.

Brookover, W. B., Beady, L., Flood, P., Schweitzer, J., & Wisenbaker, J. (1979). *School social systems and student achievement: Schools can make a difference.* New York: Praeger.

Brown vs. Board of Education, 347 U.S. 483 (1954).

Burrell, G., & Morgan, G. (1982). *Sociological paradigms and organizational analysis: elements of the sociology of corporate life.* London: Heinemann.

California Commission on Educational Quality. *Report to the Governor,,* (1988, June). Sacramento, CA: Califronia Commission on Educational Quality.

Carnegie Forum on Education and the Economy. (1986). *A nation prepared: Teachers for the 21st century.* Princeton, NJ: Carnegie Foundation.

Carnegie Foundation for the Advancement of Teaching. (1988). *Report card on school reform: The teachers speak.* Princeton, NJ: Carnegie Foundation.

Cohen, D. K. (1982). Policy and organization: The impact of state and federal educational policy on school governance. *Harvard Educational Review, 52,* 474–499.

Coleman, J. S., Campbell, E. O., Hobson, C. J., McPartland, J., & Mood, A. M. (1966). *Equality of educational opportunity.* Washington, DC: Department of Health, Education and Welfare.

Coleman, J. S., & Hoffer, T. (1987). *Public and private high schools: The impact of communities.* New York: Basic Books.

Committee for Economic Development. (1985). *Investing in our children.* New York: Committee for Economic Development.

Cubberly, E. (1916). *Public school administration.* Boston: Houghton Mifflin.

Cusick, P. A. (1983). *The egalitarian ideal and the American high school: Studies of three schools.* New York: Longman.

Darling-Hammond, L. (1984). *Beyond the commission reports: The coming crisis in teaching.* Santa Monica, CA: RAND.

Darling-Hammond, L. & Berry, B. (1988). *The evolution of teacher policy.* Santa Monica, CA: RAND.

Education for ALL Handicapped Children Act of 1975, 20 USC 1400–61.

Elmore, R. F. (1980). Backward mapping: Implementation research and policy decisions. *Political Science Quarterly, 94,* 601–616.

Elmore, R. F. & McLaughlin, M. W. (1988). *Steady work: Policy, practice, and the reform of American education.* Santa Monica, CA: RAND.

Foster, W. (1986). *Paradigms and promises: New approaches in educational administration.* Buffalo, NY: Prometheus.

Fullan, M. (1982). *The meaning of educational change.* New York: Teachers College Press.

Good, T. L., & Brophy, J. E. (1987). *Looking in classrooms.* New York: Harper & Row.

Grant, G. (1988). *The world we created at Hamilton High.* Cambridge, MA: Harvard University Press.

Hampel, R. L. (1986). *The last citadel: American high schools since 1940.* Boston: Houghton Mifflin.

Hanson, E. M. (1985). *Educational administration and organizational behavior* (2nd ed.). Boston: Allyn & Bacon.

Heyns, B. (1988). Educational defectors: A first look at teacher attrition in the NLS-72. *Educational Researcher, 17,* 24–32.

Kaestle, C. F., & Smith, M. S. (1982). The federal role in elementary and secondary education, 1946–1980. *Harvard Educational Review, 52,* 384–408.

Kanter, R. M. (1977). *Men and women of the corporation.* New York: Basic Books.

Lazerson, M., McLaughlin, J. B., McPherson, B., & Bailey, S. K. (1985). *An education of value: The purposes and practices of schools.* New York: Cambridge University Press.

Lipsky, M. (1980). *Street level bureaucracy.* New York: Russell Sage.

Lortie, D. C. (1975). *Schoolteacher: A sociological study.* Chicago: University of Chicago Press.

McDill, E. L., Natriello, G., & Pallas, A. M. (1986). A population at risk: Potential consequences of tougher school standards for student dropouts. *American Journal of Education, 94,* 135-181.

Metz, M. H. (1978). *Classrooms and corridors.* Berkeley, CA: University of California Press.

Mitchell, D. E., Ortiz, F. I., & Mitchell, T. K. (1987). *Work orientation and job performance: The cultural basis of teaching rewards and incentives.* Albany, NY: State University of New York Press.

Moss, J. K. (1986). Teaching in America. *Learning,* October, 66-68.

Mozert vs. Hawkins County Public Schools, 877 F. 2d 1058 (6th Cir. 1987).

Ouchi, W. (1981). *Theory Z.* Reading, MA: Addison-Wesley.

Powell, A. G., Farrar, E., & Cohen, D. K. (1985). *The shopping mall high school: Winners and losers in the educational marketplace.* Boston: Houghton Mifflin.

Purkey, S., and Smith, M. (1983). Effective schools: A review. *Elementary School Journal, 83,* 427-52.

Ravitch, D. (1983). *The troubled crusade: American education 1945-1980.* New York: Basic Books.

Rosenholtz, S. J. (1989). *Teachers' workplace: The social organization of schools.* New York: Longman.

Rutter, M., Maughan, B., Mortimore, P., & Ouston, J. (1979). *Fifteen thousand hours: Secondary schools and their effects on children.* Cambridge, MA: Harvard University Press.

Schwartz, A. J. (1987). *Socialization to school: A study of low-income and minority children in an early childhood setting.* Los Angeles: University of Southern California, Institute for research in Educational Administration. (ERIC Document Reproduction Service No. ED290 531.)

———. (1988). *Principals' leadership behaviors in gang-impacted schools and their effects on pupil climate.* Paper presented at meeting of AERA, Division A, New Orleans. (ERIC Document Reproduction Service No. ED396 451.)

———. (1989). Middle-class educational values among Latino gang members in east Los Angeles County high schools. *Urban Education, 24,* 3.

Scott, W. R. (1987). *Organizations: Rational, natural, and open systems* (2nd ed.). Englewood Cliffs, NJ: Prentice-Hall.

Sizer, T. R. (1984). *Horace's compromise: The dilemma of the American high school.* Boston: Houghton Mifflin.

Stedman, L. C. (1987). It's time we changed the effective schools forumla. *Phi Delta Kappan, 69,* 215–224.

Sumner, W. G. (1906). *Folkways.* Boston: Ginn.

Timar, T. B., & Kirp, D. L. (1988). *Managing educational change.* New York: Falmer Press.

Waller, W. (1932). *The sociology of teaching.* New York: John Wiley & Sons.

Weick, K. (1983). Educational organizations as loosely coupled systems. In J. V. Baldridge & T. Deal (Eds.), *The dynamics of organizational change in education* (pp. 15–37). Berkeley, CA: McCutchan.

Wise, A. E. (1979). *Legislated learning: The bureaucratization of the American classroom.* Berkeley: University of California Press.

_____. (1983). Why educational policies often fail: The hyperrationalization hypothesis. In J. V. Baldridge and T. Deal (Eds.), *The dynamics of organization change in education.* (pp. 93–113). Berkeley, CA: McCutchan.

Wolcott, H. F. (1977). *Teachers versus technocrats.* Eugene, OR: Center for Educational Policy and Management, University of Oregon.

9 Centralized Curriculum Decision Making: The View from the Organized Teaching Profession

Robert M. McClure

*B*ecause of the impact on practice, teacher professionalism, teachers' standing with the public, and individual rights, teacher organizations are concerned about the shift of decision-making authority away from the practitioner, school, and school district. Of particular concern to them is the massive shift of authority to the state capitol for making critical curriculum decisions—whether that power shifts to the state's department of public instruction, the legislature, or the governor's office.

After a brief review of the involvement of teacher unions in these matters, four issues of concern to them are discussed. The chapter concludes with a description of a current activity of a teacher organization which aims to affect the substance, nature, and locus of curriculum decision making.

A Historical Perspective

The organizational structure of both of the major national teacher unions affects their stances on issues related to educational decision making. Both organizations reflect the basic structure of American public education, with its roots in local schools and school districts which operate within a structure and context determined by the state (Cameron, 1988).

There is a strong teacher organization presence in all state capitals, but their programs are largely devoted to legislative and political action and not directly to the substantive issues of curriculum and instruction. It is at the local level that teachers, on a day-to-day basis, can most effectively influence curriculum and instructional decisions. Within the National Education Association (NEA), the state affiliates exert considerable influence over policy and program, but state leaders often take their lead on these matters from leaders in local affiliates.

Historically, the national teacher organizations have an interest in the matter of where decisions are made and by whom. The two major curriculum pronouncements in the first part of the century were brought about by the NEA. Both the *Cardinal Principles of Secondary Education* (Commission on the Reorganization of Secondary Education, National Education Association, 1918) and *The Purposes of Education in American Democracy* (Education Policies Commission, National Education Association, 1938) called for dynamic leadership from the national and state levels but insisted that local schools and districts decide how to interpret and implement their proposals. Said the chair of the committee which produced the *Cardinal Principles*, "It seemed desirable that the reviewing committee should outline in a single brief report those fundamental principles that would be most helpful in directing secondary education... The translation of these cardinal principles into daily practice will of necessity call for continued study and experiment on the part of the administrative offices and teachers in secondary schools" (Commission, 1918, p. 5). The body of that report contains extensive directions as to how local faculties can organize to interpret and implement the commission's recommendations.

In the 1960s the NEA mounted another national effort to focus public and professional attention on the quality of education and the relationship of decision-making processes and locus to school quality. In the Project on Instruction (commonly referred to as *Schools for the Sixties*), a separate volume, *Deciding What to Teach* (National Education Association, 1963a), spelled out an ideal process: use the knowledge base undergirding teaching and learning to make decisions about schooling. In an effort to help the public understand the nature of desirable decision-making practices in the schools, the authors prescribed a rather simple formula:

Decisions about what to teach, how to teach, and how to organize for teaching are made daily. Many people are involved in the process. All are entitled, by virtue of their citizenship in a democracy, to make certain kinds of decisions; some are authorized by law to make other kinds. Some are

qualified by education, experience, and position to make still
other decisions. The quality and validity of the judgments that
are made depend, in part, upon clarification and observance of
the differing roles of the various people involved. (p. 12)

. . . Decisions that affect the instructional program are made at
three levels of remoteness from the student. Close to students,
teachers make daily *instructional* decisions. At a more remote
level, teachers and administrators make *institutional* decisions.
At a still more remote level, school-board members, state
legislatures, and federal officials make *societal* educational
decisions. (p. 13)

Following an explication of a rational, knowledge-based view of
decision making, the association called for a model which emphasized
the distinctions and responsibilities between professional and lay
authority and for greater authority being vested in those closest to the
learner.

The educators and lay citizens who prepared *Schools for the Sixties*
(NEA, 1963b) for the association were highly specific about what the
state should do and not do to ensure school quality. Paramount in their
view were the benefits of local control and the importance of the state
respecting and nurturing decisions made within those communities.
They recommended a strong leadership role for the state but a weak
regulatory one: establish standards and provide leadership for the
improvement of programs at the local level to "lift the schools of every
community from the potential limitations of provincialism and
mediocrity" (National Education Association, 1963b, p. 18). They also
saw the state as partner in funding basic education, financial supporter
of innovation, publisher/collector of cutting edge curricular and
instruction *advice,* statistician, and an important provider of professional
development programs.

Such was the view of unions in the heady days of the sixties, when
optimism about schools was high and when so many federal and state
resources were directed toward school improvement. In the two
decades that followed, bureaucrats and policy boards far removed from
where instruction took place became increasingly powerful decision
makers. Even as the *Schools for the Sixties* reports were being issued, the
states were increasingly taking more and more curriculum authority
unto themselves. This was, after all, the beginnings of the accountabilty
movement and the advent of massive state testing programs which
were, in just a few years, to be vigorously opposed by the NEA.

Observers of the great shift of curriculum authority to the state capital can only conclude that the 1960 recommendations of the NEA went not only unheeded but were even reversed over a twenty-year period. As the reform movement which dominated the 1980s matured, however, and the idea of professionalization of teaching took hold, the ideas contained in the three NEA reports provided important historical perspective. Their treatment of the most useful and productive sources of data for decision making and the advice to move decisions closer to learners and their teachers is consistent with much of the literature of the late eighties.

There is a resurgence of interest in the matter of curriculum and instructional authority within the organized teaching profession. The reasons for that interest and an example of how it is played out is the subject of the next two sections.

Union Issues

Why should it matter to leaders of teacher organizations that decisions about curriculum are shifted from the individual teacher, the local school, and the district to the bureaucracies and political machinations of the state? The proposition is often made, after all, that teacher unions are in a better position to influence curriculum decisions when they are centralized at a place where the state teacher organization already has considerable experience and muscle. And, along with other proponents of state control, they could justify it in the name of efficiency, accountability, and cosmopolitanism. There is a counterargument, however, which is causing teacher unions to more actively resist state centralization of authority over education. It has four parts.

Impact on Professionalism

Organized teachers, through their professional societies and unions, have traditionally perceived themselves—and been perceived by the public—as important actors in curriculum making. Indeed, such authority was seen as one of the hallmarks of a profession and of the professional.

Active involvement in curriculum making meant interpreting goals, selecting content to achieve those goals, establishing objectives, designing learning opportunities, determining the ways in which student learning would be assessed, and communicating with parents and the community about achievement. These responsibilities required that participants continually develop expertise in the pedagogical— the fundamentals of curriculum planning—and, more importantly, keep abreast of substantive developments in the content of the curriculum.

Moving curriculum authority to the state meant that others would now assume the major responsibility for curriculum making. It meant that the profession's norm of valuing involvement in curriculum development and of building and maintaining one's expertise was no longer as important. And, in the view of many, it meant the "deprofessionalization" of teaching, a job increasingly prescribed by state mandates, which, at the least, defined the program of study, even defining the ways in which the teacher was to deliver that program. (For an excellent case study of the impact of state mandates on the professional culture of a single school, see Livingston, Castle, & Nations, 1989.)

Today's teachers often found their way into the American middle class by entering what was perceived at the time of their entry as a *profession*. Removing one of the chief characteristics of a profession, that is, the authority to make an educated judgment about the nature of the program the client is offered, suggests that the country's teaching force is not entirely satisfied with its place in society. Further, the number and nature of future teachers, the pool from which the unions will seek their next generation of members, is in jeopardy in part because of this change of condition and status.

Traditionally, the resolution of fundamental dissatisfactions of this kind is seen by unionists as a way to strengthen the organization. This "organizing opportunity" cannot be lost on the leaders of America's teachers' unions. The pronouncements of both the American Federation of Teachers (AFT) and NEA presidents continually send the message that strong teacher professionalism is good for students, the educational system, society, and, somewhat more subtly, for the health of their unions.

Impact on Competent Practice

Local control of the content of the program of the school, although sometimes beset with territorial conflicts, often produced a program of studies tailored for the students the school served. The authority to make these decisions imbued the school's staff with a credible client relationship; that is, they assessed the needs of those students assigned to them and made professional decisions based on professional knowledge. Decision-making authority, delegated to the practicing professionals by the local public's representatives, meant that expertise was coupled with responsibility and that curriculum could be personalized for a particular, unique student body. In this setting, by and large, practitioners believed that their professional knowledge was being used to help clients; they felt an ownership of the program they were implementing; and, consequently, they perceived that their practice was competent.

When curriculum authority shifted to the state, programs became standardized and, according to many teachers, trivialized. When individual teachers lose confidence in the substance of the program they are teaching and when they lack essential ownership of the creation of that program, then they are less committed, perhaps even less competent, in its delivery.

In other endeavors in which unions are present—public health in the public sector or with several professional groups in the private sector, for example—professional decision making would be considered a "condition of work" and subject to action. That, of course, is not the case with organized public school employees because scope-of-bargaining rules limit union action on behalf of members to issues of time, compensation, and working conditions. There are places where matters related to curriculum and instructional decision making are interpreted as a part of working conditions, but those instances have become rarer since the early sixties, when the collective bargaining movement in education began.

Members of teacher unions   and 85 percent of American teachers belong to one—often see their organization as capable of improving their conditions of work even when they lack the legal authority to do so. In the past, problems that affected practice—class size, professional development opportunities, preservice preparation programs, entry programs, and student evaluation measures—have been taken on by the unions and often ameliorated in ways that protected and even encouraged good practice.

From acquiescence to the continuing shift of authority to the state level, state and national teacher organizations have moved toward greater advocacy for professional decision making at the local level. Through their various school improvement programs, which focus on site-based decision making and shared governance at the school and district level, the unions are assuming greater leadership in decentralization of authority. Much of the motivation for the launching of these new programs is to satisfy member demands for a reversal of the trend toward making their jobs routinized and less satisfactory.

Union leaders recognize a close relationship between organizational strength and a membership that sees itself as able to define the conditions of professional practice. Attention to the relationship of where decisions are made and the ability of members to conduct their work in a professional manner will become reinstitutionalized within teacher union programs.

Impact on Individual Efficacy

Individually as well as collectively, teachers in the past were seen by their community as expert in planning, knowledgeable about curriculum, and skillful at executing curriculum decisions. In the recent past, three perceptions supported this view.

- Teachers' personal and professional qualities were seen as positive: unbiased, future directed, student motivated, and goal oriented. School boards and district administrators, therefore, turned to teachers, particularly those with experience and those who were thought of as "scholar teachers", as important advisors about the goals of the school district.
- Teachers were seen as technically proficient at interpreting the goals of the system at the school and classroom levels; indeed, great numbers of teachers served on district curriculum committees, which produced countless guides, manuals, and in-service education programs to accomplish that translation.
- And, of course, teachers were seen as key decision makers in creating learning opportunities, selecting or developing instructional material, and devising teaching strategies to put the district's program into practice with their students.

Many of these activities continue in school districts today. The amount is considerably less, however, than when state accountability programs began to grow and caused curriculum decision making to shift to the state level. More importantly, the nature of the tasks has changed from invention to interpretation, from beginning with an attempt to blend state goals with local curricula and the needs of these students to figuring out how to align local practice with the state's curriculum. The perception is that one is now doing low-level bureaucratic work, mostly unrelated to the needs of the students. For the most part, such work is not profoundly satisfying to individual teachers.

When dealing with such huge numbers on the membership rolls of the major teacher unions, it is tempting to think of these organizations exclusively as collectives. In democratically governed organizations, and both teacher unions are decidedly so, it does not take large numbers of members to bring about policy and program review, however, and a critical mass needed to achieve change does not necessarily begin with majorities. Given that (1) the current state is not satisfactory to a significant number of individual union members; (2) members see the union as a source of potential influence on state education policy; and (3) individual and institutional memories are sufficient to remember a time in which curriculum planning was more professionally satisfying than it is today, the unions will continue their recent aggressiveness to return major aspects of curriculum decision making to the local level.

Teacher as Citizen

Finally, there is the argument that in the public schools there ought to be the right of citizen participation in the development of the curriculum. Current practices in many states, however, deny those at the local level reasonable access to that involvement. Although states constitutionally have responsibility for schooling, considerable research, precedence, and public opinion support the state's delegation of those decisions so that they can be made in reasonable proximity to those affected. (See, for example, Carnegie Forum on Education and the Economy, 1986; Peters and Waterman, 1982; National Governors' Association, 1987.)

Concomitantly, upon meeting standards set by the state, local communities should have the right to delegate to those they hire and oversee the making and implementing of professional and technical decisions. In the many states where centralized decision making has become the norm, educators at the local level have become second-class citizens in two respects. First, along with others in the community, they no longer have ready access to the most basic decisions about what the community's students will be expected to learn. And second, they also have lost what many perceive to have been their right by way of education and license to be participants in the process as professionals.

The NEA and AFT have been in the forefront of the movement to strengthen licensing requirements and to make the license to teach represent a meaningful right. If that license only enables one to qualify for a job with little decision-making authority, then its acquisition becomes a meaningless accomplishment and consequently affects the status, compensation, and security of the union's members. Similar threats, such as those that have come through imposition of certain personnel evaluation procedures or diminutions of the rights pertaining to the license, have caused the unions to react vigorously in the past.

There are indications that arguments such as these are affecting the priorities of the unions. The AFT's support of decision-making innovations at the local level, such as in Dade County, Florida, Rochester, New York, and Toledo, Ohio, suggests that the union is trying to provide an alternative to the shift of decision making to the state level. The NEA has launched a major training program for its twelve hundred field staff to help them gain the skills necessary to bargain contracts and in other ways help members deal constructively with site-based decision-making initiatives. Many NEA state affiliates—Washington, Iowa, and Kansas, to name three of the most visible—have strong programs to assist local associations, school districts, and individual schools in reversing the trend toward state oligarchy. The NEA Learning Laboratories program, establishing a school restructuring demonstration in a school district in each state, will rely heavily on the autonomy of the district's community to make basic curriculum and instructional decisions.

The most systematic, researched-based program mounted by a national union to examine the effects of faculty-led school renewal and its impact on learning and teaching is the NEA's Mastery In Learning Project (MIL). This effort began with the assumption that every decision about learning and instruction that can be made by a local school faculty must be made by that faculty (Goodlad, 1984, in particular, pp. 272–279; see also Bentzen, 1974; Bentzen, Goodlad, et al., 1968; and Sarason, 1971). The MIL program was developed to help union officials, state and local policy makers, and the research community understand the efficacy of investing greater authority in the local school faculty—to observe and report the effects of such empowerment and its impact on curriculum, teaching, and student learning.

Lessons from Union Members at the School Level

Twenty-six demographically representative schools make up the network of cooperating schools in the Mastery In Learning Project. Selected for their representativeness from a pool of several hundred applicants, the faculties in these schools engage in school renewal activities designed, ultimately, to restructure curriculum, learning, teaching, and the context of the school—its climate and culture.

Key to this form of local decision making is an emphasis on using the knowledge base to inform the decision-making process. In the NEA's Mastery In Learning Project, that means attention to research, to examples of good practice in schools, and to the literature which describes new approaches to schooling (Livingston & Castle, 1989; Mastery In Learning Project, 1988). Schools in the network are electronically connected with each other, major universities, the regional education research and development laboratories, selected schools in the two other national networks engaged in school renewal, and the project's resource center. This system allows the knowledge base to be interactive and therefore to grow because information and insights are constantly shared, critiqued, and tested in several contexts.

Among the curriculum topics that have been addressed by Mastery In Learning Project faculties through a computer network are writing across the curriculum, whole-language approaches, integration of subject matter, "less-is-more" conceptions of scope, instructional materials tailored for students with special needs, thinking skills programs, and alternative forms of student evaluation. Decision making in these schools, therefore, is based on data more often than is usual (Livingston & Castle, 1989).

Faculty members in these schools are beginning to feel ownership of their decisions. They are increasingly skillful at interpreting information, shaping decisions for their students, and establishing criteria for measuring success. And, in those places where the states exert considerable control over curriculum, they are developing strategies to substitute local school responsibility for state-mandated accountability. These strategies range from testifying before state committees to enlarging the number and nature of instructional materials that can be used with students and to convincing state authorities to support pilot projects on new forms of student assessment measures. In one case, the state and the local school administration have cooperated to remove many of the requirements from the school and to permit the faculty to develop policies and implement practices more appropriate to their community and student body.

As experimentation with new curricula has come in conflict with state requirements, MIL Project faculties are increasingly interested in how the system can be altered to accommodate and support greater school-community autonomy. A few faculties in the project are now ready to challenge state practices which curtail the faculty's ability to shape the program to match student need. Through the project, these school staffs and their communities are gaining the skills, knowledge, and dispositions to test the limits of what is appropriate for them. In the future, these schools and those in other endeavors will have assembled a record that is likely to demonstrate the reasonableness of the idea that schools are best when critical decisions about learning, teaching, and curriculum are made as close to the learner as possible.

Faculties and individual teachers associated with the Mastery In Learning work are beginning to approach the issues discussed in this chapter differently than those who have not had the empowering experiences which they have. Through documentation of the Mastery In Learning Project reports (McClure, 1988; Livingston & Castle, 1989), reports from those working in other school improvement networks (see for example, Coalition of Essential Schools, 1988–1989) and from observations made by NEA leaders working on such efforts as the National Board for Professional Teaching Standards, five trends emerge:

- The *faculty*—teachers, site-based administrators, counselors, librarians, and others who work with students—are seen as critical and, too often, neglected participants in the decision-making process.
- To become more central in decision making, teachers must become more secure, explicit, and assertive about using their knowledge of students to make instructional decisions.
- Teachers must see themselves as sources of important understandings about pedagogy and curriculum content before they can convince others to grant them the authority to use that expertise.
- Students and parents are clients—persons to whom the faculty is accountable—and district and state rules, regulations, and policies which interfere in that relationship must be changed.
- The great importance of teaching to the society, to clients, and to the individuals who do it must become realized; only then can teaching be more satisfying, involving less "burnout," stress, and frustration.

To move in these directions requires a paradigm shift within the educational establishment, including major changes in the ways staff and leaders of unions see their work and that of the members. Since there are significant numbers of people within all levels of the teacher unions now working to "challenge the regularities" (Sizer, 1987), it is clear that, in the future, union programs designed to move decision-making authority to the local level will expand and increase in effectiveness.

References

Bentzen, M. M. (1974). *Changing schools: The magic feather principle.* New York: McGraw-Hill.

Bentzen, M. M., Goodlad, J. I., et al. (1968). *The principal and the challenge of change.* Los Angeles: Institute for the Development of Educational Activities.

Cameron, Don. (1988). *Collective bargaining, teacher professionalism, school restructuring* (Occasional Paper No. 3). Washington, DC: NEA Mastery In Learning Project.

Carnegie Forum on Education and the Economy. (1986). *A nation prepared: Teachers for the 21st century.* New York: Author.

Coalition of Essential Schools. (1988–89). *HORACE,* (newsletter) Cushman, K., editor. Providence, RI: Brown University.

Commission on the Reorganization of Secondary Education, National Education Association. (1918). *Cardinal principles of secondary education.* Washington, DC: United States Department of the Interior, Bureau of Education.

Education Policies Commission, National Education Association. (1938). *The purposes of education in american democracy.* Washington, DC: National Education Association.

Goodlad, J. I. (1984). *A place called school: Prospects for the future.* New York: McGraw-Hill.

Livingston, C., & Castle, S. (Eds.). (1989). *Teachers and research in action.* Washington, DC: National Education Association.

Livingston, C., Castle, S., & Nations, J. (1989). *Testing, curriculum, and the limits of empowerment.* Paper presented at the annual meeting of the American Educational Research Association, San Francisco.

Mastery In Learning Project. (1988). *Information statement.* Washington, DC: Author.

McClure, R. M. (1988, November). The evolution of shared leadership. *Educational Leadership, 46,* (3), 60–62.

National Education Association. (1963a). *Deciding what to teach.* Washington, DC: Author.

————. (1963b). *Schools for the sixties.* New York: McGraw-Hill.

National Governors' Association. (1987). *Results in education: 1987.* Washington, DC: Author.

Peters, T. J., & Waterman, R. H., Jr. (1982). *In search of excellence: Lessons from America's best-run companies.* New York: Harper & Row.

Sarason, S. B. (1971). *The culture of the school and the problem of change.* Boston: Allyn & Bacon.

Sizer, T. (1987). An agenda for change. In R. M. McClure & G. Obermeyer (Eds.), *Visions of school renewal* (pp. 6–7). Washington, DC: National Education Association.

10 Issues from Curriculum Theory in the Centralization of Curriculum

M. Frances Klein

In recent years there has been a pronounced shift in educational control from the local district to the state. It has occurred because of a number of factors; among them are changes in the way public schools are funded, calls for greater accountability for education tax dollars by the lay public, low student achievement on standardized tests, and a general dissatisfaction with the curriculum offered. The common perceptions basic to this change were that the schools must be improved, even reformed; that the local districts had failed to produce good schools; and it was, then, up to the state to ensure that the needed changes would occur.

Significant changes have occurred in education as a result of this power shift, and to some educators, legislators, and lay publics, the changes have been good ones. This is particularly true for the curriculum; the changes are proclaimed as major accomplishiments by some, but at the same time condemned by others as repressive moves which are damaging to the quality of education that students now receive. These different views of current curriculum practices stem from the particular value perspective that is held about what curricula ought to be and do for students and who should make curriculum decisions—topics which are central to curriculum theory. This chapter focuses upon a personal value perspective on curriculum theory by briefly summarizing some typical characteristics and the impact of state-mandated curricula, examining four issues debated within curriculum theory which can enlighten the discussion occurring about state control over the curriculum, and concluding with curriculum theory and decision making within the context of three more general educational issues currently being discussed.

Characteristics and Impact of State-Mandated Curricula

State-mandated curricula have some similar characteristics, and have had a major impact on the type of curriculum offered to and experienced by students. There is little question that the movement to state-mandated curricula has strengthened and improved the traditional view of curriculum and centralized basic decisions in curriculum development. Curricula that emanate from the state are characterized by such concepts and practices as curriculum alignment, widespread achievement testing, extensive use of direct instruction, higher academic standards and more rigorous courses, a teacher-dominated classroom, increased time on task, increased homework assignments, more rigorous, demanding texts, and high teacher expectations for student achievement. (It is interesting to note that Cuban, 1986, has documented some of these as being persistent patterns of curriculum and instruction for some time, and therefore they cannot be considered the exclusive result of recent moves by state legislatures and state departments of education for greater control. It is clear, however, that these characteristics have been legitimatized and strengthened to a much greater extent with the shift in power and decision making to the state.)

A technological process for curriculum development is normally used: goals and objectives are stated, texts are chosen which support them, teachers are trained to deliver the desired content, and tests are administered to determine the success of the curriculum in terms of student achievement. All aspects of curriculum planning and practice are aligned as closely as possible so that decisions made about the various elements of curriculum planning and implementation are compatible. In this approach to curriculum development students are often viewed as the raw materials, teachers are the workers, schools are the assembly line, the curriculum as defined by the state is the process, and the educated, economically productive citizen is the finished product.

This view of curriculum assumes that the outcomes of curriculum and the content to be taught as identified at the state level are appropriate for every student throughout the state, that teachers have flexibility in determining how best to teach the expected outcomes and content, and that all students are expected to work diligently toward the desired outcomes, showing ever-higher degrees of achievement on standardized tests. In the process, school practices across the state become more prescribed and standardized as district and school curricula are aligned to closely reflect the state expectations and particularly the achievement tests used for assessment.

In this process it is often not recognized that one curriculum decision affects potential decisions about all others. When a decision is made about one element of curriculum planning, there is often a direct impact on the array of possible decisions which can be made about the other elements (see Chapter 2). Even those curriculum elements which are not dealt with explicitly in state mandates receive certain pressures which cause the school districts to make uniform decisions about them. A domino effect occurs in curriculum planning; as decisions are made at the state level, they have effects, sometimes far-reaching ones, on other decisions which are thought to be reserved for the local level.

In the state of California, a major leader in the movement of state-mandated curricula, these are very familiar concepts and practices to educators. Documents have been developed and distributed extensively by the California State Department of Education which specify goals and objectives, identify specific content to be taught, name the textbooks which are "recommended" for the elementary school (but carry the benefit of state money only if districts buy from those listed), and describe the testing program developed for determining the success of the curriculum and students. Model curriculum standards are issued by the State Department of Education and sent to every school district to assist them in curriculum alignment and program evaluation. Districts too often use the standards as firm external criteria in order to comply with state expectations rather than as guidelines or suggestions for developing or improving their own curricula at the local level.

The power and interactive nature of these curriculum decisions made at the state level are illustrated by two fundamental examples. California now mandates that teachers will be evaluated on their instructional skills and that administrators must develop and be certified that they have the necessary skills for this task. Districts have been quick to comply. Most are responding by giving help to administrators in evaluating direct instruction almost exclusively, a very restricted view of teaching which will help students develop a narrow array of curriculum outcomes. A teacher who uses another teaching strategy may be viewed as not exhibiting important skills of teaching, or may be simply viewed as being "different" at best. It is the rare administrator who recognizes and rewards alternative ways of teaching and thus who encourages the teacher to address an array of curriculum outcomes in creative ways. This emphasis on teacher evaluation has created strong pressure for uniformity in teaching strategies and curriculum outcomes throughout the state.

Similarly, the quiet, orderly, "productive", time-on-task, teacher-dominated classroom being advocated by the state, both implicitly and explicitly, is always evaluated as better by many administrators than those classrooms which have some noise and movement and where students may spend some minutes off task, perhaps relating in a personal way to the teacher. The preferred type of classroom is undoubtedly good for some types of objective, measurable outcomes mandated by the state; but if classrooms are always that way, there will be many desirable classroom activities which will not be offered to students. This will leave many significant learnings left potentially unattended. Feeling the excitement of learning, making decisions and experiencing the consequences, pursuing individual interests and talents, and respecting all types of people are examples of goals which will receive short shrift in neat, orderly, quiet, teacher-dominated classrooms.

Thus, in California the move to state control over curriculum planning has been quite complete. The state now controls either implicitly or explicitly most of the elements of curriculum decision making. Local districts feel great pressure to comply with state guidelines and mandates about curriculum. There is not much left for the districts or school faculties to do in curriculum development but to monitor how well they are doing in response to state mandates.

This approach to curriculum development has considerable support. There are some proponents who believe that some of the changes which have come about, in part as a result of state-mandated curricula, successfully address the need for quality and equality in education for all students (see, for example, the argument developed by Adler, 1982). They believe that the provision of the same curriculum offered to all students resolves the problem of inequality of schooling and ensures that all students will receive a quality curriculum. Other supporters point with pride at the increased attention to the importance of education, better funding, higher standards for graduation, more students in academic courses, harder textbooks, and increased achievement scores. Legislators like it because there is some accountability for tax funds spent on education. To them, higher test scores mean that the tax dollars have been spent in effective ways with unequivocal outcomes for all to see. Some practitioners support this approach because they believe they finally know, through strong state direction, what needs to be done to build a good curriculum. (These educators should not be disparaged, because they receive very little, if any, consistent preparation in curriculum which helps them know how to plan and implement curriculum and how to effectively engage in their responsibilities.) Taxpayers like it because the success and improvement of the public schools are reported in terms of standardized test scores which they believe they understand. There is, then, considerable support for the shift in curriculum decision making to the state away from the time-honored concept in American education of local control.

At the same time, however, there are serious reservations about and condemnations of the changes in curriculum which have occurred. The opponents of state control over the curriculum believe that education for many students is not as good as the supporters proclaim, and may have become even worse than before in some ways. The changes are viewed by some as elitist and even punitive to some students, unnecessarily restricting what students could learn, contributing to the alarming dropout rate, forcing teachers to teach to the tests, and in general being a step "back to the future." These opponents of state control over curriculum decision making want much more decision making returned to the district and, often, to the teachers at the local school. They deplore the little time or effort devoted to creative work in curriculum development at the local level but recognize there is not much incentive to do so (see Chapter 7). It takes only the strongest, most determined administrators and teachers to openly challenge the strong pressures to define curriculum as some states now are doing. (It may be, however, that those are the educators that ought to be valued the most.)

An examination of some issues from curriculum theory can extend and better inform the debates by both proponents and opponents of state-mandated curricula. Specifically, it can help clarify the positions taken about curriculum decision making by theorists and practitioners, make explicit and implicit assumptions much clearer, and suggest some options to the current trends toward state control over the curriculum. The following discussion addresses four such issues from curriculum theory and reflects a personal perspective on them.

Issues from Curriculum Theory and State-Mandated Curricula

The issues addressed in curriculum theory that are related to a more centralized curriculum are fundamental, complex, value laden, and often overlooked in the shifts in decision making which occur periodically in American education (see Chapter 5). The stands taken on these issues by both theorists and practitioners have significant implications for the types of curricula that are planned for and experienced by students. Thus, the issues need to be raised for public debate and not considered lightly or overlooked. The theoretical issues discussed in this section are the nature of knowledge, comprehensiveness of the curriculum, relevancy of the curriculum, and the role of the implicit curriculum.

The Nature of Knowledge

The perceptions of what and how knowledge can be organized, taught, and learned are fundamental to the debate about centralized curriculum decision making. The issue centers around the objectivity or subjectivity of knowledge.

The nature of knowledge assumed by the proponents of greater state control (or for greater district control by others, also a form of centralized curriculum at another level) is that knowledge is objective, exists independently of a student, can be carefully defined in advance of classroom interaction, can be organized logically and sequentially, is best represented in the traditional disciplines, can be presented effectively to students through the use of a well-organized textbook, and can be successfully evaluated by standardized achievement tests.

It is assumed that since knowledge is objective, all students can and will learn the same content and will experience the same curriculum to the best of their abilities as measured by standardized achievement tests. Once the curriculum has been determined, in large part by the state, it can and will be implemented with a considerable degree of fidelity in all schools throughout the state. This view of knowledge is held by many curriculum theorists, and they are likely to support some degree of centralization in curriculum (see, for example, Hunkins, 1980; McNeil, 1985).

Other theorists reject this objective view of knowledge and subscribe to a much more subjective view (Klein, in press). They believe that until students attach personal meaning to knowledge, it is meaningless or nonexistent, that although knowledge can be defined objectively, it is only learned when internalized by students. Knowledge, thus, ultimately becomes subjective since it is learned in relation to what else the student knows as a result of his or her life experiences (see, for example, Macdonald, Wolfson, & Zaret, 1973; Zaret, 1986).

These theorists reason that the appearance of specific content in the formal curriculum in a logically organized way does not ensure that all students will achieve that particular view of it. As teachers and students interact with the formal curriculum (if they must), changes will be made—some content deleted, added to, and modified. Further, students may well have personal associations which affect their understanding of the content being learned, additional knowledge beyond what was specified, or gaps which exist in their understanding of the content. These conditions ensure that not all students will conclude their studies with exactly the same knowledge base or educational experience from the curriculum as all other students.

The view of knowledge as being objective is both a rational and reasonable one for some purposes, particularly in curriculum planning at some levels of decision making remote from the students (which I believe is important for broad directions of the curriculum). To the degree that the objective view of knowledge ignores the dynamic interaction between teachers and students and the personal interaction of each student with the content being learned, however, it is sterile and naive. An overemphasis on the objective view of knowledge easily leads to useless memorization, teaching and learning only content which can be tested, considerable frustration with schooling by some students, and the gap that most students consistently see between school and the rest of their lives. Students must be encouraged to reflect upon and internalize what they are taught in school if it is to be remembered and related to their lives in meaningful ways.

Comprehensiveness of the Curriculum

A second issue from curriculum theory has to do with the comprehensiveness of the curriculum. There are two basic concepts which are essential in a discussion of this issue: the explicit curriculum and the null curriculum (Eisner, 1985). These two curricula will always exist no matter who plans the curriculum; they are inescapable consequences of curriculum development. The explicit curriculum is that which is carefully and deliberately planned, taught, and evaluated—at any level of curriculum decision making. The comprehensiveness of the explicit curriculum is defined by the expectations for what students will learn and what they do learn—what content students study, the outcomes students are expected to and do achieve, and all the decisions which are related to these two fundamental elements of curriculum development. Such questions as the following are usually addressed and help define the comprehensiveness of the explicit curriculum. What are the major goals of schooling? Will students be introduced to the major disciplines (since they represent humankind's organized and transmitted wisdom) so that they will be able to identify their particular interests and abilities and be adequately prepared as educated citizens? Do students study the subjects frequently enough and long enough at a time to learn what is important in them? By answering such questions, a state-mandated curriculum typically emphasizes the attainment of a carefully defined body of knowledge and skills, based largely on the disciplines, which is thought to encompass the requirements of a good education.

A second essential concept in determining the comprehensiveness of the curriculum is the null curriculum. Eisner (1985) defines this as what is not taught. Regardless of how carefully the explicit curriculum is planned, a null curriculum will always exist because the school cannot teach all that students need to know in order to lead personally satisfying, productive lives in this complex, diverse society.

The time students spend in school is very limited, therefore careful choices must be made about what students should learn while they are there. Some school subjects are much more important than others, and those which are most important must be featured. Then, decisions must be made as to how much this curriculum will be "watered down" by the introduction of such subjects as drivers education, home economics, and physical education. Those subjects considered less important may well be relegated to the null curriculum. Basic decisions such as these determine what the explicit curriculum will be and what the null curriculum will be as a result. The null curriculum must be as consistently examined as the explicit curriculum in any aspect or level of curriculum development in order to determine whether the curriculum is as comprehensive as it needs to be to ensure an effective education for young people. It rarely is carefully examined, however.

The debate about a state-mandated curriculum is clarified when the comprehensiveness of the explicit curriculum and what is relegated to the null curriculum are considered. For example, the explicit curriculum is carefully defined by the state in terms that primarily represent the disciplines. Other areas may be included in the curriculum but typically do not receive the emphasis in either theory or practice as the traditional subjects of math, science, reading, literature, and history. A few disciplines, such as the arts, may be a part of the formal state curriculum but actually become a part of the null curriculum in practice.

With the emphasis on the traditional disciplines defining the explicit curriculum, many important outcomes of schooling desired by teachers, parents, and the general lay public are likely to fall into the null curriculum in a state-mandated curriculum (see for example, Klein, 1989). Open-ended exploration of interesting, socially relevant ideas and complex, controversial issues, for example, is not likely to occur. Pursuit of individual interests and talents within areas not represented by the disciplines will not occur, and most content not included in achievement tests will be noticeably absent in classrooms. Students will potentially receive little direct help in attaining such important goals as learning how to learn, respecting people who are different from themselves, appreciating the arts and their importance to daily life, learning to resolve conflict, and developing a commitment to the importance of life-long learning. These types of outcomes are consistently valued and desired as being very basic to everyday life and are included in virtually all statements of curriculum goals and expectations. Under state control with accountability by achievement test scores, however, they are not likely to be addressed because they are not amenable to testing. They will be relegated to the null curriculum and will receive little or no attention. The resulting explicit curriculum is narrowly defined and imbalanced in what is expected of students. A comprehensive curriculum must attend to all aspects of student development, not just that which represents only the disciplines or is easily tested.

As suggested above, one basic curriculum element and a very powerful force currently affecting how the explicit and null curricula are defined in a state-mandated curriculum is evaluation through standardized tests. (See also Chapter 8 for a discussion of the impact of testing upon the curriculum.) Standardized testing is the major way schools are held accountable to the public for spending tax moneys wisely, and an extensive program is often mantained in selected subject areas with a state-mandated curriculum. It is generally agreed that standardized tests currently are driving the curriculum. When one of my doctoral students wanted to do some research on the social studies curriculum for the primary grades, she was hard-pressed to find teachers who taught social studies. Most teachers she contacted for the study indicated that they spent their day on reading and math because of the visibility and importance of test scores in those two subject areas. Testing was clearly driving the curriculum for those teachers.

Thus, with strong state control over the evaluation of student learning through standardized testing, only those content areas and curriculum outcomes which can be tested are likely to be in the explicit curriculum. What is included in the tests required by the state (and district) becomes the content of the explicit curriculum; all else is minimized or deleted, becoming the null curriculum. The curriculum will be restricted to those outcomes which can be easily measured—factual knowledge, low-level thinking skills, and basic skills in reading and math. Even those outcomes which can be evaluated by other means, but not easily tested, will not receive much emphasis from a centralized curriculum with a strong standardized test component. Few would consider this to be a comprehensive curriculum for the kind of education needed by today's students.

Relevancy of the Curriculum

One of the most fundamental concepts in curriculum development is relevancy—the relationship to and importance of the curriculum to the lives of students. A relevant curriculum helps ensure that students will become engaged in what they are expected to learn and will thus learn what they and others deem to be important and necessary. As curricula are planned at levels further away from students, the chances increase that they will not be as relevant as those planned with specific groups of students in mind. As relevancy decreases, students (and teachers) are likely to become less involved in learning activities and not achieve the desired outcomes of the curriculum.

In a state-mandated curriculum, students often have to be persuaded to learn from a curriculum which has been developed (and will be assessed) by adults often far removed from the classroom. The curriculum will reflect adult views of what is important for students, not necessarily what students perceive as relevant. Most teachers are able to successfully entice some of their students to become involved in the curricula by offering external rewards such as grades, admission to college, parental approval for success at school, teacher respect and approval, and tangible rewards in the classroom. But today there are many students, in fact, frighteningly large numbers of students, who are not willing to stay engaged in state-mandated curricula. One significant factor in the increasing dropout rate may well be the curriculum being offered—it is too often perceived as irrelevant by too many students, even to some who remain in school to "suffer through" the requirements for high school graduation (Association for Supervision and Curriculum Development, 1989). The dropout rate is one of the most serious problems confronting the nation today, and it must be dealt with from many different aspects, one of them being the critical examination of the relevancy of the curriculum offered to students.

Further, a state-mandated curriculum with great emphasis placed on student growth as measured by standardized achievement tests and a curriculum planned and expected to be implemented with fidelity leaves little hope that it will be relevant for all students in the state. In a state with a student population as diverse as in California, for example, it almost ensures that for good numbers of students, the curriculum will not be as relevant as one planned closer to a group of specific students. The content of a science curriculum, the stories in a literature program, the topics of the social studies curriculum, and the textbooks selected for math at a state level will not be appropriate for all students in the state. There must be more freedom than there is in a state-mandated curriculum for teachers and students to engage in aspects of curriculum development for themselves, for some opportunities to select what they will study in order to achieve the important broad goals of schooling which should be mandated at the state level. Only when they have these opportunities to select for themselves some areas and materials of interest to study can the curriculum attain an adequate degree of relevancy. Then perhaps students will be more encouraged to stay in school through involvement in a relevant curriculum, and perhaps even attend more closely to those areas of the curriculum over which they may have little control.

The Implicit Curriculum

There is much discussion in the recent literature about the implicit curriculum, another issue in curriculum theory. The implicit curriculum consists of those messages which students learn, often affective in nature, but which may not be deliberately intended or examined. They are typically communicated through the values of the educators who run the school, the expectations of teachers, the classroom rules and regulations, the way schools are structured and organized, and the quality of the interactions with adults and other students, for example. Any curriculum must be carefully examined to determine what students are learning from the implicit curriculum (as well as the explicit and null curricula).

The implicit curriculum cannot be determined unless students are directly consulted, but some potential messages students might receive from a state-mandated curriculum are the following:

1. What is important to be learned is determined by someone else, and learning means to comply with the expectations of others. Learning also does not often mean thinking for oneself about the meaning of what is being learned and the relevance of it to one's life.
2. What is really important in school is measured by achievement tests. If what is learned is not tested or reported to parents, it obviously cannot be of much importance.
3. Those in authority, the state or district officials, know what is best for all students regarding what should be learned. Individual interests and talents are unimportant unless they are taught as organized subjects and tested in school.
4. Compliance, orderliness, memorization, and respect for authority are important characteristics of good students.
5. Teachers and administrators are only concerned with what is to be learned and tested, not with other developmental aspects or the lives of students outside of the school and classroom.

These messages, if they are, indeed, communicated to students through state-mandated curricula, are very undesirable ones which need to be revised or countermanded, even in a centralized curriculum.

Too often curricula are planned and implemented with no attention paid to what students might be learning from the implicit curriculum. It is very possible that some of the potential messages of the implicit curriculum could function to counteract and negate some of the important learnings desired in the explicit curriculum. It is very hard, for example, to learn about democracy in a totally adult-controlled school environment.

An implicit curriculum will exist just as surely with a curriculum developed at the local level as with a curriculum developed at the state level. It might not be any different with local control over the curriculum, especially when similar assumptions are made about the explicit curriculum as currently are expressed by the proponents of a state-mandated curriculum. But it would be much easier to challenge and correct the undesirable messages from the implicit curriculum with control at the local level rather than at the state level. The state level is too far removed from the individual school to be challenged effectively by a faculty concerned about the messages their students might be receiving from the implicit curriculum. Thus, undesirable messages are more likely to persist in a state curriculum than in a locally controlled one.

Curriculum Theory and Decision Making within the Current Educational Context

Curriculum development never occurs in a vacuum. Both the processes and substance of curriculum theory and decision making are always embedded in the larger issues and concerns of American education. Three broad educational issues with which curriculum theory interacts will be briefly discussed in this final section: how curriculum change occurs in schools, the professionalization of teachers, and the function and contributions of curriculum theory to the quality of education offered to and received by students.

Curriculum Change

The belief that significant curriculum change will occur through a strategy which imposes a curriculum upon teachers and students such as occurs in state mandates must be seriously questioned. This so-called top-down approach is not the most effective strategy for curriculum change (McLaughlin & Marsh, 1978), and in fact, the changes (if any) made with this strategy are usually disappointingly small and too often temporary. Change efforts using the strategy of top-down reform often are blunted on the classroom door (Goodlad, Klein, & Associates, 1974).

Teachers and site administrators must be directly involved in proposals for change and must develop ownership of them if they are to become a reality, even those emanating from powerful sources such as the state. Significant curriculum change will not occur if teachers are simply technicians waiting to carry out "orders," to implement with high fidelity curricula planned by people remote from classrooms and without teacher participation. Even teachers who may be supportive of state-mandated changes, or at least not resistant to them, do not necessarily implement them in their classrooms as planned.

The belief that successful state-mandated, top-down approaches to desired curriculum change will being about commonly shared perceptions, goals, and actions among all the educators who must be involved in curriculum reform reflects a very naive view. The debate occurring about state-mandated curricula strongly suggests that the perceptions and values of the different participants in curriculum decision making are not shared and that the participants are not in agreement about what changes are needed. Curriculum reform, like other educational movements, is conducted in a political arena, often a complex array of competing ideas, and is subjected to the reality of different values about education, funding which is too limited, and the different vested interests of many who are concerned about the curriculum (see Chapter 1). The desirability and efficacy of the top-down change strategy being used in state-mandated curricula must be seriously questioned.

Professionalization of Teachers

A second general issue is about the degree of professionalization that teachers should be expected to develop and exhibit. Many are arguing that the teacher must be a professional decision maker (see, for example, Wise & Darling-Hammond, 1984/1985), and this is expected to occur particularly in regards to the curriculum of the school and classroom (Klein, 1985). The move to a state-mandated curriculum leaves few areas in which teachers can exercise professional judgment. Through the kinds of curriculum decisions made, the states have defined the role of the teacher as a technician. The major task left to the district, local school, and teachers is to align the curriculum, that is, to make sure the instructional curriculum offered by the teacher is in agreement with the formal curriculum which the state expects, provides, and evaluates. This approach to curriculum development demands little creativity or professional skill from the classroom teacher.

Before teachers can be expected to engage in curriculum development as professionals, however, they must develop the needed knowledge and skills. Depressingly few opportunities exist for teachers to become skilled in making curriculum decisions (see also Chapter 6). Few preservice programs include any course work in curriculum development; most assume that the curriculum will be given to them through state and district documents or at least by the textbook. Nor are staff development programs noted for their rigorous offerings in curriculum development—or even for ways to modify curriculum expectations to meet the needs of specific groups of students. Teachers, unfortunately, are not prepared to engage in curriculum development in any serious way.

As long as curriculum development is not a part of the teacher's basic preparation, right, or responsibility, it is difficult to see how teachers will ever become professionals. Teacher education and staff development programs must include curriculum development as an important aspect, or strong centralized control over most curriculum decisions will likely ensure that teachers perform as good technicians and not as professionals.

Contributions of Curriculum Theory

Curriculum theorizing—or any theorizing—is sometimes thought to be an ineffectual or useless activity. A consideration of curriculum theory in a time of state control over the curriculum—or any time of change—can be a very clarifying endeavor, however. An urgent task to which curriculum theory can contribute is a consideration of who should make what kinds of curriculum decisions. That is not an insignificant question, but the decisions are too frequently made without a full understanding of their fundamental nature.

Questions from curriculum theory regarding who makes curriculum decisions have been answered in many states by the trend toward much more state involvement and control than in the past. Whether this is a desirable condition will continue to be debated in the future as the issue of who makes curriculum decisions is reconsidered and the success of the state in curriculum change is determined. The question is not whether the state should make curriculum decisions—or the district, or the teacher. The answer must be that all of the above are deeply concerned about the curricula which are developed for students, and, therefore, must be involved in the process. An effective and appropriate role must be developed for all those participants who must be involved in the process, and any imbalance which exists must be corrected.

Schooling clearly is a concern of the state, the local community, professional educators, and the student, among others. The state must ensure that all students will receive an effective, relevant, balanced, current curriculum. The district must be held accountable to the local community that its students are receiving an equitable curriculum and one which includes all that is considered to be important in the educational process. The school faculty and each teacher with his or her students must have the freedom to develop some curricula or at least to modify curricula which are planned beyond the school and classroom to make them more relevant to the students. All of these fundamental and interactive responsibilities must be coordinated and compatible decisions made, or difficulties with the curriculum will occur. When one group usurps the right of the others to be involved in curriculum decisions, the resulting curriculum will be less effective than it could be.

The shift to state control of the curriculum has not been a benign transfer of power. It has had many significant implications for other educational issues and has had a profound impact on the type of curricula offered to and experienced by students. Whether this shift is to be modified or intensified must become an essential debate for all those concerned about the nation's schools. It will not be an easy debate to resolve, and it will require the best efforts from curriculum theorists and of even more powerful educators and lay citizens. The decision as to who will make curriculum decisions and what type of curriculum will thus be offered to students will have a significant impact on the future.

References

Adler, Mortimer J. (1982). *The Paideia Proposal: An educational manifesto.* New York: Macmillan.

Association for Supervision and Curriculum Development. (1989, August). Helping underachievers succeed: Opting for acceleration, not remediation. *ASCD Update, 31* (5), 1-2.

Cuban, Larry. (1986, September). Persistent instruction: Another look at constancy in the classroom. Phi Delta Kappan, 68 (1), 7-11.

Eisner, Elliot W. (1985). *The educational imagination: On the design and evaluation of school programs.* New York: Macmillan.

Goodlad, John I., Klein, M. Frances, & Associates. (1974). *Looking behind the classroom door.* Worthington, OH: Charles A. Jones.

Hunkins, Francis P. (1980). *Curriculum development: Program improvement.* Columbus, OH: Charles E. Merrill.

Klein, M. Frances. (1985, September). The master teacher as curriculum leader. *The Elementary School Journal, 86* (1), 35-44.

Klein, M. Frances. (1989). *Elementary school curriculum reform: Creating your own agenda.* New York: Teachers College Press.

Klein, M. Frances. (in press). Approaches to curriculum theory and practice. In James T. Sears & J. Dan Marshall (Eds.), *Teaching and thinking about curriculum: Empowering educators through curriculum studies.* New York: Teachers College Press.

Macdonald, James, Wolfson, Bernice, & Zaret, Esther. (1973). *Reschooling society: A conceptual model.* Washington, DC: Association for Supervision and Curriculum Development.

McLaughlin, Milbrey W., & Marsh, David D. (1978, September). Staff development and school change. *Teachers College Record, 80* (1), 69–94.

McNeil, John D. (1985). *Curriculum: A comprehensive introduction.* Boston: Little, Brown.

Wise, Arthur E., & Darling-Hammond, Linda. (1984/1985). Teacher evaluation and teacher professionalism. *Educational Leadership, 42* (4), 28–31.

Zaret, Esther. (1986, Winter): The uncertainty principle in curriculum planning. *Theory into practice, 25* (1), 46–52.

Index